Co-operative Struggles

Studies in Critical Social Sciences

Series Editor
David Fasenfest
(*Wayne State University*)

VOLUME 203

New Scholarship in Political Economy

Series Editors
David Fasenfest
(*Wayne State University*)
Alfredo Saad-Filho
(*King's College London*)

Editorial Board
Kevin B. Anderson (*University of California, Santa Barbara*)
Tom Brass (*formerly of SPS, University of Cambridge*)
Raju Das (*York University*)
Ben Fine ((*emeritus*) SOAS *University of London*)
Jayati Ghosh (*Jawaharlal Nehru University*)
Elizabeth Hill (*University of Sydney*)
Dan Krier (*Iowa State University*)
Lauren Langman (*Loyola University Chicago*)
Valentine Moghadam (*Northeastern University*)
David N. Smith (*University of Kansas*)
Susanne Soederberg (*Queen's University*)
Aylin Topal (*Middle East Technical University*)
Fiona Tregenna (*University of Johannesburg*)
Matt Vidal (*Loughborough University London*)
Michelle Williams (*University of the Witwatersrand*)

VOLUME 13

The titles published in this series are listed at *brill.com/nspe*

Co-operative Struggles

Work Conflicts in Argentina's New Worker Co-operatives

By

Denise Kasparian

Foreword by

Julián Rebón

Translated by

Ian Barnett

BRILL

LEIDEN | BOSTON

Cover illustration: Bust of Karl Marx, 1939, by S.D. Merkurov, at the Fallen Monument Park (Muzeon Park of Arts) in Moscow, Russia. Photo courtesy of Alfredo Saad-Filho.

Library of Congress Cataloging-in-Publication Data

Names: Kasparian, Denise, author. | Rebón, Julián, writer of foreword. | Barnett, Ian (Translator), translator.
Title: Co-operative struggles : work conflicts in Argentina's new worker co-operatives / by Denise Kasparian ; foreword by Julián Rebón ; translated by Ian Barnett.
Other titles: Lucha ¿sin patrón?. English
Description: Leiden ; Boston : Brill, [2022] | Series: Studies in critical social sciences, 2666-2205 ; volume 203 | Includes bibliographical references and index.
Identifiers: LCCN 2021043027 (print) | LCCN 2021043028 (ebook) | ISBN 9789004468580 (hardback) | ISBN 9789004468641 (ebook)
Subjects: LCSH: Cooperative societies–Argentina. | Labor policy–Argentina. | Social conflict–Argentina.
Classification: LCC HD3468 .K3713 2022 (print) | LCC HD3468 (ebook) | DDC 334.0982–dc23
LC record available at https://lccn.loc.gov/2021043027
LC ebook record available at https://lccn.loc.gov/2021043028

Typeface for the Latin, Greek, and Cyrillic scripts: "Brill." See and download: brill.com/brill-typeface.

ISSN 2666-2205
ISBN 978-90-04-46858-0 (hardback)
ISBN 978-90-04-46864-1 (e-book)

Copyright 2022 by Koninklijke Brill NV, Leiden, The Netherlands.
Koninklijke Brill NV incorporates the imprints Brill, Brill Nijhoff, Brill Hotei, Brill Schöningh, Brill Fink, Brill mentis, Vandenhoeck & Ruprecht, Böhlau Verlag and V&R Unipress.
All rights reserved. No part of this publication may be reproduced, translated, stored in a retrieval system, or transmitted in any form or by any means, electronic, mechanical, photocopying, recording or otherwise, without prior written permission from the publisher.
Authorization to photocopy items for internal or personal use is granted by Koninklijke Brill NV provided that the appropriate fees are paid directly to The Copyright Clearance Center, 222 Rosewood Drive, Suite 910, Danvers, MA 01923, USA. Fees are subject to change.

This book is printed on acid-free paper and produced in a sustainable manner.

Contents

Foreword
The Democratisation of Conflict   VIII
   Julián Rebón
Acknowledgements   XI
List of Illustrations   XII

Introduction   1
1   The Question of Work Conflicts in New Co-operatives   3
2   Dimensions of New Social Conflicts in Co-operative Socio-productive Contexts   9
3   The Challenge of Comparing Paradigmatic but Non-equivalent Experiences: Studying a Whole That Acts as a Whole   15
4   The Structure of the Book   18

1   **Co-operatives 'Made in Argentina'**
The Process of Enterprise Recuperation by Their Workers   20
   1   The Socio-genesis of the Processes of Enterprise Recuperation   21
      1.1   *When Worker Resistance Becomes an Offensive Movement*   21
      1.2   *The Widespread Crisis of 2001–2002, or Adding Fuel to the Fire*   23
      1.3   *The Movement of the Flames*   26
   2   The Evolution of Enterprise Recuperation Processes   29
      2.1   *The Fuel of the Growing Economy Keeps the Flames of Production Moving*   31
      2.2   *The Moral Economy of Work in the Continued Presence of Enterprise Recuperations*   33
      2.3   *"Argentina Is One Big, Recuperated Factory": Public Policies for Recuperated Enterprises*   36
      2.4   *The Movement's Fragmentation, Co-operative Convergence and Union Rapprochement*   42

2   **Incubated Co-operatives**
Co-operative Formation under the Argentina Works Programme   48
   1   Social Schemes with Work Requirement: From Workfare to the Argentina Works Programme   50
   2   The Mediation of Unemployed Workers' Organisations: Civil Associations, Productive Units and Co-operatives   56

3	The Dual Logic of the Argentina Works Programme's Socio-genesis: Creating Jobs and Co-ordinating Local Politics 60	
4	Induced Co-operatives? The Struggle of Unemployed Workers' Organisations 62	
	4.1	*The Evolution of the Argentina Works Programme* 65
	4.2	*The Intensity and Dynamics of Contentious Action* 67
	4.3	*The Demands and Forms of Contentious Action* 70

3 Keeping and Having a Job
A Milestone in Constitutive Conflicts 76

1. 'Occupy, Resist, Produce' … and Have! 76
2. From 'Induction' to the 'Co-operative without Brokers' 89
3. A Comparative Lens on Constitutive Conflicts 97

4 The Recuperated Enterprise and Social Power in Production 105

1. Recuperators, Activists and the 'Born and Bred' 106
2. Property Relations: Social Possession and Differential Appropriation of the Fruits of Labour 110
3. The Logic of Production and the Issue of Sustainability in Recuperated Enterprises 120
4. The Political Dimension: Between Self-management and Delegation 125
5. Social Groupings and Potential Antagonisms: Opportunity Hoarding, Enterprise Projects and Work Generations 134

5 The Argentina Works Co-operative and State Power in Production 139

1. The Labour and Socio-spatial Precarity of Argentina Works Programme Workers 140
2. Property Relations: Social Possession and Autonomy 142
3. The Logic of Production: Between Subsistence and Political Accumulation 148
4. The Political Dimension: State Power and Co-management 156
5. Social Groupings and Potential Antagonisms: State Officials, Co-operative Members and Activists 162

6 The Production of Co-operative Conflict 166

1. Board Removals: Conflicts over the Running and Expansion of the Productive Process 168
2. Regulations, Sanctions and Exclusions: From 'Founder Members' to '*Founderer* Members' 182

    3   "We Fought over the River Module": The Conflict over Autonomous
        Work   190
    4   Between Subsistence Consumption and Political Accumulation in the
        Social Organisation   199
    5   A Comparative Lens   206

7 **Conclusions**   210
    1   The New Twenty-First-Century Co-Operativism and Its Struggles
        Around Work   210
    2   What Patterns of Conflicts Are There without Bosses? Towards a
        Theory of Unrest in Worker Co-operatives   214
    3   From Prelude to Present: A Toolbox for New Research
        Questions   222

Bibliography   225
Index   242

Foreword

The Democratisation of Conflict

Julián Rebón

In terms of prospects for emancipation, the dawn of the twenty-first century is framed by the waning of the main alternatives that sought during the twentieth century to transform the capitalist system. The crisis of real socialism and social democracy, and the power of the expanding neoliberal system with its negative consequences for social inequality, promoted a search for new alternatives. These included various ways of recreating the traditions of co-operativism and self-management.

Argentina's 2001 neoliberal crisis became a genuine social laboratory in the search for a solution 'right here, right now' to the exclusion created by the system. Direct action and autonomy came to be the hallmarks of a citizenry that ceased to delegate the defence of its social identities to the institutional authorities. Worker-recuperated enterprises began to spread during this widespread crisis. Against a backdrop of high unemployment and social dislocation, groups of workers stood up and defended their jobs. To do this they had to change the patterns of what was pre-established. A far cry from passiveness and the individualisation of suffering as a way to deal with unemployment, these workers occupied the factories and got them into production.

Rather than being restricted to an exception or anomaly of the crisis, these processes of social innovation and conversion of capitalist enterprises built on workers' associated production continued and developed over the following years. Limited as they are in numbers (about 400), they have had a significant impact in the public arena. Social sciences and political debate were no strangers to this tendency and gave rise to an abundance of research and articles, while also sowing the seeds of local and international debates that varied in the fruits they bore. While the phenomenon spread to other countries in Latin America and the rest of the world, in their degree of development and form – as a social movement – *las recuperadas* (recuperated enterprises) have remained closely associated with Argentina.

At a local level, they involved a heterodox renovation of old-school Argentinian co-operativism. Workers disobeying unemployment advanced on production. In ways more adaptive than utopian, workers put together new co-operatives, which, unlike a significant part of traditional co-operativism, did not split property and work. Instead, they formed worker co-operatives, the associational form with most ruptures as compared to capitalist enterprises. In contrast to past experiences, these enterprises were not born from scratch steered by the ideals of the old co-operative movement, but from the conversion of capitalist enterprises by groups of employees seeking to preserve their jobs, even at the expense of having to change their employment category.

A few short years later, in the wave of Latin American progressive governments – one of the most significant critical responses to the global neoliberal hegemony – the creation of co-operatives took on a new role. During the so-called political cycle of Kirchnerist governments,[1] co-operative creation was used as a meaningful tool in the social policy of inclusion and the fight against extreme poverty. In this context, various programmes incorporated association in worker co-operatives as a prerequisite for their beneficiaries.

Unlike recuperated enterprises, this wave of co-operativism promoted the formation of co-operatives more through the initiative of the state than civil society. This enabled this organisational form to spread, and mitigated or circumvented the problem of market insertion, but with widely differing and complex results, particularly in relation to the ventures' autonomy and their capacity to innovate for social change. Thus, whether the initiative comes from workers or from governments critical of neoliberalism, worker co-operativism has emerged in latter-day Argentina as an alternative to unemployment, but its very development fuels the hope in the area of theory and action at the global level that it will play a prominent role in the field of alternatives to capital.

Denise Kasparian's book, *Co-operative Struggles: Work Conflicts in Argentina's New Worker Co-operatives*, is one of the most original and polished pieces of research into these issues. It sets out to chart the new experiences of co-operativism from an unprecedented angle, at the intersection of the organisation of the socio-productive process and social conflict. Revisiting the old Marxist axiom that every mode of production is a mode of confrontation, the book poses the question of conflict in the new forms of work.

Unlike the mainstream of labour conflicts, it sets out to broaden the study of contentious events towards non-wage relations. Unlike the dominant approaches to the field of social and solidarity economy, conflict appears not only as a struggle for self-management but as a result of it. Far from being a territory where contradictions and tensions are extinguished, in self-management,

---

1 I refer to the government cycle ushered in by the presidency of Néstor Kirchner (2003–07) of the *Partido Justicialista* [Justicialist Party] (PJ) and the *Frente para la Victoria* [Front for Victory] (FpV), and continued by Cristina Fernández de Kirchner (PJ-FpV, 2007–11 and 2011–15).

they acquire new forms and are structured by new cleavages. Conflict presents itself as an operator inherent to the social organisation, and its character changes with the organisation. The thesis developed by Kasparian proposes that the democratisation of production implies the democratisation of conflict, not its disappearance. The class cleavage around working conditions tends to be displaced by a more horizontal, less stratified and aggregated conflict more diversified in the themes of its claims.

Based on comparative case studies complemented with different data sources, Kasparian adopts a critical stance to develop the analysis of the various socio-productive forms taken by the new co-operatives, as well as how they structure and are structured by social conflict. On the way, she steeps herself in a rich use of social theory. Her touchstone is Erik Olin Wright and his neo-Marxist approach but, with the heterodoxy required by the research, this is enriched by the use of other approaches from social theory. Diverse perspectives on economic sociology, the social and solidarity economy, social conflict and collective action are deployed on the way. The thesis is developed and specified masterfully and readably as we turn the pages, inviting us to read and to press ahead in this field of research with open minds.

Denise Kasparian is a sociologist, with a Ph.D. in Social Sciences, and a researcher at the *Consejo Nacional de Investigaciones Científicas y Técnicas* [National Scientific and Technical Research Council] (CONICET). She set out on her adventure of knowledge at the *Instituto Gino Germani* [Gino Germani Institute] of the *Universidad de Buenos Aires* [University of Buenos Aires] (UBA), where she still passionately pursues her research and teaching work today. Her work focuses on the fields of self-management, co-operativism, and the social and solidarity economy. She is, without a doubt, one of the most promising young writers in Argentinian sociology. *Co-operative Struggles* is her first magnum opus. The book is drawn from her doctoral thesis, first published in Spanish in 2020 by Editorial Teseo and the Faculty of Social Sciences, UBA, in Argentina, and defended with the highest honours at the UBA in 2017. This new English version of the book will surely facilitate circulation of the knowledge contained in Kasparian's work to new frontiers. I firmly believe that reading it will broaden the horizons of understanding of the challenges faced by co-operativism and self-management through its identification of the problems, dilemmas and strengths of 'working without bosses.' As a rigorous and unequivocal exponent of emancipatory social science, she expands our toolbox for social change. I would therefore extend this invitation to the reader to explore her pages and enjoy your reading.

Acknowledgements

This book draws on my Ph.D. in Social Sciences, earned at the University of Buenos Aires in Argentina. I would like to acknowledge the institutions and people who made the thesis as well as this book possible. I thank the *Consejo Nacional de Investigaciones Científicas y Técnicas* [National Scientific and Technical Research Council] (CONICET), the University of de Buenos Aires, the Gino Germani Research Institute, the *Centro Cultural de la Cooperación* [Cultural Centre of Co-operation] and the *Agencia nacional de promoción de la investigación, el desarrollo tecnológico y la innovación* [National Agency for Promotion of Research, Technological Development and Innovation] (Agencia I+D+i) for funding the research.

I am particularly grateful to my advisor, Julián Rebón, and to my co-advisor, Rodrigo Salgado. I would like to thank also María Maneiro, and the examining committee members María Inés Fernández Álvarez, Verónica Maceira and Malena Hopp. I am also thankful to my colleagues and friends from the *Observatorio Social sobre Empresas Recuperadas y Autogestionadas* [Social Observatory on Recuperated and Self-Managed Enterprises] (OSERA), the *Taller de investigaciones sobre cambio social* [Research Workshop on Social Change] of the Department of Sociology, UBA, and the Gino Germani Research Institute. Specially, Juan Miguel Ainora, Natalia Bauni, María Eugenia Díaz, Gabriel Fajn, Leandro Gamallo, Candela Hernández, Eugenia Mattei, Agustina Súnico, Melina Tobías and Fabio Troncoso.

I am indebted to Erik Olin Wright; whose untimely and sad death left the *Pathways to a Cooperative Market Economy* project unfinished. Different parts of this book were inspired by this work and presented during the Buenos Aires and Johannesburg meetings of the project. I would like to thank the Series Editor, David Fasenfest, the Production Editor, Judy Pereira, and Michelle Williams for the orientation during the preparation of the manuscript. A special acknowledgement to all those people whom I interviewed during the course of the research and, in particular, to the workers of the two co-operatives that I analyse in depth in the book.

I wish to thank Pablo Alí and Ian Barnett for their expertise and commitment with this book, and to Alejandro, Ana and Miguel for their love and support during the laborious years of research to earn the Ph.D.

I end by thanking Diego, for his supportive guidance, suggestions and insights, and above all, for his love and for taking care of me.

Illustrations

Figures

1. Frequency of annual enterprise recuperations: Argentina, 1996–2015   30
2. Percentage distribution of knowledge and assessment of enterprise recuperation: AMBA, 2012   34
3. Nominal annual Argentina Works Programme budget implementation deflated to 2009 Argentinian pesos (millions of Argentinian pesos): Argentina, 2009–2015   55
4. Nominal monthly evolution of Argentina Works Programme's individual subsidies, minimum living adjustable wage, and salaries for private household workers: Argentina, August 2009–September 2015   67
5. Number of collective actions by unemployed workers' organisations under Argentina Works Programme by month and period: Argentina, September 2009–June 2012   68
6. Claims made during collective actions by unemployed workers' organisations under Argentina Works Programme by period (in percentages): Argentina, September 2009 – June 2012   71

Tables

1. Numbers of recuperated enterprises and recuperated enterprise workers: Argentina, 2004, 2010, 2013, 2016   31
2. Percentage distribution of assessment of enterprise recuperation by class position and economic activity status: AMBA, 2012   35
3. Main policies for associational and self-managed work from the ministry for social development and the ministry for labour, employment and social security: Argentina, 2003–2015   40
4. Total Argentina Works Programme and co-operatives per annum: Argentina, 2009–2015   54

Images

1. The co-operative's location   112
2. The co-operative's neighbourhood   141
3. Composition of the co-operative by 'cumpas' and 'recursos'   146
4. The co-operative's activity   193

Introduction

Let us begin at the end. On 20 July 2016, in an adverse social and economic climate (increased public utility rates, falling domestic consumption, public works at a standstill, dwindling social schemes), 10,000 co-operative workers occupied the length and breadth of 9 de Julio Avenue, one of the busiest arteries in Buenos Aires, and thereby succeeded in obtaining an audience with the officials of three ministries to deal with their demands. This and so many other protests demonstrate these co-operatives' power to mobilise, formed as a result of the recuperation of enterprises and the implementation of the *Programa Argentina Trabaja* [Argentina Works Programme] (PAT). Even more thought-provoking, it shows their ability to voice demands as a united front and – for all their particularities and differences – stands as proof of common interests and objectives.

That said, this collective action is a clear example of an emerging reality in early-twenty-first-century Argentina: new forms of worker co-operativism that become actors not just in production but in social struggle. The protest described above is the end point of the processes addressed in this book. The research it contains unfolds in the prelude that leads up to it.[1]

Argentina has a long history of co-operativism linked to European immigration from the mid-nineteenth century to the early twentieth. Most of the twentieth was dominated by co-operatives in agriculture, public utilities and consumption. Worker co-operatives, on the other hand, got off to a slower start, and it was not until 1990 that they saw significant growth against a backdrop of rising unemployment and precarisation from neoliberal reforms. At the start of the twenty-first century, the strain on the model of accumulation emerging from neoliberal reforms (Basualdo, 2013) expressed itself in a severe and generalised crisis. It was under conditions like these that worker co-operatives gained unprecedented momentum and restructured the co-operative sector as a whole.

---

1 This book is based on my doctoral research carried out at the Faculty of Social Sciences, University of Buenos Aires (UBA), between 2012 and 2017, and published virtually by Teseo Publishers (Kasparian, 2020a), and on a series of articles containing partial advances or thematic demarcations, published between 2013 and 2020 in academic journals in Argentina, Brazil, Chile, Spain, the United States and Venezuela. For more information, see Kasparian 2013a, 2013b, 2014, 2017a, 2017b, 2017c, 2019a, 2019b, 2019c and 2020b. Also, Rebón and Kasparian 2015 and 2018 and Rebón, Kasparian and Hernández 2015 and 2016.

By around 2011, when the ideas for this research were beginning to take shape, the exponential rise of worker co-operatives and the increasing role of their members in various popular protests and demonstrations was conspicuous. This new twenty-first-century worker co-operatives was driven mainly by two processes: recuperation of enterprises by their workers and state incubation of co-operatives by promoting a social and solidarity economy. Between 2001 and 2002, according to National Institute of Associations and the Social Economy (INAES) data, co-operativism encompassed 16,059 co-operatives, 42% of which were worker co-operatives; a decade later in 2012, the picture was different: out of a total of 21,002 co-operatives, the number of worker-run co-operatives reached 72% (Acosta, Levin and Verbeke, 2013; Montes and Ressel, 2003).

This specific sector of the co-operative movement became far more heterogeneous (Rebón and Kasparian, 2015). Co-operative formation since the start of the twenty-first century has fallen under the umbrella-term 'new social economy,' in contrast to the historical experiences of co-operativism and mutualism that make up the 'traditional social economy' (Pastore, 2010). Mirta Vuotto (2011) points out that there are three models of co-operative, gauged by their performance as businesses and associations: 'integrated,' 'claims-based' and 'state-induced.' While the 'integrated' model would be close to the experiences of the 'traditional social economy,' the 'claims-based' and 'state-induced' models belong to the twenty-first century as co-operatives respectively formed through enterprise recuperation processes or backed by public policy. In 'claims-based' co-operatives, the worker collective shares previous experience of wage labour in a non-co-operative organisation, whereas 'state-induced' productive units are promoted by public policy and made up of excluded individuals, for whom need is the prime motive.

Given this state of affairs, my initial question was what forms of work and production do these new twenty-first-century worker co-operatives produce? Certain normative, doctrinaire definitions from international bodies and the Argentine state and legislation helped to outline a first, tentative answer. Co-operatives represent an organisational form of the economy aimed at meeting such social needs as providing access to health services, housing and public utilities, organising financing schemes, and many other needs. This type of organisation is founded on the voluntary association of people, collective ownership and democratic control.

To what extent is this formal definition consistent with the various prevailing socio-productive forms? How to move forward in conceptualising them sociologically, particularly seeing that these co-operatives' special feature is that they address a specific need: namely, to provide their members with work?

They are in fact a socio-productive form not structured on wage relationships, where workers are at the same time members of the organisation. In other words, they are co-operative workers without bosses.

Although this increase in co-operatives went hand in hand with renewed labour disputes (Etchemendy and Collier, 2008), neither academic research nor public debate had taken an interest in exploring and tackling these issues within the field of co-operativism. My central concern then was to identify the patterns of conflict in these co-operative enterprises without bosses: why, how and by what cleavages and groupings does the labour force come into conflict in socio-productive units not structured on wage relations? This book looks at the configuration and dynamics of work conflicts in co-operatives in Argentina between 2003 and 2015, and particularly at two paradigmatic types of the new co-operativism: enterprises recuperated by their workers and co-operatives backed by social policy.

To this end, I describe both types of co-operatives in terms of their socio-geneses and socio-productive characteristics. I identify the main cleavages and divides in the formation of social groups in both types of co-operatives and describe the work conflicts on the basis on their forms, demands, actors and impacts. Finally, I break new ground by comparing paradigmatic but not equivalent experiences of the new co-operativism.

1 The Question of Work Conflicts in New Co-operatives

Certainly, even in the context of the objectivity needed for any scientific contribution, research must not detach itself from its political implications and horizons. I therefore set out to produce knowledge from the perspective of an emancipatory social science. The goal of such a science is to build knowledge to create the conditions for an equal, democratic post-capitalist social order (Wright, 2006).

First, referring to this enterprise in terms of science rather than social criticism or philosophy aims to produce systematic scientific knowledge about how the world works and to subject it to a constant open dialogue. Second, to describe this science as 'emancipatory' is to declare its moral purpose: to eliminate oppression and create conditions for human flourishing. So, given the goal of producing knowledge from this position, there are three overarching tasks for any emancipatory social science: 1) to develop a systematic, critical diagnosis of the world as it exists; 2) to imagine and conceive viable alternatives; 3) to understand the obstacles, possibilities and dilemmas of social transformation (Wright, 2006).

The idea – and the practices surrounding it – that an alternative mode of production is needed to eliminate all forms of exploitation and domination has been around for two centuries (De Sousa Santos and Rodríguez, 2011; Quijano, 2011). More recently, since the late twentieth century and the early twenty-first, the debate around alternative forms of production has mainly been reflected in the notions of 'social economy,' 'solidarity economy,' 'popular economy' and others. In what elements would the alternative, emancipatory nature of the experiences of the social economy lie? The alternatives are viewed as ways of increasing social power – or the power of civil society; pathways trodden with concrete institutional innovations (Wright, 2006). Even under the preponderance and domination of the capitalist mode of production, considering the heterogeneous nature of all social formation (Hobsbawm, 2009; Marx, 2009) allows us to posit that the development of institutional alternatives to increase social power deepens its socialist character and erodes dominant capitalism in the here and now.

In this framework, Erik Olin Wright (2012) identifies the social economy as a way to boost social empowerment. Worker co-operatives are a concrete institutional proposal notable because it reverses the very foundation of the capitalist mode of production: the dispossession of the direct producers of their means of production. Paul Singer (2007) argues that the solidarity economy, whose typical unit is the worker co-operative, is a mode of production that, though at first glance forming a hybrid between capitalism and small-scale commodities production, is in fact a synthesis that exceeds both. When there is a deliberate attempt to join up isolated experiences into more structured alternatives to capitalism, worker co-operatives and organisations of the social economy may form interstitial anti-capitalist emancipatory strategies: that is, they develop in the gaps or cracks in society. This is so regardless of the fact that, taken individually, they may not constitute systemic challenges, since they depend on and relate to capitalist markets (Williams, 2014).

These analyses are intended to map the ways open to social processes or their potentialities. They are not intended to replace research into social reality with the researcher's wishes. I do not therefore approach co-operatives based on normative or doctrinaire models that put us on the level of the 'ought-to-be.' Nor do I take a systemic view, as this would only enable these experiences to be conceptualised as activities within a political economy of poverty aimed at deepening precarity and marginalisation. In contrast, I approach the analysis of worker co-operatives based on the certainty of the heterogeneity of social reality. The definition of 'worker co-operative' presented at the opening of this book, as Fernando Balbi (1998) notes, thus delimits a universe in terms of formal levels of organisation and so is simply a starting point.

INTRODUCTION

In short, from the twenty-first century onwards, worker co-operativism was driven primarily by two processes: the recuperation of enterprises by their workers and the promotion of worker co-operatives by social policy. On one hand, recuperated enterprises are productive units in crisis whose workers take up the reins of production, usually by forming worker co-operatives. These social processes spread like wildfire after Argentina's extensive crisis of 2001–2002. Their central importance to the universe of worker co-operatives does not lie in their scope: by the end of 2015, the number of recuperated enterprises did not exceed 400. We contend that their importance rests first and foremost on their installation in the social imaginary. In 2012, the research groups I belong to[2] conducted a door-to-door survey entitled "Alternative Economic Forms,"[3] representing the population over eighteen years of age in the Buenos Aires Metropolitan Area (AMBA), Argentina's main urban area. The data from the survey supported the hypothesis that, while there are relatively few recuperated enterprises, they are widely known among the population: 83% of respondents had heard of recuperated enterprises, while 87% identified that this conceptualisation refers to an enterprise in crisis whose workers take over production (Rebón and Kasparian, 2015).

Second, a large number of recuperated enterprises are the result of closures of major factories in their sectors (Fasinpat, formerly Zanón; Renacer, formerly Aurora Grundig; Cristal Avellaneda, formerly Durax; and others). This is not only important in itself when it comes to determining the centrality of recuperated enterprises but also gives rise to a third major element. Set up on previous productive processes, recuperated enterprises have possession –though not necessarily ownership – of the means of production.

Co-operatives included in public policies, however, are central in terms of their numbers. In 2003, the national state launched a series of schemes to

---

[2] The *Taller de Investigación sobre Cambio Social* [Research Workshop on Social Change] of the Department of Sociology, UBA, led by Professor Julián Rebón, and the *Observatorio Social sobre Empresas Recuperadas y Autogestionadas* [Social Observatory on Recuperated and Self-Managed Enterprises] (OSERA) of the Gino Germani Research Institute, coordinated by Rodrigo Salgado.

[3] We worked with a probabilistic, stratified, multi-stage sample design. The main aim was to collect perceptions and assessments about alternative economic forms. The sample contained 599 cases with a 4% margin of error. The survey was conducted as part of the UBA research project, "*La cultura de la recuperación de empresas. Representaciones y valoraciones de los trabajadores sobre el proceso*" [Enterprise Recuperation Culture: Workers' Representations and Assessments of the Process], jointly with the *Centro para el Desarrollo de la Economía Social y América Latina* [Centre for the Development of the Social Economy in Latin America] (CEDESAL).

promote worker co-operativism in the social and solidarity economy as a job creation strategy. The establishment of worker co-operatives through government schemes has altered the shape of the sector. By 2012, 76% of active co-operatives fell under public policy (Acosta, Levin and Verbeke, 2013). These co-operatives' activities are grounded in state demand and focused on housing, social infrastructure and maintenance of public spaces (Vuotto, 2011). Among the various schemes to set up co-operatives, the *Programa de Ingreso Social con Trabajo* [Social Income with Work Programme], commonly known as *Argentina Trabaja* [Argentina Works], created in 2009 by the national state, stands out for its mass outreach, territorial expanse and large budget.

The new angle expressed in this book is that it asks itself about work conflicts in these socio-productive forms not structured on wage relations and therefore traditionally relegated from studies on labour disputes. To ask this research question involves revising the notions of 'work' and 'labour disputes.'

The notion of 'work' refers to the ability of human action to transform reality according to a premeditated plan or end. During the twentieth century, two theoretical conceptions related to the advance of industrial capitalism and wage labour encouraged a restricted view of this concept. Whereas the neoclassical conception only looks at work that is bought and sold for a paid wage, the classical Marxist conception, while not restricting the concept of work to the wage earner, favours its analysis and believes that the working class – in a restricted sense – is called on to undertake a historical task (De la Garza Toledo, 2009).

Where labour disputes are concerned, from a classical Marxist perspective, the unique feature of the labour force is that it not only transfers its own value to the commodity it produces but has the ability to create value or surplus value during the productive process (Marx, 2011). The difference between the exchange value paid by the capital and the labour force's use value in capitalist consumption, made viable through the capital's function of management, is a structural antagonism that is key to understanding social conflict in the capital–labour relationship (Marx, 2011). Indeed, the structuring elements of the confrontation take shape in the productive process. Accordingly, the concept of 'labour conflict' has traditionally been used to designate oppositions and confrontations between capital and work in capitalist social formations.

By the 1960s, labour relations formed an object of study in modern social sciences based on the 'industrial relations system' devised by John Dunlop (1958). This functionalist approach, which regarded conflicts as a pathological fact and denied the contradictory character of production relations (Bauni, 2011), while concerning itself with "conflicts exclusively from a control perspective in a situation of normality and balance" (Kohler and Artiles,

2007: 138), predominated for a time. By the 1970s, Harry Braverman triggered the so-called 'labour process debate' by positing that the changing shape of worker–employer relations was primarily motivated by issues of control and class power, not by apparently abstract principles of organisational efficiency, neutral technological imperatives or an inevitable modernising dynamic (Smith, 1995). From a neo-Marxist perspective, the basic premise then was that labour relations in contemporary capitalist societies are an inevitable source of conflict – and provisional pacts – given the opposition of interests between the owners of the means of production and the workers as vendors of the labour force in the relations of control, domination and exploitation in the labour process (Hyman, 1981).

The central importance of Braverman's contribution lies not only in his premises but in the studies he prompted. According to Vicki Smith (1995), by granting capitalists a preponderant power to design labour processes and organisations to maximise the extraction of surplus value and the exercise of control, Braverman underestimated the interests, resilience and co-operation of workers as transformative factors in labour processes and conflicts. By the 1980s and 1990s then, a series of studies began to analyse the feedback between workers' resistance and the diversification of forms of labour control (Edwards, 1978), and the contribution of workers' consent to domination in capitalist enterprises, as conceptualised in terms of hegemony (Burawoy, 1989).

To study conflict in labour relations, P.K. Edwards (1990) proposes three levels of analysis. The first and most basic level is structured antagonisms, which refers to the basis of conflicts in labour relations and, as I have mentioned, expresses a group's appropriation of the surplus value created by the labour force. The second level is the organisation of labour relations in the workplace, where the co-existence and intertwining of conflict and co-operation in the organisation of the productive process becomes intelligible. The last level, that of concrete behaviour, where there is variation in the forms of expression of the conflict, refers to manifest and planned actions but also to hidden forms of deliberate resistance enshrined in widespread collective practices. Ultimately, labour disputes involve inter-class struggles, which may be directed against capitalists or the state as an intermediary or agent of capital (Silver, 2005).

That said, as I have pointed out, these theoretical tools are based on the conception of work as a social relation of employment: in other words, a specific social form of work that is paradigmatic in modern and contemporary societies. Work, however, is a social relationship that goes beyond employment (Castillo, 2000; Quijano, 2013), and so, to analyse forms not restricted to wage earning, such notions as 'control over the labour process,' 'labour market,' 'labour regulations' are limited, especially when it comes to settling worker-boss conflicts (De la Garza Toledo, 2009). This broader way of conceiving work is not grounded in an ideal-type definition of a labour relationship but on a conception of the labour relationship as an interaction between key actors in the productive process.

In summary, this book applies some of the theoretical tools presented thus far: forms of control in relation to worker resistances (Edwards, 1978), the identification of the central and oft-forgotten role of consent in domination (Burawoy, 1989), as well as the three levels of conflict analysis, identifying their structuring factors and the interactions between conflict and co-operation, as well as the concrete forms of the conflict (Edwards, 1990).

From this point, I apply the notion of 'work conflicts' in order to distance myself from the concept of 'labour disputes,' used to designate oppositions and confrontations between capital and labour around consumption and exchange conditions of the labour force in the capitalist mode of production. This book then posits that 'work conflicts' refer to struggles over the conditions of access to, consumption of and remuneration for work, a perspective that goes beyond the classic social relationship of employment. It goes without saying that these struggles vary from one socio-productive form to another.

Approaching the subject through the study of social formations allows us to grasp the complexity introduced – even under the preponderance and domination of the capitalist mode of production – by the combination of multiple modes of production in actual societies. In particular, I highlight the suggestion made by Wright (1994) regarding the various types of contradictions and potential confrontations that can be triggered by different modes of production and their combinations. It is therefore relevant to problematise the many socio-productive forms and modes of work conflict in contemporary Argentina's social formation, especially in worker co-operatives.

Among the book's findings, I suggest that the socio-productive characteristics of the recuperated enterprises and co-operatives in the Argentina Works Programme impact the configuration and dynamics of work conflicts. The book's central thesis thus contends that the way production is socially organised affects work conflicts. I argue that, in both types of co-operatives, compared to productive organisations structured on wage relations, labour relations are democratised and the function of management is politicised. There emerge in this field lines of work conflicts[4] founded on elements that are not expressed in traditional capitalist enterprises with equal importance, such as workers' various

---

4 One line of conflict involves competing actors, forms of action and reasons for the dispute, as well as demands made.

perceptions of their own work, the emergence of numerous enterprise projects, the generations of workers in the productive unit, lattices of comradeship and labour hierarchies.

In addition to the above conditions of possibility bestowed by the co-operative form, there is a politicisation of the conflict that goes beyond the productive unit and differs in nature and intensity from one co-operative to the next. Whereas such politicisation in recuperated enterprises is linked to the fact that the productive process – and hence its management – involves any political actions necessary for the co-operative's sustainability and the formal possession of the productive unit, in the Argentina Works Programme its management is linked to the presence of formal state institutions.

Regarding conflicts that extend beyond the productive unit, I notice that the class cleavage does not necessarily go away. Some politicisation is also apparent in such conflicts inasmuch as the state takes a central role. Again, depending on the type of co-operative in question, both the character and the importance of the state varies in such conflicts. That said, alongside this meaningful link between socio-productive form and conflicts, the analysis of the specific conflicts described requires the incorporation of other elements in the chain of causality that are not to do with the socio-productive form. I refer both to the specific socio-geneses, histories and cultures of co-operatives and their members, and to the political opportunity structures and organisational resources available for contentious action. In short, I argue that actual conflicts are the result of a barrage of factors: the mode in which production is socially organised is a key to understanding the way these conflicts are structured, but it is not the only one.

2   Dimensions of New Social Conflicts in Co-operative Socio-productive Contexts

This thesis does not take an anomic or pathological view of the conflict. I believe it is impossible to conceive of a social configuration free of conflict. Quite the reverse, following Georg Simmel (1904), conflict is a form of socialisation as inherent to social life as co-operation, as constitutive of unity as harmony. Similarly, Lewis Coser (1970) suggests that it can become a catalyst for creativity and innovation. Specifically, all social conflict refers to a certain type of social relationship, namely, configurations of reciprocally corresponding actions (Piaget, 1986), in which the actions of at least one of the actors aim to hamper the other (Rebón, 2007). As a result, conflict furnishes a thought-provoking sociological productivity, coming to form a topic that prompts us to explore the configuration of the conflicting social groups, and their power relations, inequalities and hierarchies, on the one hand, and the innovation and social change in the worker co-operatives that arise from the conflicts on the other.

To analyse the causal link between socio-productive characteristics and work conflicts, we draw on the contributions of Wright (1994, 2012, 2015) on social forms of production and the degrees to which they enable social empowerment in the economy. Two entailments of this theoretical perspective are particularly important. First is its description of social forms of production as inevitably mixed, complex or hybrid, formed from various patterns of articulation and interpenetration of modes of production. Second, and related to the first premise, the social relations of production structure contradictions and potential confrontations.

In this way, in tackling my object of study, I use Wright (1994, 2012, 2015) to profile the co-operatives.[5] This socio-productive profiling explores the set of social relations that order such a process (Rebón, 2007; Salgado, 2012). Indeed, the socio-productive process is dealt with in all its social dimensions, and the social includes the economic, the political and the ideological (Wright, 1994). I thus identify cleavages and divides in the formation of social groupings and potential confrontations which are the result of the combined presence of elements characteristic of different modes of production in the co-operatives.

Wright's first dimension concerns property relations, insofar as ownership of the means of production is a condition for its use and control, and thus for the appropriation of the fruits of its utilisation, assuming therefore the exclusion of others (Marx, 2009). The character of the ownership of the means of production makes certain types of social relations likely to develop rather than others. So, for example, in productive units whose ownership relies on direct producers, collective self-appropriation of the fruits of labour may occur, built on democratic, participative decisions regarding work-rates, modes of distributing and utilising any income, and other issues.

---

[5] To avoid decontextualising the theoretical tools I use, I should mention that the schema in Wright (1994) is designed to study social formations in transitional societies and post-capitalist futures. This text was first published in 1979 and, as the author clarifies, is marked by the intellectual and political context of the day. However, the schema is clearly sufficiently rich and apposite to handle worker co-operatives on a micro scale, with the necessary local adaptations and contributions of the research team I belong to (Rebón, 2015; Salgado, 2012), by considering the exemplifications and suggestions in Wright's text, where the author makes use of the scale of productive units, as well as dimensions of the schema in subsequent texts to analyse specific institutions and cases, including co-operatives (Wright, 2012, 2015).

Ownership of a productive unit may be private, state or social. While private ownership is based on the established right of individuals or groups of individuals over a commodity, state ownership refers to such a right as exercised by the state. Finally, in social ownership, appropriation is the product of a collectivity or community – not isolated individuals or associated shareholders – that engages interdependently in economic activities. That said, the extent to which any particular social ownership moves away from or draws near to its full or abstract notion – namely, that encompassing the whole human species – can be addressed in three variables: its depth, breadth and inclusiveness or level of social aggregation. The first variable concerns the scope of rights effectively under social control and varies from full ownership to limited forms of possession or usufruct (Rebón, 2015). The second observes the scale or importance of the set of activities or commodities involved in the ownership relation. The third variable focuses on the type of people who control and use the means of production and may include anything from a small community to an entire nation, via a state with significant levels of democracy (Rebón, 2015).

Wright's second dimension concerns the analysis of the logic of production in the sense of the criteria, principles and purposes guiding the allocation of resources and the disposition of any surpluses in the socio-productive units. On one hand, there is the immediate destination of production and, on the other, the destination of the surplus – if any – or the purpose of production in the sense of its ultimate goal. The immediate destination of the production may have two values, namely those of exchange or use. In exchange, goods are produced that can be exchanged in traditional capitalist markets, whereas, in use, products are geared to meeting needs and their production is therefore linked to criteria of need and use. Strictly speaking, market buying and selling is not the sole principle of exchange in our societies, and even usable goods can be bought and sold. Here, I draw on Karl Polanyi (2007) to go deeper into the various principles of behaviour – beyond the mercantile one – that may guide the exchanges and circulation of goods, services and persons in societies. On the one hand, I wish to reinstate this author's suggestion that the market principle can give rise not just to markets with a claim to self-regulation, but also – and primarily, throughout human history – to regulated markets immersed in general social relations. On the other hand, Polanyi (2007) introduces two principles of behaviour not usually associated with the economy that provided food for thought: namely, reciprocity and redistribution.

The principle of reciprocity has to do with exchanges between symmetrical pairs in a gift–counter-gift dynamic or, in other words, forming a circuit of obligations to give, receive and give back (Mauss, 2010). This involves offering others a good or a service with no assurance of reward but with expectations of reciprocation (Caillé, 2009) or countergift, understood as an obligation to give back. This principle thus also constitutes circuits for the exchange of goods, albeit in the framework of trust-based relations or alliance-building.

The principle of redistribution has to do with the distribution of goods organised through a central authority that collects, stores and redistributes the social production to avoid the disintegration of society. This principle is analysed in the context of a society's political regime. A clear example of this are Welfare States as conceptualised by Gøsta Esping-Andersen (1993), which provide goods or services as rights. As a result, they withdraw from the market, and the importance of the principle of market exchange is played down via inter-generational, inter-class and other redistribution mechanisms.

The destination of the surplus or the purpose of production can either target the accumulation of means of production in order to increase productive capacity and obtain greater surpluses, or else individual or collective end consumption to meet needs. Wright (1994) also introduces another type of accumulation, characteristic of the statist mode: politico-bureaucratic accumulation focused on the accumulation of usable goods. On this basis and articulated with specific contributions on social policy, the sustainability of social and solidarity economy ventures, and the territoriality of political practices in the popular sectors, this book outlines a specific kind of non-bureaucratic political accumulation.

Wright's third dimension is the political aspect of production relations in approaching the ways power organises itself during the productive process, where political relations may take one of two forms: domination or self-determination. Therefore, to explore this dimension, I analyse the degrees of both the internal democracy and the autonomy of co-operatives in light of extra-unit productive powers. Specific developments regarding self-management are important here, as are the above-mentioned tools specific to the study of labour conflict in terms of forms of control and the production of consent. Also important are works on social movements and their links with the state based on a dynamic of bargaining and conflict.

Wright's fourth and last dimension is to do with the nature of groups determined by production relations. It allows us to analyse the characteristics set by the other three dimensions' structural properties in the formation of social groupings, their principal social relations and potential conflicts between them. To this end, it is necessary to determine, in the event there are any such groupings, who makes up the ruling groups and who the subordinate ones, as well as the source of power – or what the ruling groups control or monopolise – that defines the mechanism of appropriation by certain groups and the exclusion of others. Throughout the analysis, I make use of the notion of 'cleavage'

INTRODUCTION

to refer to lasting, stable divides of confrontation among groups, which tend to organise the conflicts (Lipset and Rokkan, 1967).[6]

I also revisit theoretical developments regarding collective action and social movements. In particular, contributions on resistance movements to commodification provide tools to analyse the processes of socio-genesis in the new types of co-operatives I deal with. Specifically, I reinstate the developments of Beverly J. Silver (2005) regarding global labour movements and their long-term dynamics, and those of Michael Burawoy (2008, 2015) regarding new social resistance movements to commodification. Both authors make an association between Marx's *Capital* and Polanyi's *The Great Transformation* when characterising contemporary social and labour struggles.

According to Silver and Burawoy, the background to the struggles lies in the fictitious nature of work as a commodity: it is not a good that has been produced for sale on the market. The fiction suggested by the transformation of work into a commodity is that, according to Marx, it may lose its use value under certain conditions of exploitation for the extraction of surplus value or, according to Polanyi, of exchange in the labour market. In other words, excessive exploitation during the labour process or a deregulated exchange of the labour force produces worker resistance, insofar as such commodification may even mean the death of the human bearer of this labour force. The singularity of the labour force thus lies in the fact that its commodification and productive consumption simultaneously presupposes the creation of the conditions to resist them.

Burawoy (2008, 2015) utilises this schema to understand contemporary social movements. These are formed as modes of resistance to the commodification of both work and other fictitious commodities: land, money and knowledge. In relation to the workers' movement, he argues that it takes on a new character in that the focus is placed on marginalised workers and on the impossibility of guaranteeing social reproduction, rather than on the conditions of exploitation in the workplace. This is because, paradoxically, the problem in today's societies is the disappearance of the guarantee of exploitation and, taking its place, the rise of precarity. Thus, the unlimited commodification of the labour force – in other words, the deregulation of this market – implies not only a lack of protection in the face of forms of recruitment and dismissal, and wages below the cost of social reproduction, but also its disuse. Indeed, the struggles

---

6　Although Seymour Lipset and Stein Rokkan (1967) coin this concept in order to account for the cleavages that organise lasting social conflict at the macro-social level in Western European political systems, its use is relevant as it enables us to distinguish persistent divides from more flexible, changeable ones.

tend to include wage earners, people who have no access to wage labour and people facing other types of commodification (access to public utilities, land and so forth).

In addition to Burawoy and Silver's contributions, to analyse the shift from grievance to collective action, first and foremost in the case of enterprise recuperation, it is necessary to delve into the cultural fabric surrounding work in Argentinian society. To do this, I make use of the notion 'moral economy of work' (Rebón, Kasparian and Hernández, 2016), which join up conceptualisations of E.P. Thompson (1979) and Thomas C. Arnold (2001). In Thompson, 'moral economy' refers to a popular consensus anchored in the past that allows people to distinguish economic practices according to their legitimacy and establish a cultural framework to inspire and legitimise collective action. The author analyses the cultural mediations between deprivation and collective action that operate as legitimising notions. This concept helps then to explain how popular consensuses around the legitimacy of certain practices in relation to certain goods stand as inspiration for collective action when there is a marked inequality or break regarding such practices and therefore also as potential limiters of commodification processes.

Our proposed notion of the 'moral economy of work' takes up the importance of the cultural framework in collective action from Thompson (1979). The moral economy stands as a legitimising notion in turning deprivation into grievance and in inspiring action, which works – even with the threat of it in times of inequality – as a limiter and shaper of social relations of production. Unlike Thompson's perspective, this legitimising notion does not boil down to a criterion founded on a pre-capitalist past but may have its origins in another stage of capitalism, operating in a new way in the current context. Similar to Arnold's conceptualisation (2001) of 'social goods,' we refer to a specific good, the labour force, which in the context of a cultural configuration takes on a set of social attributes that limit its commodification and, in the case of recuperated enterprises, leads to social innovations in production relations.

Put succinctly, the moral economy of work is defined by the specific ways a historical form of work is socially valued in conjunction with and opposition to other values. In this sense, it opens up a field of possibility for the conflict. In particular, it helps us understand the moments when the forms taken by the commodification of work tend toward social dislocation. In these situations, the moral principle associated with work may expand and temper other values – such as private property – to become a significant legitimiser of collective action, even when this goes beyond the institutional channels for processing social conflict.

In examining the contentious dimension of these new co-operatives' socio-geneses and the specific constitutions of the ones we deal with as case studies, the literature on social movements and collective action produced by the angle of the study of the political processes, referenced in Charles Tilly and Sidney Tarrow, has been particularly fertile. This contentious dimension was expressed in the public space and took the form of a social movement. This angle therefore provides tools that help to describe the contentious public nature of socio-genesis, to conceptualise the notion of social movement and to comprehend the interaction of conflicts with institutionalised politics and wider political-social contexts.

3 The Challenge of Comparing Paradigmatic but Non-equivalent Experiences: Studying a Whole That Acts as a Whole

The design of the research is based on a multiple instrumental case study (Stake, 1994/2013). Guided by the logic of complementarity, this combines quantitative and qualitative sources and methodologies (Vasilachis de Gialdino, 1992), predominantly qualitative. This strategy proved the most appropriate from the moment I began to couch my embryonic research question, as it helps to gain a deep, meticulous, contextualised grasp of work conflicts in co-operatives. This is true even after they have been established or consolidated, at which point their public dimension tends to diminish, and immersions in specific cases become necessary. This methodology enabled me to characterise the co-operatives in socio-productive terms. It also helped to identify the main cleavages and divides in the formation of groupings, and to characterise work conflicts.

I selected an enterprise recuperated by its workers and a co-operative from the Argentina Works Programme, both within the AMBA. This spatial cross-section is in response to the fact that the Metropolitan Area is home to half of all recuperated enterprises (Programa Facultad Abierta, 2014) and that the periphery of Buenos Aires is the principal geographical space targeted by this scheme. It is also a region of major importance in the study of social conflict given its centrality in Argentinian political processes.

In the time dimension, I looked at work conflicts over the period 2003–15, in response to a criterion anchored in the political processes (Tarrow, 1999). This period is characterised by the Argentinian government's development of a reformist policy that, in various areas, establishes breaks with the regressive trends of the previous period. I concentrate primarily on the policy of promoting worker co-operatives and their consequent increase.

The recuperated enterprise selected was formed in 2003 in Buenos Aires. It is a medium-sized enterprise in the services sector, with a fairly equal ratio of men and women, predominantly from the traditional working class and having a heterogeneous bag of career paths. The co-operative sells its services in the marketplace, which is the source of its workers' income. Framed in the Argentina Works Programme, the other co-operative was formed in 2010 in the Buenos Aires Conurbation.[7] It is a small-scale operation in the service sector and, unlike the first, consists primarily of women from similar work backgrounds, characterised by precarity and instability, and workers receive their income solely from the public policy subsidy. After I finished writing this book, major changes took place in these co-operatives. With the beginning of the presidency of Mauricio Macri in 2015, public policies aimed at co-operatives lost momentum and, in 2018, the Argentina Works Programme was shut down. That same year the co-operative I analysed decided to dissolve. In the case of the recuperated enterprise, in October 2020, in the context of the crisis of the COVID-19 pandemic, the enterprise had to leave its premises and relocate.

The case studies' representativeness is not bound by any statistical criterion representing a certain type of co-operative. Following the suggestions in the case-study literature, I have tried to ensure they respect a thematic, conceptual representativeness, capturing aspects, attributes and themes that I feel are crucial to exploring work conflicts. I have also taken up the observation by Robert Stake (1994/2013) about case selection for social research into consideration: the most important criterion should be to choose cases that allow us to learn more. He therefore suggests that the case selected should offer a variety of attributes and themes while providing better opportunities for learning. Finally, insofar as this book adopts a comparative approach, its potential for learning necessarily involves being mindful of the benefits of cases for comparative study. In this sense, if they are to be compared, cases must have both similar variables that remain constant and other dissimilar variables whose contrast is of interest (Lijphart, 1971).

My strategy is instrumental because I do not look at the individual cases for their intrinsic interest; rather, it is of secondary interest because it serves to understand a broader problem (Neiman and Quaranta, 2006): the phenomenon of work conflicts in co-operatives. Taking up Claudia Fonseca (1999), I suggest that "each case is not (only) a case." Research in qualitative social sciences observes and analyses specific empirical cases to reach conclusions with

---

7   The name '*conurbano bonaerense*' (literally 'Buenos Aires Conurbation') refers to twenty-four districts in Buenos Aires Province that make up an area linked to the city of Buenos Aires. Taken together they form the 'Metropolitan Area of Buenos Aires.'

a degree of generalisation. The cases are therefore classified in sociological and historical terms, with the focus on the social dimension of the processes in order to develop systems that go beyond the individual cases (Fonseca, 1999). From the case to the social, from the particular to the general: this is the way generalisations are built up. In connection with this, I have chosen to maintain the anonymity of the co-operatives, the social organisations in which they are embedded, the informants and the geographical locations (streets and addresses), without, however, losing their contextual, historical and sociological setting.

This is also a multiple case study and therefore enables an 'analytical generalisation' by predicting contrasting results for explicit reasons, which gives rise to 'theoretical' replications (Neiman and Quaranta, 2006). In this vein, my case study sets out to build a 'theoretical' replication through a comparative approach to case analysis. This approach describing similarities and differences aims to explain phenomena and processes by identifying probable links – more than necessary – between the different factors comprising the phenomena (Valdueco, 2012).

While my methodological strategy is based on the case study, when characterising the socio-genesis and development of co-operative formation, I also take a nationwide purview. Accordingly, I explore the social processes in which they are embedded and therefore go beyond the catchment of the AMBA.

Deploying qualitative and quantitative methodologies, and a variety of sources and techniques, I described the socio-geneses and development of both processes in latter-day Argentina. To this end, I collected and systematised literature on the subject, as well as public policies, regulations and legislation regarding new worker co-operatives at the national and sub-national levels. I also carried out documentary analyses of reports prepared by Argentina's Ministry for Social Development, international worker co-operative organisations and social organisations. I conducted interviews with an authority of the Federation of Worker Co-operatives of the Argentinian Republic (FECOOTRA) and a leading figure in the recuperated enterprises movement. Finally, to address certain specific dimensions, I turned to such complementary techniques and sources as the preparation of a catalogue of collective actions connected with the Argentina Works Programme undertaken by unemployed workers' organisations, and a systematic search for news about collective actions by recuperated enterprises. To these actions I applied qualitative content analysis.

In the case studies, I turned primarily to the technique of in-depth interviewing, using semi-structured guides, and of participant observation. We conducted a total of thirty-four interviews with co-operative members and key informants (leaders and leading social figures, public officials): nineteen for the case of the recuperated enterprise between 2006 and 2017; and fifteen with the case of the co-operative under the Argentina Works Programme between 2009 and 2016. The interviews were conducted as part of my doctoral research and together with colleagues in various group projects.[8]

I decided to add participant observation to the interview technique, as it allows access to a fragment of social reality beyond what is expressed by interviewees. Between 2011 and 2016, I observed daily work activities and routines in co-operatives, in both the workplace and elsewhere: demonstrations, events and demonstrations on public thoroughfares, social or political activities organised by co-operatives or the social organisations they are part of, as well as meetings of social organisations. Last, I make use of documentary analysis of primary sources (photographs taken during field-work) and secondary sources such as co-operative documents (statutes, internal regulations and organisation charts) and audio-visual recordings (documentaries on experiences).

4   The Structure of the Book

The book offers a structure that starts with global processes and goes on to analyse work conflicts in co-operatives through the strategy of the case study. The first two chapters describe the socio-genesis and development of the two main forms of worker co-operativism in twenty-first century Argentina. Chapter 1 deals with the formation of worker co-operatives through enterprise recuperation, while Chapter 2 explores the establishment of co-operatives by public policy. Both forms of co-operativism are characterised by highly conflictive socio-geneses anchored in demands and claims over work. I argue that this element is a cornerstone of the socio-productive features of co-operatives.

Chapter 3 looks at the conflicts in the origins of the two case studies and establishes a dialogue with the national scale provided in the first two chapters. Additionally, I note that the prolonged lack of definition of the problem of occupancy of the premises in the recuperated enterprise – typical of the early days of recuperations – means that the conflict remains open to some extent, even after the co-operative stabilises financially and productively. In the Argentina Works co-operative, the analysis of the constitutive conflict nuances the 'induced' character attributed to these experiences (Vuotto, 2011).

---

8 Detailed information can be found in the reference section, but I would like here to mention that these are publicly-funded research projects coordinated by Julián Rebón, Rodrigo Salgado and María Maneiro. I thank them for their mentoring and support.

INTRODUCTION

Chapters 4 and 5 provide a socio-productive description of the two worker co-operatives. This involves both the analysis of the social relations of production and the attributes of the workers making up each co-operative. On the one hand, in Chapter 4, I contend that the recuperated enterprise constitutes a form of workers' self-managed production in its interpenetrating elements of socialist and capitalist modes of production, with a predominance of social power. On basis of this observation, I identify an array of cleavages and divides in the establishment of groupings and potential conflicts.

In Chapter 5, I maintain that the Argentina Works co-operative constitutes a hybrid social form in which the statist mode of production dominates, subordinating the workers' self-managed production. I then present the cleavages and potential groupings at loggerheads shaped by this social form of production.

Chapter 6 looks at work conflicts in the recuperated enterprise and the Argentina Works co-operative once they are up and running. I establish linkages between these conflicts, the constitutive disputes and the co-operatives' socio-productive characteristics by identifying the structural divides and oppositions activated in the disputes. In the case of the recuperated enterprise, I elaborate on two work conflicts over the running of the co-operative and its regulations. In the Argentina Works co-operative, I investigate two other conflicts over the definition of its activity and the purpose of its production.

The conclusions take a coherent look at each chapter's main findings in light of my research question. Finally, I pose new questions and suggest lines of future study in order to contribute to emancipation and social empowerment in today's economies. This horizon of new forms of work will not be without its struggles, even if no bosses are involved.

CHAPTER 1

Co-operatives 'Made in Argentina'

The Process of Enterprise Recuperation by Their Workers

"A successful worker-recuperated enterprise is one that makes a successful stand for workers' dignity," said Mariano, a co-operative member at a food factory founded in 1971 and recuperated by its workers in 2002. These were the words with which he closed an interview I did in 2017. Although it had been fifteen years since the recuperation, Mariano's passion was still intact when recalling the events of 2002.

The convulsions of December 2001 were still being felt, not only in terms of the economic and political havoc they wrought, but in terms of the street demonstrations and renewed practices of political participation and organisation. It was January 2002, and overnight, while the factory workers were going through a period of suspension brought on by the economic crisis, a notice posted on the front door informed them of the enterprise's bankruptcy and the loss of all their jobs. There was nowhere for the workers to turn after thirty years in the same factory and a country lying in ruins.

The sudden closure was followed by six months' camping out at the factory gate. But the workers were not alone. That summer, activists from the incipient recuperated enterprise movement, together with the factory's workers, outlined the project needed to apply for a co-operative license. During the protest, neighbours, popular assemblies, university students and lecturers, trades union delegates and local shops donated food, supplies and services to the campers. State legislators and government officials provided subsidies and backed the adoption of a law expropriating the factory. Their situation was widely reported in the media. However, the judiciary were reluctant to rule in favour of a co-operative in the bankruptcy hearing:

> We went down on bended knee to the judge, begging him like to give us the factory to work in. [...] We fought for it, and we won the arm-fight thanks to this appeals judge who listened to the conversation, and the fireworks and drums outside. He called us in to see what our beef was. We handed over all the files and told him, "This is what we want: to W-O-R-K." A week later he called us and said, "*Muchachos* [Lads], the factory's yours."
>
> MARIANO, member of the recuperated food factory, October 2017; interviewee's emphasis

Finally, on 14 June 2002, they were able to return to the plant. They had won their dignity. And then began another story. Mariano's account contains all the ingredients of the enterprise recuperation process that spread throughout Argentina in the early twenty-first century: a bankrupt enterprise, a country in ruins, and a wide range of social actors supporting the workers.

This chapter describes the socio-genesis and evolution of enterprise recuperation, beginning with the widespread crisis of 2001–2002 and lasting until 2015. In terms of socio-genesis, I analyse the factors that enabled the process to spread and expand: the crisis of the productive unit as a structuring element at the enterprise level, the events of 2001 and 2002 as economic, political, and cultural amplifiers at the macro-social level, and the recuperated enterprise movement as a promoting agent.

Regarding the second moment, I identify the components that contributed to its evolution: the economic and political recovery after the generalised crisis; the cultural incorporation of recuperation in the workers' toolbox and the social imaginary; the impact of this cultural element on public policy, and the development of the recuperated enterprise movement.

Based on these co-ordinates, I outline a specific type of worker co-operative defined by the conflictual dimension of its socio-genesis and its roots in work-related protest. Exploring these origins lays the groundwork for analysing the constitutive conflict of the case study selected in Chapter 3 and its socio-productive characteristics in Chapter 4.

1   The Socio-genesis of the Processes of Enterprise Recuperation

1.1   *When Worker Resistance Becomes an Offensive Movement*

The main element informing the socio-genesis of the processes of enterprise recuperation is the crisis at the productive unit level (Rebón, 2007). These are triggered when, faced with the collapse of the reproduction of capital, the boss or business owner engages in various methods of undermining the wage relationship: wage cuts, arrears and partial payments, suspensions, bankruptcies followed by owner abandonment or fraudulent asset-stripping.

Whatever form it takes, this undermining of the wage relationship threatens the reproduction of the worker's life, not to mention their very identity, rooted as it is in stable salaried employment. It also paves the way for disobedience by provoking the boss's loss of legitimacy. Faced with this situation, ceasing to be a salaried employee is seen as the only way of continuing to work. The collective action of workers' recuperation is therefore not the result of a collective project devised according to ideological motivations with the aim of organising production under an associational, self-management model. On the contrary, it is a mechanism of resistance and defence of jobs, in other words, the way workers find to reproduce their identity (Fajn, 2003; Fernández Álvarez, 2007; Rebón, 2007). However, the defensive nature of this collective demonstration, understood as a response and resistance to the threatened or actual loss of jobs, introduces offensive elements into its development, namely, taking opportunities to encroach on opponents' properties, territories, and prerogatives (Tilly, 1978).

On one hand, the most emblematic – although not exclusive – way to carry out this defence is to occupy the productive establishment.[1] This constitutes an effective means of appropriating the enterprise's premises in order to prevent them from being asset-stripped and restart production. On the other hand, the occupation is followed by the start of production. The resulting productive process gives rise to changes in relation to the original capitalist enterprises. These include the transfer of the function of management from capital to the self-managed workers' collective and the alteration of property relations, creating fresh articulations between associated labour and ownership of the means of production (Rebón and Salgado, 2010). In short, the collective action of resistance involves an alteration of property and power relations within the productive units. In the terms of Mirta Vuotto (2011), recuperated enterprises conform to a claims-based co-operative model, insofar as they contain a logic of action akin to that of union claims. While there are precedents for this process,[2] the recuperations of enterprises spread and attracted public attention, as well as higher degrees of organisation from 2001 onwards, reaching their peak in 2002, when the economic depression deepened.

---

[1] In the field of labour conflict, the occupation of productive establishments has been a tool of struggle regularly used in Argentina since the mid-twentieth century (Cotarelo and Fernández, 1997). In general, occupations in the labour sphere have been associated with defensive disputes that seek to preserve the wage relationship (protests against lay-offs, workplace closures and others).

[2] Julián Rebón (2007) reviews the experiences between the late 1980s and early '90s which led to the formation of fifteen co-operatives by salaried employees in crisis-hit enterprises. Spearheaded by the Quilmes Branch of the Metal-Workers' Union (UOM), this process was concentrated in the south of the Buenos Aires Conurbation. Eventually it petered out and did not spread any further. Besides these experiences, some of the most emblematic cases in the recuperation process also emerged prior to the crisis of 2001 and 2002. This is the case, for example, with the Buenos Aires metal-working enterprise *Industrias Metalúrgicas y Plásticas Argentina* [Argentina Metal-Working and Plastics Industries] (IMPA).

1.2 The Widespread Crisis of 2001–2002, or Adding Fuel to the Fire

The late twentieth and early twenty-first centuries in Argentina saw the consolidation and subsequent waning of an economic model of accumulation based on financial valorisation. This model, which had started to take shape in the civil-military dictatorship that lasted from 1976 to 1983, was based on financial speculation sustained by external debt and favoured by differential national and international interest rates. From the 1990s, this model was consolidated by an unheard-of privatisation of state-owned enterprises, the restructuring of the state, deregulation of the economy and the labour market, the Convertibility Plan,[3] the opening of borders to imports and external debt (Basualdo, 2013).

By the mid-1990s, the golden age of convertibility (1991–1994) had come to an end, and the social and economic havoc wrought by the model became inescapable. As a result of the external opening of the commodities market, the process of deindustrialisation intensified, marking a transition from an industrial to a financial, agricultural and service-based economy. This deindustrialisation against a background of job-market deregulation precipitated an expulsion of the labour force which, added to the one caused by the privatisation of public services, increased levels of unemployment and contributed to the decline of real wages for workers. By the mid-1990s then, unemployment had risen to two figures, reaching 18.3% in 2001 (Basualdo, 2013). In this context, the process of expropriation unleashed on the Argentinian working classes was evident not only in unemployment and falling income, but also under-employment and labour precarisation, significantly impoverishing Argentinian society.

In 2001–02, this model erupted into an unprecedented, full-blown crisis. The context of this crisis created the economic and labour-market conditions on the one hand, and the cultural and political conditions on the other that spread enterprise recuperation processes (Rebón, 2007; Salgado, 2012). In economic and labour terms, the significant growth of enterprise closures and bankruptcies during this period increased the presence of the structuring element in the process (the crisis at the level of the productive unit). In addition to this, the deregulation of the labour market weakened the institutional mechanisms

---

3 The Convertibility Plan, popularly known as '*el uno a uno*' (the 1-to-1), established a fixed exchange rate for the Argentinian peso, in which one peso was the equivalent of one US dollar. In other words, an over-valued peso was pegged to the dollar. It was introduced in March 1991 and lasted until 2002. Its main aim was to curb inflation and stabilise prices. At first, it succeeded in stabilising prices and drove economic growth. However, as idle capacity fell, it began to be evident that convertibility was incapable of developing a sustainable economy in terms of progressive income distribution and economic growth (Basualdo, 2013).

to offset dismissals, namely, the possibilities of claiming indemnities as legally established compensation paid by employers to dismissed workers. In other words, there was an escalation of the commodification of work. The economic and labour-related context was the engine driving the spread of this means of defending jobs during the crisis of the productive unit.

To analyse the transition from the deprivation caused by job losses to the action of recuperation, it is not sufficient to simply refer to the economic and labour-market conditions created by the widespread crisis. To understand the moral ammunition that transforms deprivation into grievance and triggers the action of recuperation, along with support and tolerance for it, we explored the cultural framework around work in Argentinian society. To that end, in previous studies we used the concept of the 'moral economy of work' (Rebón, Kasparian and Hernández, 2016).

Work as an element inherent in identity has played an important social and political role in Argentina. Connected to the emergence and consolidation of Peronism, work as a value came to be significantly institutionalised, taking a specific form – full-time, salaried, stable and socially beneficial – as a key element of identity. In the context of the regressive restructuring of Argentinian capitalism, work was subjected to profound alterations: precarisation, heterogenisation and growing unemployment. However, work as an element that informs social identity continued to leave a deep impression on working-class culture, representing the organising factor of life in contrast to other reproductive alternatives codified as indecent and irresponsible (Fernández Álvarez, 2007).

In enterprise recuperation, work as an identity-forming element was a legitimising notion (Thompson, 1979): the deprivation of work as a result of the closure of a productive unit became a serious grievance that fed into a sense of disgruntled moral opposition. Therefore, the activation of this criterion of justice, a principle of the workers' moral economy, found fertile ground: logs to throw on the dying embers of bankrupt enterprises.

The selective recreation of the culture of work created the moral conditions for the workers to recuperate enterprises and for these actions, despite challenging, undermining and relativising the value of private property – the means of production – to find support and tolerance of diverse social groups. These characteristics allow us to hypothesise the existence of a moral economy of work in the socio-genesis of the recuperation process and in its subsequent evolution, as we will see in the up-coming sections.

In addition to this cultural dimension, I argue that the widespread crisis shaped a structure of political opportunities for worker recuperations to spread. A structure of political opportunities refers to the moment when opportunities open up for social agents who lack regular access to political institutions to raise new or unaccepted demands (Tarrow, 1999). In the context of a marked political crisis, an unprecedented process of demonstration and social protest was unleashed. *Escraches* (individually targeted protests),[4] *cacerolazos* (pot-banging protests), *puebladas* (popular uprisings), roadblocks, assemblies and demonstrations manifested different social sectors' dissatisfaction with the existing institutional mechanisms, and direct action thus became a way to express social dissent (Rebón, 2007). These forms of expression were met with a greater degree of tolerance and even acceptance in society and, in particular, among state authorities and the media.

Loss of work therefore became intertwined with a set of grievances, and workers could rely on the support of political entrepreneurs, disseminators and key allies to defend their jobs when carrying out recuperations. This social alliance was a product of the way the crisis altered the reproduction conditions of multiple social identities (Rebón, 2007). Karl Polanyi (2007) suggests that the profound social dislocation which the stages of widespread commodification, especially of work, lead to, along with the dispossession of its stabilising elements, is experienced by society as a looming social catastrophe. In response to this experience, social resistance often emerges which cannot be reduced to the interests of one social class – although this is not without importance, and there may be sectors that mobilise to a greater degree than others – but which generally adopts the form of movements of resistance to commodification that bring together different social sectors as participants or supporters (Burawoy, 2008).

In the Argentina of the early twenty-first century, the unique character of the recuperated enterprise movement lies in the fact that not only does it possess elements of Polanyian struggles but also incorporates elements of Marxian struggle. On the one hand, it can be understood as a social movement of resistance to commodification, a product of a moment of profound social dislocation caused by the generalisation of commodification, which gives rise to Polanyian alliances and social conflicts. On the other hand, it also possesses a low-level Marxian character insofar as it unites the enterprise's workers, who, through collective action, transform the relations of exploitation in the

---

4 *Escrache* is a form of direct action unique to Argentina in which a group publicly denounces a person in their home, workplace or other space with the aim of promoting social condemnation of them. This form of action began to be used in the 1990s by the human rights group HIJOS to denounce the impunity of the perpetrators of genocide and the repressors of Argentina's civil-military dictatorship of 1977–1983.

productive unit, thus posing an obstacle to the capitalist character of the relations of production.

1.3   *The Movement of the Flames*

As John McCarthy and Mayer Zald (Pérez Ledesma, 1994) note, the role of organisation is central to collective action. In this sense, the political and cultural context described above contributed decisive resources for the wave of recuperations that took shape in the heat of the process. Even though worker recuperations represent a new development, it should not be forgotten that they are bound up with the forms of struggle and organisation of the Argentinian working classes. Reviving such traditions of struggle as the factory occupations and self-management that developed in the early 1980s in response to the first impacts of deindustrialisation (Palomino, 2003), enterprise recuperation can be understood as another chapter in the struggle of Argentina's working classes in a context of widespread crisis framed by transformations to the repertoire of labour protests. Precedents for these working-class struggles can be traced back to the return of democracy in 1983 and from the 1990s onwards, as Marina Farinetti's (1999) analysis suggests.

This framework differs in that the unions played no significant role in the enterprise recuperations. With some exceptions,[5] the workers who led the recuperations encountered indifference and neglect from trades unionists. In the context of the economic conflicts generated in crisis-hit enterprises, the loss of the leadership role usually played by trades unions brought about an autonomisation of worker collectives. The lack of an organisational form providing guidance to workers in terms of what strategy to adopt in defence of their jobs thus led to the emergence of what came to be termed 'recuperated enterprise movements' (Rebón, 2007).

While the first recuperations were relatively sporadic, the confrontations later went beyond conflicts between bosses and employees to encompass a wide range of social relations, in which judges, lawyers, state officials, legislators, members of neighbourhood assemblies, university students and lecturers, workers from other recuperated enterprises, and party-political activists promoted and drove the recuperations forwards. Strictly speaking the recuperation strategy did not arise spontaneously from the workers in an act of parthenogenesis but from their articulation with other actors. The interaction between these political entrepreneurs and the workers, coupled with the

---

5 In the socio-genesis of the recuperation process, the main exceptions were the Quilmes Branch of the Metal-Workers Union, the Greater Buenos Aires Graphics Federation, and the Neuquén Ceramics Union.

conflict and the negotiation with other actors, gave rise to various recuperated enterprise and factory organisations.

In 2000, the *Movimiento por la Economía Social* [Movement for the Social Economy] (MOPES) was founded through an initiative from the *Instituto Nacional de Asociativismo y Economía Social* [National Institute of Associativism and Social Economy] (INAES). At its core were opposing two positions. While one group led by the recuperated enterprise *Industrias Metalúrgicas y Plásticas Argentina* [Argentina Metal-Working and Plastics Industries] (IMPA) proposed the formation of an all-embracing recuperated enterprise organisation, regardless of their legal form, the other, represented by the recuperated enterprise Yaguané and the *Federación de Cooperativas de Trabajo de la República Argentina* [Federation of Worker Co-operatives of the Argentinian Republic] (FECOOTRA), advocated a grouping based on legal status so that the new co-operatives emerging from recuperated enterprises could join this traditional co-operative Federation, set up in 1988 (Rebón, 2007). In 2001, the first group founded the *Movimiento Nacional de Empresas Recuperadas* [National Movement of Recuperated Enterprises] (MNER), whose slogan 'Ocupar, resistir, producir' [Occupy, Resist, Produce] encapsulates the movement's strategy.

The literature indicates that recuperated enterprises are experiences of adaptive co-operativism, given that, far from adopting a co-operativist approach grounded in doctrine, the workers discovered in the organisational and legal form of the co-operative the most suitable and effective means to defend their jobs (Palomino, 2003; Rebón, 2007). Early in the spread of these processes, this form coexisted with other strategies, notably worker-controlled nationalisation. This proposal consisted of the state expropriating the enterprise and placing it under the management and control of its workers while guaranteeing their working conditions. The aim was to establish forms of social ownership and put self-management at the service of productive activity that was in line with society's needs. The weakening of this strategy at the expense of forming co-operatives to pursue the subsequent expropriation of the enterprises was down to the fact that nationalisation did not take into account the need for transitional legal coverage (Rebón, 2007). The formation of co-operatives[6] and the struggle for expropriation, with intermediate judicial settlements, eventually prevailed. Under these conditions, the adoption of this legal form was negatively interpreted by traditional co-operativism. The

---

6 By 2004, 94% of the recuperated enterprises had obtained the legal status of 'worker co-operative' (Programa Facultad Abierta, 2010).

second of the above groups – represented by Yaguané and FECOOTRA – therefore played a secondary role in the recuperations.

In the context of the socio-genesis of the recuperation process, roughly between 2001 and 2003, recuperated enterprises and related organisations bypassed Argentina's working classes' form of aggregation – the union – to form a social movement. Charles Tilly and Lesley Wood (2010) define social movements as a type of contentious politics that, with a degree of stability over time, develops a public campaign of a joined-up set of collective claims aimed at state authorities through a defined repertoire of collective actions. The recuperated enterprise movement, both on the public stage and before state authorities, succeeded in establishing the strategy of recuperation (which, paradigmatically speaking, involved the occupation of the productive premises) as a valid form of action in defence of jobs. Although workers from recuperated enterprises were the linchpin of the movement, it was the product of an embryonic social alliance that transcended the identities present in the enterprises.

This 'movementist' period saw major collective actions featuring a range of social actors. The collective actions surrounding the recuperation processes usually create fairly minimal disruption in the public space, as they tend not to feature mass protests that disrupt public order and block traffic. Consequently, the media does not systematically report on them. Apart from this low-level coverage, recuperated enterprise organisations tend to take less collective action in public spaces than other sectors, such as unemployed workers' organisations. Therefore, to analyse the collective actions surrounding enterprise recuperations, I conducted a systematic search for press articles in the digital archives of two alternative news agencies that tend to cover this type of event: the *Agencia de Noticias RedAcción* [Network-Action News Agency] (*ANRed*) and the *Centro de Medios Independientes Indymedia Argentina* [Indymedia Argentina Independent Media Centre]. I conducted a qualitative analysis of the content of the articles surveyed and identified the most significant and most extensive actions during the period studied.

As a rule, the movement tended to take collective action to resist evictions and maintain occupations in defence of fresh recuperations, while also getting expropriation laws passed. Its repertoire was based on two forms of action. First, to recuperate the enterprise and make a stand against their former employers, worker collectives occupied productive premises with the support of political entrepreneurs and other social groups. Second, they made use of demonstrations to put their demands to the state authorities regarding the emblematic and most conflictual cases, and also to raise such broader claims concerning the regulation of recuperated enterprises as the expropriation of all the recuperated factories, the allocation of working capital and the development of lines of credit.

That said, the movement was characterised by its low levels of penetration in enterprises, relying primarily on a handful of activists and leaders, and by its weak capacity to mobilise.

> That's a problem and a key one at that. […] When there's production, it's difficult to get them up and moving. If there's a lot of work on, sometimes they [the *compañero* (fellow worker)] can't go. Not cause they're not allowed, but cause they've got to get their work done. […] When the Recuperated Enterprise Movement was getting started in IMPA, me and this other compañero, who'd also retired, used to go every Saturday, but we did it cause we enjoyed it. And when we used to come here nobody give us the time of day. We'd go to the recuperated enterprise movement, then report back to the Board, and nothing would happen. And if you turned up with a problem, there were ten more serious problems, so yours ended up being shelved. […] That's why it was always so hard to mobilise. […] When a conflict starts in a company, the workers are all mobilised but then, once everything gets started, it's way more difficult. You can't just stop production and go off to a protest when you have to deliver an order in two or three days. So, they send you a few from one co-operative, a few from another, but it's tough.
>
> RAÚL, leading figure in the recuperated enterprise movement, September 2016

This peculiarity of the movement is associated with the imperative to keep production running and with the consequent difficulties posed by involving the whole labour force in collective actions. The process of enterprise recuperation is, in short, the direct result of the 2001–2002 crisis, both because of the economic devastation it wrought, and because of the political and cultural transformations it brought with it. However, the process proved not to be bounded by the crisis. Instead, it took hold and became a trademark 'Made in Argentina.'

2   The Evolution of Enterprise Recuperation Processes

Once the cycle of recession and social turmoil had subsided, recuperations carried on evolving apace. According to the latest data, by March 2016, there were 367 recuperated enterprises employing 15,948 workers. Mainly small and medium-sized enterprises (SMEs), recuperated enterprises produced their

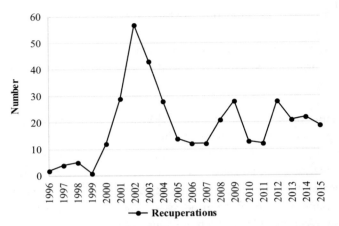

FIGURE 1   Frequency of annual enterprise recuperations: Argentina, 1996–2015
Note. Prepared by author using data from the Programa Facultad Abierta (2016).

wares in metalworking, food production, printing presses, textiles, catering and the meat industry. Just over half were concentrated in the Buenos Aires Metropolitan Area (AMBA) (Programa Facultad Abierta, 2016).

Although at a more relaxed tempo compared with the early twenty-first century, up until 2015 – the end of the period analysed here – there were new recuperations, and these continued apace at relative high rates compared to pre-crisis levels. As shown in Figure 1, approximately 60% of recuperations occurred after 2004 after the widespread crisis had subsided.

Most firms carried on operating as recuperated enterprises. According to data from the *Programa Facultad Abierta* [Open Faculty Programme] (2016), by March 2016 only 43 out of 411 of enterprises recuperated since 2002 had been forced to close for legal or financial reasons – evictions or auctions – or had ceased to be worker co-operatives due to the sale of the enterprise to private capital or, in one case, as a result of its nationalisation. Recuperated enterprises also preserved jobs and even – albeit insubstantially – created new ones. Table 1 shows that, while, over the years, the number of recuperated enterprises and workers has shown similar growth, the number of workers was been slightly higher, with the number of enterprises increasing by 128% and the number of workers by 131%.

In short, the recuperation process not only achieved an expanded reproduction, forming new recuperated productive units, but a simple reproduction as well. This is demonstrated by the productive and organisational-legal

TABLE 1 Numbers of recuperated enterprises and recuperated enterprise workers: Argentina, 2004, 2010, 2013, 2016

Survey year	Recuperated enterprises		Recuperated enterprise workers	
	Absolute numbers	2004 Base 100	Absolute numbers	2004 Base 100
2004	161	100	6,900	100
2010	205	127	9,362	135
2013	311	193	13,462	195
2016 (March)	367	228	15,948	231

Note. Prepared by author using data from the Programa Facultad Abierta (2005, 2010, 2014, 2016).

continuance of the experiences, and by the preservation of jobs with the incipient creation of new posts.

In the previous section, I remarked that, during the tumultuous years of the crisis, Argentina endured this rise in unemployment and poverty which hindered labour reinsertion in the against background of enterprise closures. I also suggested that the political, social and cultural climate set the stage for the formation of a social movement based on a multi-actor alliance of resistance to the commodification of multiple spheres of life. That said, as of 2003–04, there were signs of economic growth. In this context, it is worth asking how there could be fresh recuperations.

2.1 The Fuel of the Growing Economy Keeps the Flames of Production Moving

From 2003 on, employment and wage levels recovered, and the proportion of formal workers rose (Groisman, 2008). While, in the first quarter of 2003, unemployment rose to 20.4%, by the same quarter the following year, this had dropped to 14.4% and continued to fall steadily until it reached 7.1% by the first quarter of 2015 (Encuesta Permanente de Hogares [EPH], INDEC).

This improvement was related, first, to the change of relative prices introduced in the Argentinian economy in early 2002 with the abandonment of the new peso's '1-to-1' peg to the US dollar. The contraction of economic activity starting in 1998 halted as a result of these price changes, which restored the competitivity of local production. The relative increase in prices of imported goods stimulated a substitution of imports by local production, which proved to be a determining factor in interrupting the negative downward trend in economic activity (Damill and Frenkel, 2015). A favourable context was thus created for recuperated enterprises, primarily SMEs producing for the domestic market. Although this recovery might be interpreted as an obstacle to fresh recuperations, relaxing as it did the social dislocation of the start of the century, I maintain that not only did it contribute to the simple reproduction of the process, namely the preservation of enterprises already recuperated, but it also had a positive impact on the expectations of worker collectives in crisis-stricken enterprises. It is important to remember that business closures are a structural feature of capitalism and continued to happen after 2001, albeit to a lesser degree.

Between 2003 and 2007, Gross Domestic Product (GDP) grew by an annual average of 9%, fiscal and external surpluses were maintained, real wages and employment levels rose significantly, and income distribution improved appreciably. In 2008, Argentina began to feel the shockwave of the global crisis triggered in mid-2007 by the sub-prime mortgage market in the United States triggered by falling commodity prices, which in turn affected tax revenues from exports (Damill and Frenkel, 2015). As Figure 1 above shows, this period corresponded to a slight rise in the number of enterprise recuperations from 2008–09.

Nevertheless, at that particular juncture, Argentina was in a relatively stable position to weather the crisis: it had substantial reserves, a sizeable current account surplus and a financial surplus in the public accounts. For that reason, the crisis did not severely affect living standards or prospects for economic growth (Damill and Frenkel, 2015). Moreover, this was related to the government's expansionary and inclusive policies,[7] which absorbed the worst shocks of the crisis and maintained levels of growth, economic activity and domestic consumption.

In this context, the 2009 launch of the *Programa de Recuperación Productiva* [Programme for Productive Recovery] (REPRO) – still in place at the time of

---

7 These notably include the nationalisation of the private pensions system in 2008, which allowed the state to obtain resources to confront the negative effects of the global crisis and stimulate economic recovery by maintaining increased public spending, the extension of the number of people covered by pensions and the implementation of the *Asignación Universal por Hijo* [Universal Child Allowance] in October 2009. The latter introduced social protection for the children of the unemployed or informal workers, or people earning the legal minimum wage or less. By 2015, more than 3,500,000 children were receiving this allowance.

writing – proved fundamental. This scheme consists of a fixed monthly sum up to the equivalent of the legal minimum wage, paid to workers employed by enterprises in financial difficulty for a period of twelve months in order to top up the income corresponding to their job category. In practice, the benefit tended to be renewed and even extended to self-managed enterprises, which included worker-recuperated enterprises, by means of Line 1 of the *Programa de Trabajo Autogestionado* [Self-Managed Work Programme] of the Ministry for Labour, Employment and Social Security. This income was essential to keep recuperated enterprises running.

By October 2011, increasing inflation, exchange-rate appreciation, subsidies for public services, the depletion of fiscal and external surpluses, international financial isolation and other factors painted a complex economic picture, when the then president, Cristina Fernández de Kirchner, was re-elected (Damill and Frenkel, 2015). The depletion of the Central Bank reserves intensified as a consequence of the mass flight of capital. However, a series of policies attempted – and succeeded relatively well – to sustain aggregate demand in order to mitigate the adverse economic climate. Schemes launched towards the end of our period to encourage consumption drove demand. Last, other relevant factors included the uninterrupted continuation of collective bargaining for formal workers, the *Asignación Universal por Hijo* [Universal Child Allowance] and legally required increases to different components of social security (including pensions) and the legal minimum wage.

Recuperated enterprises thus continued to enjoy a context relatively favourable to reproducing themselves as productive units, which built up positive expectations for a fresh wave of recuperations, even in the absence of general crisis. Fuelled by the recovery of the economy, production and the domestic market, the process of enterprise recuperation, which got under way during 2001–02, managed to strengthen its hold.

That said, if the labour market could offer opportunities – or at least reasonable prospects – for labour reinsertion, what other elements tipped the scales in favour of recuperations of crisis-hit enterprises rather than prompting the break-up of worker collectives in search of new employment opportunities? Here it is necessary to turn our attention to the cultural dimension.

2.2　*The Moral Economy of Work in the Continued Presence of Enterprise Recuperations*

Recuperation as a repertoire of actions has become a significant feature in the culture of the workers' struggles. Its positive assessment as a way of confronting business closures is a central factor in the continued existence of enterprise recuperations after overcoming the crisis (Rebón, 2007; Salgado, 2009). In

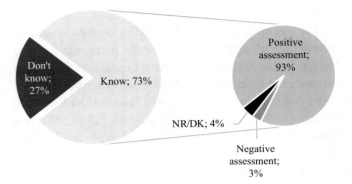

FIGURE 2   Percentage distribution of knowledge and assessment of enterprise recuperation: AMBA, 2012
Note. Data from "Alternative Economic Forms" survey.

spite of being limited in quantitative terms, recuperated enterprises are widely recognised in society and, even more relevantly, have aroused wide-ranging approval (Rebón, Kasparian and Hernández, 2016). In this sense, we can identify the cultural incorporation of the recuperation repertoire at the societal level. Figure 2 shows that 83% of the survey's respondents were familiar with the phenomenon of recuperated enterprises, and 87% of them affirmed that this concept refers to an enterprise in crisis run by its workers. Almost three quarters of all respondents then demonstrated knowledge of the process: in other words, they were able to identify both the concept and its main attributes. What is more, this social knowledge tended to be accompanied by a positive assessment of 93%.

In Table 2, we can see that the level of legitimacy attributed to the recuperation process is evenly distributed across society as a whole and does not vary significantly according to socio-economic status. The socially diverse composition of this legitimacy is a typical feature of the resistance to the effects of social dislocation produced by the advance of commodification (Polanyi, 2007).

This favourable assessment is fundamentally based on the representation of these experiences of self-management as a method used by workers to preserve their jobs rather than as a way of democratising the workplace. Of the survey's respondents, 80% prioritised the preservation of jobs as their criterion for positive assessment: 'dignified work' as the labour activity that builds positive social esteem. By contrast, only a fifth of the population approves of the experience for the democratic running of the productive unit by its workers. Here the legitimising factor is not the preservation of the previous situation – no doubt perceived as the defence of a right already acquired – but as

TABLE 2   Percentage distribution of assessment of enterprise recuperation by class position and economic activity status: AMBA, 2012

	Class position		Economic activity status			Total
	Middle class	Working class	Employed	Unemployed	Inactive	
Positive	89	94	91	100	94	93
Negative	4	2	3	-	4	3
NR/DK	7	4	6	-	2	4
Total	100	100	100	100	100	100

Note. Data from "Alternative Economic Forms" survey.

a progressive social innovation in the field of power: self-management within the productive unit.

The 'moral economy of work' thus emerges as an explanatory key with which to analyse knowledge and opinions about the recuperation process and its general features. The depth of the crisis early this century was such that numerous social experiences of resistance and self-organisation are still anchored to it, the experience of worker recuperations included. Even though the context of widespread crisis has passed, the legitimacy attributed to the process persists, rooted as it is in Argentinian society in the value of work as a form of social, material and symbolic reproduction. Work is a good binding together different values, meanings and ideas that help us to discriminate between justice and injustice, and to promote collective action and tolerance of it when they are considered under threat. This cultural configuration around work, which we term the 'moral economy of work,' thus imposes limits on its commodification: under certain conditions, defending it may even relativise or subordinate the private ownership of the means of production as a social value (Rebón, Kasparian and Hernández, 2016).

Indeed, Rodrigo Salgado (2012) and we contend that knowledge about and positive assessment of the 'recuperation' form partially offset the reversal of the crisis period. In other words, we assign a multiplying role to the cultural installation of the 'recuperation' repertoire, as long as this repertoire is not challenged, and the political context does not become openly hostile (Salgado, 2009). This cultural installation provides the conditions for fresh recuperations, not only through the role of knowledge and positive assessment in making them viable, but also because of its implications for the dominant norms and institutionality.

2.3 "Argentina Is One Big, Recuperated Factory": Public Policies for Recuperated Enterprises

In March 2010, in the recuperated factory *Envases Flexibles Mataderos* [Mataderos Flexible Packaging], President Cristina Fernández de Kirchner announced the draft amendment of a project to reform the *Ley de Concursos y Quiebras* [Competition and Bankruptcy Act], eventually approved by the Argentinian Congress in 2011. In her speech, she said: "For me, Argentina is one big, recuperated factory." The cultural installation of recuperation, in other words, its spread, knowledge and social legitimacy, has had significant repercussions at the political, juridical, and institutional levels. This institutionalisation, albeit partial – in that enterprise recuperation is not legally recognised as a right of workers facing business closure – has also been a significant factor in terms of feedback into the recuperation process after its socio-genesis against a background of widespread crisis.

As I mentioned above, the recuperation strategy primarily involved setting up co-operatives and demanding expropriation laws in order to obtain, in principle, the granting of a commodatum on the productive units for the co-operatives' use and to start production with certain legal safeguards. The first step was facilitated by active participation of the INAES, the national institution responsible for licensing co-operatives and friendly societies.

The expropriation stage proved more complicated, as it implied a move on private property. However, the crisis of political legitimacy early this century significantly limited the stances that relatively weakened governments were able to take. In this context, governmental structures at various levels were inclined to recognise expropriation claims. Furthermore, given that these laws stipulate deferred payments, they do not at first entail high financial costs for the state. The most substantive action performed by the executive and legislative powers then was the expropriation of crisis-stricken enterprises and the granting to worker co-operatives of a commodatum deferring specific moves on private property.

In this connection, now that several years have elapsed since the first laws were passed, we can observe a tendency not to implement the expropriations: few recuperated enterprises[8] have obtained ownership of their

---

8 Among the successful cases in terms of the transfer of ownership are two iconic recuperated enterprises: the ceramic tile factory *Fábrica sin patrón* (FaSinPat) [Factory Without Bosses], formerly Zanon, and the textile factory *Textiles Pigüé* [Pigüé Textiles], formerly Gatic. In

productive establishments and the moveable assets. In summary, although this partial institutionalisation facilitated the continuation of production and a degree of legal protection, it did not grant the co-operatives ownership and left them vulnerable to changes of government.

In spite of their limitations, by reaching settlements in the legislative sphere, expropriations provided political and institutional solutions to the difficulties and the prolongation of the conflicts raised by obtaining productive continuity in the judicial and institutional arena, namely in bankruptcy hearings for failed enterprises presided over by commercial judges. The characteristics of this state power mean that it is less receptive to the demands and needs of society. Furthermore, the goals of worker collectives were opposed to the spirit of the Competition and Bankruptcy Act, which was oriented towards the rapid liquidation of the enterprise in order to use its assets to settle debts, mainly with the banks rather than the state or the workers affected.

In mid-2002, the amendment of Competition and Bankruptcy Act Article 190 introduced the possibility of worker co-operatives appearing before the bankruptcy judge and petitioning for the continuity of the enterprise as trustees of the assets. The judge might accept or reject the petition. In the event of acceptance, the productive unit would be handed over for a specific time period, generally two years, which is the length of time usually taken by bankruptcy proceedings. The worker collectives would thus provisionally remain in charge of the enterprise under the authority of a commercial judge until the ownership of the property of the bankrupt enterprise had been defined. Luis Caro, a lawyer specialising in enterprise recuperation and a representative of the *Movimiento Nacional de Fábricas Recuperadas por sus Trabajadores* [National Movement of Worker-Recuperated Factories] (MNFRT) explains it as follows:

> The Bankruptcy Act was there to liquidate, you might even call it destructive. The thinking was that if it went bust it was for a reason, you had to sell it, auction it off and that was it. That's why it said it had to be sold in four months [...] I had this far-fetched idea in 2004 of being able to reform the law to get Article 190 extended, because the judges themselves told me they didn't have no legal tools. What were we doing? How did we

---

January 2014, after thirteen years of self-management, the 450 FaSinPat workers obtained the documentation needed to establish the co-operative as owner of the ceramics factory. The formalisation of the ownership of *Textiles Pigüé* occurred in April 2014, when the provincial government submitted the deed of conveyance of ownership to the co-operative after a process initiated ten years earlier.

> get round it? With demonstrations, petitions, expropriation laws to stall the sale.
>> LUIS CARO, leading figure in the MNFRT, cited in the *Observatorio Social sobre Empresas Recuperadas y Autogestionadas* [Social Observatory for Recuperated and Self-Managed Enterprises], OSERA, 2011

Worker collectives were thus in thrall to the peculiarities of the procedures of each failed enterprise, the arbitrariness of judges and their own capacities to mobilise. Several years later, in early 2010, Argentina's president announced the proposed draft of an amendment to the Competition and Bankruptcy Act, and the National Congress passed Act 26,684 in June 2011, amending the existing law. This new amendment marked a fundamental difference from its predecessor: the continuation of production in the hands of workers organised in co-operatives was no longer under the control of the Judiciary.

> With the reform, workers can stay on in the premises with immediate effect and have got to notify a judge: they've got a period of 24 hours to do so. And they can do so with a co-operative that's still taking shape as well. The immediate continuity is really important. The Executive's explanation when it proposed the reform says precisely that the objective is for the enterprise to keep running so the productive unit and the labour force aren't wasted, and all that wasn't a directive in the previous law.
>> LUIS CARO, leading figure in MNFRT, cited in OSERA, 2011

The main amendments include the possibility of workers organised in co-operatives – even those still taking shape – to be awarded immediate continuity of production, non-suspension of any interest accrued on wages owe, and priority in bidding for and gaining access to the direct allocation of assets using their labour credit notes. Act 26,684 thus enables workers to become predominant actors in eventual bankruptcy proceedings, guaranteeing the preservation of jobs and the continued running of the enterprise.

This reform opened up a new channel for institutionalisation by stipulating that, in the event of bankruptcy, workers could use their labour credits to purchase the enterprise. However, much as the reform represented an important landmark and narrowed the gap between the legitimacy and legality of the recuperation process, contrary to initial assumptions, the intensity of the conflicts and collective actions around recuperations did not wane. On this point, the Open Faculty Programme (2014) posits that the reform has not facilitated recuperation processes. On the one hand, by udicializing recuperations, it has tended to prolong conflicts. On the other hand, by creating expectations of resolution, it has in many cases blocked the legislative channel for expropriations.

For example, in the recuperation processes started in Buenos Aires between 2011 and 2015, after the amendment to the act, workers began to occupy productive premises to a greater degree than in the recuperations that took place before it. We ascertained that, in 52% of enterprises recuperated between 1992 and 2010, worker collectives had turned to occupation as a mode of action; whereas, after the amendment to the act, in other words, enterprises recuperated between 2011 and 2015, that percentage rose to 70%. That said, this does not account for the fact that the amendment brought about an escalation of occupations of productive units. It is important to consider that in 50% of new recuperations in Buenos Aires the premises are not the property of the failed enterprises' management.[9] For that reason, the workers have to confront eviction notices issued by the property's owners – to whom months of rent are owed – a problem that lies beyond the scope of both the bankruptcy proceedings and the law.

We can see then that the amendment to the law has not entirely succeeded in institutionalising recuperations and the conflicts this involves. Nevertheless, it has, in some cases, furnished workers with legal instruments to institutionally channel recuperations. Some examples in Buenos Aires are the recuperated restaurant *Los Chanchitos* [The Little Pigs], and the graphics enterprise Jetcoop. In 2015, in the context of bankruptcy proceedings, both enterprises' workers managed to offset their labour credit notes and benefits with moveable assets from the failed enterprises. Similarly, in 2016, the metal-working co-operative Famel succeeded in securing full ownership of the fixed and moveable assets using their labour credit notes. This is consistent with the amendment to the law granting the workers of failed enterprises priority in offsetting their outstanding credit notes with the enterprises' assets.

Last, starting in 2003, the national state implemented a battery of public policies that drew on the associated and self-managed experiences that had emerged in response to capitalism's structural incapacity to create jobs (Hintze, 2013). These policies were inserted in a broader process of state construction

---

9 We conducted our initial survey in 2012 as part of a research project with the University of Buenos Aires, "*La cultura de la recuperación de empresas. Representaciones y valoraciones de los trabajadores sobre el proceso*" [The Culture of Enterprise Recuperations: Workers' Representations and Attitudes towards the Process], through telephone-based or face-to-face interviews in all the recuperated enterprises in Buenos Aires (N: 45). In 2015, we carried out a study of the media reporting on recuperation processes in Buenos Aires from 2011 to 2015 (N: 19).

TABLE 3   Main policies for associational and self-managed work from the Ministry for Social Development and the Ministry for Labour, Employment and Social Security: Argentina, 2003–2015

State body	Scheme/Project	Characteristics
Ministry for Social Development	*Manos a la Obra* [Down to Work] Socio-Productive Projects	Financing for machinery, tools and supplies, as well as technical assistance and training for individual, family or associative productive projects.
	Programa de Microcrédito [Micro-Credit Programme] – National Micro-Credit Commission	Financing for productive projects not meeting the conditions to access traditional bank loans.
	Marca Colectiva [Collective Brand]	Creation of brands or distinctive logo designs to identify products or services provided by groups of enterprises in the social economy.
	Monotributo Social [Social Monotax]	Tax regime aimed at the socially vulnerable population providing goods or services. It includes health insurance, pensions and Universal Child Allowance.
	Programa Ingreso Social con Trabajo [Social Income with Work Programme] (known as *Argentina Trabaja* [Argentina Works])	Promotion of co-operative creation among socially vulnerable sectors to carry out works for urban and community infrastructure, sanitation, housing and improvement of green spaces.

CO-OPERATIVES 'MADE IN ARGENTINA' 41

TABLE 3 Main policies for associational and self-managed work (*cont.*)

State body	Scheme/Project	Characteristics
Ministry for Labour, Employment and Social Security – Sub-secretariat for the Promotion of the Social Sector of the Economy (created 2009)	*Programa de Trabajo Autogestionado* [Self-Managed Work Programme]	Individual financial contributions for workers in self-managed productive units, when the minimum wage is not met (Line 1) and for the purchase of machinery, tools, supplies and the implementation of health and safety improvements (Line 2)
	Promoción de Empleo Independiente y Entramados Productivos [Promotion of Independent Employment and Productive Structures]	Financing of individual or associative productive enterprises, with training and technical assistance. The Line of *Entramados Productivos* [Productive Frameworks] finances productive or service centres for entrepreneurs or entrepreneurial collectives.

Note. Prepared by author based on documents from the relevant ministries.

of the social economy (Hopp, 2013a). While they promoted and institutionalised forms of production that already enjoyed significant social legitimacy, they also fostered the creation of a field of the social economy in which recuperated enterprises and other experiences converged. The main state bodies that developed policies aimed at this sector were the Ministry for Social Development, and the Ministry for Labour, Employment and Social Security.[10] Table 3 presents a brief list of the ministries' policies.

---

10   There are also some initiatives of the INAES, the *Instituto Nacional de Tecnología Industrial* [National Institute of Industrial Technology] (INTI), the *Instituto Nacional*

Following Susana Hintze (2013), two levels can be distinguished in the public system of reproduction of associational and self-managed work: the reproduction of the workers and the sustainability of the productive units. Hintze points out that most of the policies have been oriented towards reproducing the ventures rather than protecting the workers participating in them. There is then still some way to go in terms of security and social protection for the self-managed workers.

The partial institutionalisation of the enterprise recuperations is, in short, a factor in their evolution, after the context of widespread crisis. The expropriation laws, the amendment to the Competition and Bankruptcy Act and the various policies detailed above helped to preserve existing recuperations and new ones to emerge. Yet these were not sufficient to consolidate the process, as recuperated enterprises often lack the legal status needed to produce on a reliable base, and their workers have no access to the same rights as a salaried employee. In any case, these shortcomings were to an extent offset by the relative receptiveness of the government.

2.4   The Movement's Fragmentation, Co-operative Convergence and Union Rapprochement

As of 2003 and 2004, the 'movementist' character of the recuperation process was petering out. In other words, the movement began to fragment into isolated organisations. In a new social, political and economic context, the convergences in mass demonstrations gave way to the diversification both of ideas about how enterprises should organise themselves post-recuperation and of stances towards the government and, therefore, towards the appropriate forms of action for stating their demands. This diversification created splits in the original organisations and gave rise to new structures.

---

de Tecnología Agropecuaria [National Institute of Agricultural Technology] (INTA), the Ministry for Federal Planning, Public Investment and Services, the Ministry of Education's Secretariat for University Policies and the Ministry of Industry. Initiatives worth mentioning are: the Ministry of Industry's *Programa Capital Semilla* [Seed Capital Project]; the INAES's *Programa de Educación y Capacitación Cooperativa y Mutual* [Programme for Education and Co-operative and Mutual Training] and the *Programa de Ayuda Financiera* [Financial Assistance Programme]; the INTI's *Programa Recuperar el Trabajo* [Recuperate Work Programme], the *Subprograma de Asistencia en Gestión de Proyectos Productivos* [Sub-Programme for Assistance in Managing Productive Projects] and the *Subprograma de Comercio Electrónico* [Sub-Programme for Electronic Commerce]; the INTA's *Programa Pro Huerta* [Pro-Orchard Programme] and the *Programa Minifundio* [Smallholdings Programme]; and the Ministry of Education's Secretariat for University Policies's *Programa de Cooperativismo y Economía Social en la Universidad* [Co-operativism and Social Economy in the University Programme].

The first fracture in the MNER occurred in 2003, only two years after its creation, with the formation of the MNFRT. Its strategy is more legalistic than the MNER's, focusing on institutionalising the recuperation process through legislative reforms. By 2013, it combined some 60 enterprises, around a fifth of total recuperated enterprises at the time. It is the only organisation of its type to have kept up its stance of bringing together exclusively recuperated enterprises.

The second split from MNER took place in December 2006, when one of the dissident groups founded a second-tier federation,[11] the *Federación Argentina de Cooperativas de Trabajadores Autogestionados* [Argentinian Federation of Self-Managed Workers' Co-operatives] (FACTA), which, towards the close of our research, combined over 60 co-operatives comprising around 2,500 workers. After a first stage incorporating recuperated enterprises, this organisation underwent a twin-track development. On one hand, in a clear shift towards the traditional co-operative sector, it started welcoming worker co-operatives that were not from recuperated enterprises. This move was crystallised in FACTA's incorporation into the *Confederación Nacional de Cooperativas de Trabajo* [National Confederation of Worker Co-operatives] (CNCT), established in 2009, uniting more than 25 federations nationwide. The CNCT represents the link between recuperated enterprises' productive experiences and federations of traditional co-operativism like the FECOOTRA, or those linked to the social and popular economies, such as the *Federación de Cooperativas de Trabajo Unidas* [Federation of United Worker Co-operatives] (FECOOTRAUN), which brings together co-operatives from the *Programa Argentina Trabaja* [Argentina Works Programme]. On the other hand, in 2014, FACTA formalised its incorporation in a 'social movement unionism' confederation (Senén González and Haidar, 2009), the *Central de Trabajadores de la Argentina* [Workers' Confederation of Argentina] (CTA).[12]

In 2005, the *Asociación Nacional de Trabajadores Autogestionados* [National Association of Self-Managed Workers] (ANTA) was formed, belonging to another branch of the CTA. This organisation is principally based on the

---

11 Second-tier organisations are formed by the convergence of legal entities, in this case productive units forming worker co-operatives (first-tier organisations), and are called 'federations,' while third-tier organisations combine both productive units and second-tier associations, and are called 'confederations.'
12 Founded in 1992, the CTA is characterised by a network of relationships with organisations not traditionally linked to the world of work and by a membership recruitment policy based on a broad definition of the working class. It thus possesses a logic similar to 'social movement unionism' (Senén González and Haidar, 2009).

experience of the *Unión Solidaria de Trabajadores* [Workers' Solidarity Union] (UST), a recuperated waste management enterprise. Unlike others, this is a union that accepts membership through individual worker affiliations. We can see then that, while informal relationships were the norm in the original organisations, this became formalised as time went by. On one hand, the federations and confederations require co-operatives' formal incorporation; on the other, as a union, the ANTA stipulates the individual affiliation of workers belonging to self-managed organisation, regardless of their legal form.

Finally, in 2010 another organisation emerged: the *Unión Productiva de Empresas Autogestionadas* [Productive Union of Self-Managed Enterprises] (UPEA), which, like FACTA, extends beyond the world of recuperated enterprises. Formed by 25 recuperated enterprises, worker co-operatives and smaller-scale productive establishments, the UPEA was set up as an organisation whose main concern was self-management – and not the legal form as in the case of FACTA – and its primary aim was to secure the rights enjoyed by salaried employees for self-managed workers. The UPEA's main demand was the establishment of the *Estatuto del Trabajador Autogestionado* [Self-Managed Workers' Statute]. One of the striking characteristics of the organisation was its close relationship with the national government and, more specifically, the Ministry for Labour, Employment and Social Security.

In summary, among new organisations we see an expansion of forms of aggregation, with the exception of MNFRT, which stays afloat by bringing recuperated enterprises together. FACTA is a federation that opts for closer ties with the co-operative movement and 'social movement unionism' through their affiliation with the CTA. ANTA is an example of a union of self-managed workers' organisations under the auspices of the CTA and with a logic of individual membership. Last, UPEA also opens up its catchment to self-management.

Where collective action was concerned, there were no actions during this second stage on the scale of those that took place during the period of widespread crisis. Strictly speaking, the number of enterprises and co-operatives comprising these organisations should be downplayed: joining an organisation does not necessarily imply the effective participation of the workers. On the contrary, participation in these organisations and the actions they undertake often falls to just a handful of workers, mainly the leading figures.

Demonstrations continued as the form of collective action used to make an entrance on the public stage. However, between 2006 and 2007, business fairs were also held for recuperated enterprises to exhibit their wares as a way of pitching their demands, which had moved on since our first socio-genetic period. As well as those in defence of emblematic cases, mainly concerning the ownership of premises, demonstrations were held to demand a national expropriation law for all recuperated enterprises and to call for the amendment of the Competition and Bankruptcy Act, which finally took place in 2011. They also opposed the veto of expropriation laws by the then head of the Buenos Aires city government, Mauricio Macri. Press conferences with legislators and workers from recuperated enterprises were held outside the city government headquarters. Last, between mid-2011 and early 2012, the demonstrations – in some cases nationwide – were in response to the national government's intention to discontinue Line 1 of the Ministry for Labour, Employment, and Social Security's *Programa de Trabajo Autogestionado* [Self-Managed Work Programme].

In short, on the one hand, as Héctor Palomino, Ivanna Bleynat, Silvia Garro and Carla Giacomuzzi (2011) have pointed out, the original logic of association centring on recuperated enterprise organisations – which emerged from the convergence of political entrepreneurs unconnected to the productive units and workers in the recuperated enterprises – gave way to broader associational forms (federations, confederations and so on). This enabled a greater degree of liaison with organisations of traditional co-operativism and of experiences of self-management and the popular economy. I term this process 'co-operative convergence,' in that the different trajectories gradually flowed together into broad-based organisations. On the other hand, forms of associating also spoke of union rapprochement, in particular to 'social movement syndicalism.'

The cultural installation of the enterprise recuperation process, together with its repercussions at state level, was crucial in this convergence. It is important to remember that the adaptive adoption of the legal form of the worker co-operative (Palomino, 2003; Rebón, 2007) had been negatively received by traditional co-operativism, which felt it failed to conform to the values of the co-operative movement. As a result, traditional co-operativism played a secondary role during the socio-genesis of the recuperation process. However, over the years, the symbolic power of the recuperated enterprise movement ended up promoting a reinterpretation of the historical memory of traditional co-operatives, which had remained on the margins of the recuperation process and encouraged the participation of traditional co-operativsim (Palomino et al., 2011). While generally not stemming from workers' ideological and doctrinaire perceptions of co-operativism, the recuperation processes were central to the spread and symbolic recovery[13] of this legal and organisational form

---

13 The use of worker co-operatives as a way of reducing labour costs through the concealment of the wage relationship became widespread during the 1990s. However, ten years after the spread of the enterprise recuperation process, 50% of the adult population of AMBA opted for a definition of 'co-operatives' that drew on the basic principles of the

in post-crisis Argentina. The words of the former head of FECOOTRA, who even associates the first recuperated enterprises with the governments of Juan Domingo Perón in the 1940s–50s, are revealing:

> I mean, almost all the worker co-operatives are recuperated. The history of worker co-operatives started in 1918 in this country [...]. Then came the Perón process, that's when the first industrial co-operatives are recuperated. The first ones are recuperated. [...] In other words, most co-operatives always emerge from a crisis in an enterprise, and the workers recuperate it. That's common currency nowadays. They're all worker co-operatives, but the thing is, some of them ... The only one I know of that emerged through the wishes of its members is my own. [...] You've got the enterprises recuperated before 2000, and after 2000. The ones from before 2000 are old companies. [...] They're all worker co-operatives: each of them has a different formative history.
> Former head of FECOOTRA, May 2013

As part of this process, I also consider the public policies that contributed to the formation of the field of social economy and, within it, that of associational and self-managed work, to be of central importance. Where recuperated enterprises are concerned, this shift in the logics of association was driven by the need to resolve management-related issues and by the decline of more radical viewpoints opposed to co-operativism (Palomino et al., 2011). So, whereas the adoption of the 'worker co-operative' form was an adaptive strategy in the socio-genesis of the recuperation processes, nowadays the boundaries between recuperated enterprises and traditional co-operatives are becoming blurred.

On another level, alongside the new organisations, sectoral networks or clusters began to take shape. Thus, the logic of political and claim-based aggregation gradually gave rise to productive and commercial forms. The benefits of sectoral integration arise from the implementation of shared policies in issues around purchasing, storage, production, quality management, human resources, training and education, funding, marketing and dissemination. Apart from the *Red Gráfica Cooperativa* [Co-operative Graphics Network], formed in 2006, the rest were set up between 2012 and 2013. Notable among them were the *Red Textil Cooperativa* [Co-operative Textile Network], the *Red Metalúrgica Nacional Cooperativa* [National Co-operative Metal-Workers'

---

co-operative movement: democratic management and collective ownership of the means of production ("*Formas económicas alternativas*" [Alternative Economic Forms] survey, 2012).

Network], the *Federación de Cooperativas Autogestionadas de la Carne y Afines* [Federation of Self-Managed Meat Co-operatives and Related Industries] and the *Federación de Organizaciones Productoras de Alimentos* [Federation of Food-Production Organisations]. We can see that these clusters also often exemplify a process of co-operative convergence and union rapprochement. Here, the *Federación Gráfica Bonaerense* [Greater Buenos Aires Graphics Federation] was central to the formation of the Graphics Co-operative Network, just as the Quilmes branch of the *Unión Obrera Metalúrgica* [Metal-Workers' Union], as well as FECOOTRA, were key to the formation of the metal-workers' network. In the case of the textile network and the Federation of Food-Production Organisations, the CNCT played a galvanising role.

In the context of the 2015 presidential elections, driven by the possibility of a return to neoliberal policies that a change of government would bring, the organisations participated jointly in rallies and demonstrations. In this framework, I questioned whether the 'movementist' character of these organisations would resurface. It is beyond the scope of this book to answer this question. However, I would like to highlight that the change of social, economic and political context with Mauricio Macri's election as President of Argentina in 2015 prompted a revitalisation of collective action by recuperated enterprises and their organisations in the public sphere, as well as a transformation of their claims alongside the expansion of defensive union struggles in Argentina. To illustrate, on 20 July 2016, 10,000 workers from recuperated enterprises, Argentina Works co-operatives, and other social schemes, along with SMEs and consumer and user organisations took to the streets together. The aim of the demonstration was to demand a social tariff for worker co-operatives on basic utilities (electricity and gas) in response to the sharp increase in the cost of these services. The context and demands had clearly changed.

Over the course of this chapter, I have analysed the factors that explain the socio-genesis and evolution of the formation of worker co-operatives through recuperations of enterprises. I believe the contentious origins of this type of co-operative, along with its roots in work-related demands and the subsequent formation of a recuperated enterprise movement, are central nodes that will be used to analyse the socio-productive character of the resulting enterprises in the chapters that follow.

CHAPTER 2

Incubated Co-operatives

Co-operative Formation under the Argentina Works Programme

What happens when governments and their orientations change? How are public policies altered? How are new ones gestated? At the start of my research, I read an interview with two activists from the *Organización Barrial Tupac Amaru* [Tupac Amaru Neighbourhood Organisation] that caught my eye. They were discussing the political process opened up in Argentina in 2003, public policies aimed at co-operatives and the relationship between the state and social organisations.

By that time, the formation of worker co-operatives under government schemes had clearly revolutionised the co-operative sector. For the interviewees, this explosion was not down to the government having "this fantastic idea." Of course, according to them, the explosion was magnificent because it encouraged the development of co-operatives and social organisations. It was not, however, surprising:

> You can't understand Tupac without the state policy opened up by the Kirchner government in 2003. [...] Before 2003, the state didn't fund unemployed workers' co-operatives the way it does nowadays. [...] In 2003, the state opened up the way for co-operatives and self-management to make progress and develop, not because the state had this fantastic idea but because there was a process of struggle starting in the 1990s and lasting until 2003 that led to the state opening up this opportunity.
>
> MAX QUISPE RAMÍREZ and MANUEL ALZINA, activists from the
> Tupac Amaru Neighbourhood Organisation, quoted in *Observatorio Social sobre Empresas Recuperadas y Autogestionadas* [Social Observatory for Recuperated and Self-Managed Enterprises], OSERA, 2010

They replaced pipe dreams or magical thinking about the one-way genesis of public policies with the struggles of social organisations since the 1990s and their multiple overlappings with the state and its governments.

What matters is state policy and how the organisation makes the most of it, how it draws on that policy. There were lots of organisations that, even with tools provided by the state to build something with, never got round to it. In Tupac, we say the state has a responsibility to make sure there's education, work, health-care, housing, that the kids are happy. [...] When the state doesn't get there, the organisation tries to self-manage it. [...] Once you've sorted out the problems, the debate gets under way inside the organisations: whether you just paper over them and depend on the state to sort them out, or whether you get around to doing self-management and building something of your own that goes beyond the state. See, cause what happens if the state changes its orientation?

> MAX QUISPE RAMÍREZ and MANUEL ALZINA, activists from the Tupac Amaru Neighbourhood Organisation, quoted in OSERA, 2010

In this chapter, I describe the socio-genesis and development of the process of forming worker co-operatives in the framework of the *Programa Argentina Trabaja* [Argentina Works Programme] (PAT). Indeed, to understand this phenomenon, we have to retrace the connections that link the Argentina Works Programme – and social policy in general – to the practices and struggles of unemployed workers' organisations from the 1990s on. I first review social schemes with work requirement implemented in Argentina, from early workfare schemes to the launch of the Argentina Works Programme. Next, I analyse interactions between the state and unemployed workers' organisations after the launch of this type of social schemes. I identify the slowing of economic growth and the political crisis of the national government between 2008 and 2009 as elements that structure the socio-genesis of the Argentina Works Programme. Last, I describe the struggles of unemployed workers' organisations to gain access to the scheme and modify its design and implementation.

Based on this analysis, I outline the specific features of this type of worker co-operative and debate Mirta Vuotto's (2011) categorisations. She classes these co-operatives as being 'state-induced' and differentiates them from 'claims-based' experiences as represented by recuperated enterprises. As a counterpoint, I formulate the notion of 'incubated' co-operatives. I therefore stress that, as with recuperated enterprises, worker co-operativism in the framework of public policies can be defined by its contentious origins and its anchoring in work-related demands. These elements lay the foundations for analysing the constitutive conflict of the case study in the following chapter and its socio-productive characteristics in Chapter 5.

1 Social Schemes with Work Requirement: From Workfare to the Argentina Works Programme

Social policy can be defined as the set of state interventions that act on conditions of life and its reproduction (Danani, 2009). Although social interventions can be traced back throughout the history of human society, social policy was only forged in the furnace of capitalist modernity, more precisely between the late nineteenth and mid-twentieth centuries, with the rise of social or welfare states (Adelantado, Noguera, Rambla and Sáez, 1998; Gamallo, 2012). This was when the capital-labour relationship (the commodity form of labour power) becomes fundamental in the formation of the conditions of life of subjects and societies. The commodification of human labour ushered in by modernity faces society with a lack of protection. In this sense, the state's social interventions are oriented to protecting people from the risks implied by this dependency on employment-related income.

From the mid-twentieth century to the 1970s in Argentina, a state-regulated capitalist labour market had successfully been formed, guaranteeing relatively homogeneous and favourable living standards for a predominant sector of the population, along with universal access to education and basic health-care. In cases of extreme poverty, the state applied social assistance policies, which were considered a citizen's right (Soldano and Andrenacci, 2006). Over successive military dictatorships and deepening further in the 1990s with the rise of neoliberalism, this social welfare schema was gradually replaced by spaces of valorisation that recommodified the labour force and needs (Danani and Hintze, 2011). In the '90s, an assistencialisation of social policy was developed, forms of salaried employment and social security were deregulated, the quality of health-care coverage and education declined, and the system of public services disappeared as such (Soldano and Andrenacci, 2006).

Against this background, the relationship between state and society was reoriented, and the causes, effects and possible solutions to social problems were redefined (Merklen, 2013). Based on notions such as 'policies of individuation' (Merklen, 2013) or 'policies of insertion' (Castel, 1995), social scientists charted the abandonment of stable mechanisms for the integration of the subject of rights and the subsequent implementation of specific interventions based on a rationale of positive discrimination against an uncertain backdrop of rising unemployment and precarisation. The aim of these interventions was to develop skills and attitudes that encouraged autonomy, flexibility and responsibility in order to avoid dependency among particular populations (Sennett, 2003).

In Argentina, this rationale left its mark on unemployment intervention policies after 1996, with the arrival of workfare, a social policy tradition that establishes the notion of 'work requirement' (Grondona, 2012; Soldano and Andrenacci, 2006). This schema of social intervention was derived from the Anglo-Saxon welfare states and generally comprised training and temporary employment schemes. Modelled on the idea of 'the poor' – a classic concept of the Anglo-Saxon liberal welfare state – which recognises needs rather than rights associated with salaried workers, the obligatory nature of the work requirement was underwritten by a moral justification aimed at avoiding individuals' dependency on welfare (Grondona, 2012).

The first emergency employment scheme based on this schema was the *Programa Trabajar* [Working Programme], launched in 1996 during Carlos Menem's second term as president. This scheme provided a cash transfer below the level of the market minimum wage and even the basic food basket in exchange for a work requirement in community projects. Its launch implied a growing say by the World Bank in the design and assessment of social policies, which institution gave civil society organisations a leading role by incorporating them in the implementation phase of these policies (Arcidiácono, 2011).

The main successor of the Working Programme was the *Plan Jefes y Jefas de Hogar Desocupados* [Plan for Unemployed Heads of Household], started during the 2001–02 general crisis. This provided financial support to heads of households in return for attending training courses or for implementing work requirements in community projects. Initially, this cash transfer was equivalent to 75% of the minimum wage, an amount which gradually depreciated to a mere 23.8% by 2005 (Golbert, 2007). This plan marked the mass implementation of workfare throughout Argentina (Grondona, 2012): although it was intended to cover 500,000 beneficiaries, the plan was eventually extended, due to the scale of the crisis, to cover 2,000,000 homes in 2003 and reached between 7 to 8% of the total employment rate (Cortés, Groisman and Hoszowski, 2004; Groisman, 2011). By 2002, all temporary employment schemes at a national level were consolidated under the Plan for Unemployed Heads of Household. This plan therefore illustrates the transition to a mixed paradigm of social policies that, while preserving their status as welfare schemes – in other words, neither universal nor rights-creating – were relatively widespread and challenged targeted applications (Massetti, 2011).

Starting in 2003, once the general crisis of 2001–2002 had begun to abate, and with the change of government,[1] the approach shifted from cash transfer

---

1 The general crisis of late 2001 precipitated the resignation of President Fernando de la Rúa on 20 December. In the tumult that followed, there was a succession of several provisional

in response to the labour emergency to social protection strategies. A new employment regime emerged, differing from the previous one which had been underpinned by labour precarisation (Palomino, 2008). In social policy, there was a 'counter-reformation' in response to the period of neoliberal hegemony (Danani and Hintze, 2011). An important part of this process involved the changes in the pensions system and family allowances,[2] broadening social protection in four directions: sectors with no access to employment, sectors with access to informal employment, vulnerable households and elderly people with no other source of income (Massetti, 2011).

The number of beneficiaries of the Plan for Unemployed Heads of Household began gradually to fall, most notably towards 2007 (Natalucci and Paschkes Ronis, 2011). This was due to a combination of two factors: the impact of the economic recovery on the labour market and the reprofiling of the population in social policies that relocated workfare beneficiaries in other schemes. These led to an income improvement and eliminated the work requirement as it had been developed in the Plan for Unemployed Heads of Household.

Another strategy for reprofiling beneficiaries of the Plan for Unemployed Heads of Household also emerged, drawing on experiences and traditions of associativism and self-management. The designed strategy focused on the fostering of associational and self-managed work within the social economy. Some of the schemes started in 2003 and 2004 concentrated on promoting the formation of worker co-operatives for public works. These were the *Mejoramiento del Hábitat Urbano* [Urban Habitat Improvement] subprogramme, the *Programa Federal de Mejoramiento de Viviendas Mejor Vivir* [Better Living Federal Programme for Housing Improvement], the construction of *Centros Integradores Comunitarios* [Inclusive Community Centres], the *Plan Agua + Trabajo* [Water + Work Plan], and the *Programa Manos a la Obra*

---

presidents. On 2 January 2002, Eduardo Duhalde took office and called elections for April 2003. In May that year, Néstor Kirchner, the candidate for the *Frente para la Victoria* [Front for Victory], a coalition rooted in the Justicialist Party, was elected president. Subsequent to this, the political and economic systems gradually recovered from the crisis and from exceptionality. Kirchner's wife, Cristina Fernández de Kirchner, later won two consecutive presidential terms (2007–11 and 2011–15). These three 'Kirchnerist' governments were characterised by progressive centre-left policies.

2 The 2005 *Programa de Inclusión Previsional* [Pension Inclusion Programme] and the renationalisation of the funds in 2008 helped raise the quotient between pensions beneficiaries and the retirement-age population from 65.8% in December 2004 to 94% in March 2010. In addition to the expanded coverage, there was a significant increase in the minimum pension. Furthermore, as I have mentioned, the implementation of Universal Child Allowance in 2009 established a social protection insurance scheme for children.

[Down to Work Programme]. As mentioned above, the creation and promotion of worker co-operatives through government schemes altered the sector's configuration: in 2012, three quarters of all active worker co-operatives were connected to these schemes (Acosta, Levin and Verbeke, 2013).

Among them, the Argentina Works Programme, created in August 2009 by the Ministry for Social Development, was particularly significant. At the time of its launch, President Cristina Fernández de Kirchner gave an opposite diagnosis of poverty to ones that establish individual causalities, singling out instead inequality as the primary cause. She also used the opportunity to convey the message that 100,000 jobs would be created during the first stage of the scheme by the formation of co-operatives in the Buenos Aires Conurbation targeting a highly vulnerable sector of the population. The aims of the scheme were to create jobs, provide comprehensive training and encourage co-operative organisation in order to carry out low-complexity infrastructure projects. The Argentina Works Programme's regulatory framework was set up amid a deepening of public policies aimed at consolidating "a central income redistribution mechanism, thus promoting work as an instrument of social integration" and at co-operatives "as gateways to [...] dignified work" (*Ministerio de Desarrollo Social de la Nación* No. 3182/09: 1). Alongside the creation of co-operatives and their training, the Argentina Works Programme established state-subsidised workers' registration in the regime for low tax-payers called the '*monotributo social*' [social monotax], which provided health-care insurance and pension contributions. The co-operative members' income – also provided by the state – was initially set at AR$1,200, or approximately 90% of the legal minimum wage. As well as the implementation of the Argentina Works Programme, the Universal Child Allowance was also set up to integrate the scheme's beneficiaries in the system of family allowances. Last, the scheme also allocated funds to the purchase of materials, supplies and tools.

While this scheme was not the first of its kind, its central importance lies in the fact that it replicated at national level the similar smaller-scale schemes that had been under way in Argentina since 2003. This scheme stands out among social policies aimed at creating associational and self-managed work for its mass scale, territorial scope and the size of its budget. Regarding its scale, 218,870 beneficiaries[3] had been incorporated and 5,142 worker co-operatives

---

3   The category of 'beneficiary' does not necessarily refer to 'active' or current beneficiaries, but rather to people who were at some point 'incorporated' into the scheme and who may not still be 'active.' The only data available is for the percentage of 'active' beneficiaries out of the total 'beneficiaries' for 2015, when they represented almost 65% (*Ministerio de Economía y Finanzas Públicas de la Nación*, 2015).

formed under the Argentina Works Programme by August 2015 (*Ministerio de Desarrollo Social de la Nación*, 2015a).

Table 4 shows that the highest intake of beneficiaries was during the first two years after the scheme's launch. The doubling of the number of co-operatives in 2012 was due to the fact that, in that year, co-operatives, originally formed by 60 members, were required to divide in half. The number of beneficiaries in 2014 includes the beneficiaries of *Ellas Hacen* [Women Make], a line of the Argentina Works Programme launched in 2013 and aimed exclusively at women, there being no disaggregated data for the number of beneficiaries of the Argentina Works Programme's original line or for Women Make.

In terms of territorial scope, when the scheme was launched, it was stated that the initial stage would focus on the Buenos Aires Conurbation, which would later be followed by other highly socially vulnerable geographical regions. In this way, out of a total of 24, the scheme gradually incorporated beneficiaries from the following provinces or districts: Buenos Aires Province, Entre Ríos, Catamarca, Chaco, Corrientes, Formosa, La Rioja, Mendoza, Misiones, Río Negro, Salta, Santiago del Estero, San Juan, San Luis, Tucumán and the Autonomous City of Buenos Aires (the latter only in the Women

TABLE 4   Total Argentina Works Programme and co-operatives per annum: Argentina, 2009–2015

Year	Total beneficiaries (cumulative)	Total Argentina Works co-operatives (cumulative)
2009	60,000	2,224
2010	182,159	
2011	194,456	
2012	202,178	4,726
2013	208,894	5,047
2014	306,796	5,114
2015	218,870	5,142

Note. Prepared by the author based on data from the *Oficina Nacional de Presupuesto* [National Budget Office] at the *Ministerio de Economía y Finanzas Públicas de la Nación* [Ministry for Economy and Public Finances of the Nation] (2009, 2010, 2011, 2012, 2013, 2014 and 2015), *Resultados del Programa Argentina Trabaja* [Findings of the Argentina Works Programme] (*Ministerio de Desarrollo Social de la Nación* [Ministry for Social Development], 2015a), and the *Memoria Detallada del Estado de la Nación de 2012* [2012 Annual Report of the State of the Argentina Nation] (2013).

Make line). Last, in budget terms, it was also announced that the first stage would cost AR$1,500 million. As Figure 3 shows, in the following years, the funds allocated exceeded this amount and saw a slight increase, even considering the annual inflation rate. Between 2010 and 2013, the scheme represented the second highest percentage of total spending by the Ministry for Social Development, just below the budget for non-contributory pensions (Arcidiácono and Bermúdez, 2015).

On the basis of the above, I contend that the launch of this scheme consolidated the formation of worker co-operatives as a central pillar of intervention in social policy within the framework of a set of public policies that

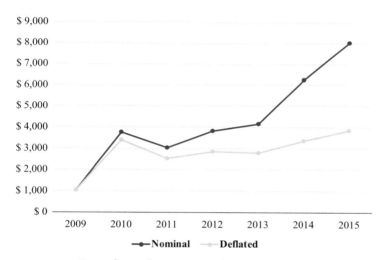

FIGURE 3   Nominal annual Argentina Works Programme budget implementation deflated to 2009 Argentinian pesos (millions of Argentinian pesos): Argentina, 2009–2015
Note. Prepared by author based on data from the National Budget Office and the Ministry for Economy and Public Finances of the Nation (2009, 2010, 2011, 2012, 2013, 2014, 2015), deflated by harmonised IMF data based on the *Índice de Precios al Consumidor del Gran Buenos Aires* [Greater Buenos Aires Consumer Price Index] (IPC-GBA) and the *Índice de Precios al Consumidor Nacional Urbano* [Urban National Consumer Price Index] (IPCNu) of the *Instituto Nacional de Estadística y Censos de la República Argentina* [National Institute of Statistics and Censuses] (INDEC). The latest available data for 2015 is from October. Taking into account the irregularities in the preparation of the INDEC's IPC, we have corroborated these figures with alternative data from the *Centro de Estudios para el Desarrollo Argentino* [Study Centre for Argentinian Development] (CENDA) and *Centro de Investigación y Formación de la República Argentina* [Research and Training Centre of the Argentine Republic] (CIFRA). According to these research centres, the trend is holding steady, albeit with a lower real budget.

encouraged associational and self-managed work. Although the Argentina Works Programme was part of this range of public policies, it must be borne in mind that it is also an off-shoot of cash transfer schemes with work requirement based on the workfare model. Nevertheless, I maintain that the Argentina Works Programme differed substantially from such schemes.

First, its fundamental principles were the central importance of work as a right and social integrator in response to the problem of inequality, as against justifications anchored in the need to provide temporary solutions and develop individual skills to integrate sectors of the population considered dependent into the job market. Second, unlike temporary employment schemes with work requirement, this one established the formation of co-operatives as a means of job-creation and social organization, while also creating instruments – mainly training-oriented – to contribute to their sustainability. Last, in contrast to the schemes that preceded it, the Argentina Works Programme made headway towards 'dignified work,' meaning work enabling workers' needs for reproduction of life to be met. This was partly due to the inclusion – though differing from formal salaried employment – of co-operative workers in social protection schemes, like the social monotax and the Universal Child Allowance, and the narrow gap between the amount of the monetary income provided and the legal minimum wage.

2   The Mediation of Unemployed Workers' Organisations: Civil Associations, Productive Units and Co-operatives

I have so far described cash transfer schemes with work requirement and pointed out that the Working Programme was the first of its kind inspired by the workfare schema of welfare policies (Grondona, 2012). Here I would like to stress that this scheme was also the first step towards the incorporation of unemployed workers' organisations as legitimate administrators of social policies (Maneiro, 2012). To develop this idea, it is first necessary to explore the emergence of these organisations in the 1990s.

In the 1980s and '90s, the forms of liaison between the state and the popular sectors began to be modified: corporative union mediations yielded to the growing weight of territorial mediations. This phenomenon was connected to a series of changes: in the labour market, they led to a decrease in unionized workers; in the sphere of social policy, the 'policies of individuation' assigned a central role to mediation by local neighbourhood leaders related with leading political and state figures; in terms of the state, the processes of decentralization transferred powers and functions from the national to the provincial or municipal levels. Taken together, these processes contributed to putting local arenas and the territorial dimension centre-stage, socio-politically speaking. In terms of the changes this entailed, Astor Massetti (2011) refers to the phenomenon of *'ingreso barrial'* [neighbourhood income] to account for the community strategies developing to meet needs (soup kitchens, community canteens and so on), while Ana Natalucci (2012) mentions the territorialisation of social conflict.

These conditions gave rise to so-called 'unemployed workers' organisations' or *'piqueteras'* [picketers], which emerged from two main sources (Svampa and Pereyra, 2004). The first refers to 'pickets' – a specific form of collective action consisting of blocking roads and other communication routes – carried out in areas of the country far-removed from Buenos Aires and linked to the decline of regional economies and the privatisation of state-owned enterprises during the 1990s. The second source alludes to territorial and organizational action in the Buenos Aires Conurbation as a result of growing poverty and the deepening of deindustrialisation ongoing since the 1970s.

Looking at the Buenos Aires Conurbation, in line with the focus of this book, the first unemployed workers' groups emerged in La Matanza, Zona Sur (the south of the Greater Buenos Conurbation) and La Plata in the latter half of the 1990s. In 1998, the *Corriente Clasista Combativa* [Combative Class Current] (CCC) and the *Federación Tierra y Vivienda* [Land and Housing Federation] (FTV) were formed as part of strategies devised by trades union confederations or by trades union elements in political parties. In contemporary terms, the *Movimientos de Trabajadores Desocupados* [Unemployed Workers Movements] (MTD) group emerged, declaring itself independent of trades unions and political parties, and advocating territorial organisation as an autonomous mode of political construction.

It is worth noting that these unemployed workers' organisations arose out of different political and organizational traditions, both in their modes of action (soup kitchens, camps, occupations of land and public buildings, and so forth) and in the forms of neighbourhood activism (co-operatives, mutual associations, neighbourhood councils, community development societies, grass-roots church communities and so on). In any event, they were all formed around the demand for work, which was considered the legitimate channel to access the means of reproduction. Against a backdrop of unemployment, poverty and the roll-out of targeted social policies, this demand for work was specified in applications for vacancies in temporary employment schemes and for the management of these public resources. Between the late 1990s and the start of the twenty-first century, these organisations formed a social movement: they waged a public campaign to instate the demand for work through road-blocks or 'pickets' as a paradigmatic form of action.

As I have suggested, the Working Programme – primarily its third stage, from 1998 to 2002[4] – represented a turning point insofar as, with the take-over of the *Alianza para el Trabajo, la Justicia y la Educación* [Alliance for Work, Justice and Education] coalition[5] in late 1999, the distribution and management of temporary employment schemes by unemployed workers' organisations deepened (Maneiro, 2012). Based on guidelines issued by the World Bank regarding the participation of civil society and as a way of weakening the territorial power of the Justicialist Party – the main adversary of the coalition then in power – the national government stipulated that productive and community projects where work requirements had been implemented could be submitted and managed by non-governmental organisations.

Accordingly, certain unemployed workers' organisations formalised civil associations to self-manage their own employment plans, and to develop community projects and productive micro-enterprises. This led to unemployed workers' movements resignifying the idea of 'work requirement' (Maneiro, 2012). These organisations' mediations in the provision of social policies meant that, as well as carrying out contentious actions, they became accustomed to undertaking different kinds of actions: in the management of the plans, to negotiating with the state around issues of, for example, the quantities and modalities of distributing subsidies; in the implementation of community and productive projects, to developing technical and administrative know-how.

With the launch of the Plan for Unemployed Heads of Household and the mass expansion of the temporary employment schemes, the ranks of social organisations swelled due to the obligatory nature of work requirement, while further entrenching their role as mediators between vulnerable populations and the state (Bottaro, 2012). Nevertheless, ultimately, the influence of unemployed workers' organisations on the Plan for Unemployed Heads of Household was fairly minor, and they only managed to administrate a small percentage of the plans (Massetti, 2011). This was a consequence of the fact that over the 2001–02 period, the successive governments formed during the

---

4 The scheme was divided into three stages: Working Programme I in 1996, Working Programme II from 1997 to 1998, and Working Programme III from 1998 to 2002.
5 The 'Alliance for Work, Justice and Education' was a political coalition formed in 1997 by the Radical Civic Union, the traditional opponent of the Justicialist Party, and FREPASO (Front for a Country in Solidarity). The main leaders of the latter came from a split within the Justicialist Party that occurred during the presidency of Carlos Menem.

widespread crisis sought to reappropriate control over those policies in order to reconstruct their political connections with local and territorial politics.

With the change of government in 2003 and the introduction of policies to encourage associational and self-managed work, the liaison between the state and unemployed workers' associations in the administration of social policy shifted. The launch of the Down to Work Programme in 2003 – and others geared towards work and production – enabled organisations to develop individual, family or associational productive ventures financed by the state. These ventures could even become state-contracted suppliers. The government's strategy in the implementation of such schemes was to encourage communication with social organisations, primarily those closest to the government's approach, and provide them with resources (Antón, Cresto, Rebón and Salgado, 2011). In this way, as indicated by the interviewees quoted at the start of the chapter, while some organisations devoted their efforts to developing political collaboration with the state, and even placing some of their leaders in positions of public administration, others remained on the side-lines.

The launch of Argentina Works Programme in 2009 was another step in the direction set out by the Down to Work Programme. Whereas organisations had to set up civil associations in order to participate in the early workfare schemes, to be accepted on the Down to Work Programme they had to create individual, family or associational productive units. The Argentina Works Programme staked everything on work in its associational format and stipulated the requirement to form co-operatives. On balance, while the participation of beneficiary sectors of the population in social policies brought no innovations, its formalization since 2003 began progressively to establish the constitution of productive units. Ultimately, the Argentina Works Programme was responsible for the 'co-operativisation' of social organisations.

As well as being set within a particular moment of social policy in Argentina, the Argentina Works Programme was driven by organisations that thought it necessary to create subsidised work through the co-operative format (Natalucci, 2012). However, responding to the claims of social organisations was not synonymous with granting them the role they hoped for. On the contrary, the national government stipulated that the implementation of the Argentina Works Programme would be entrusted to municipal governments, raising fresh question marks around the mediation of social organisations.

In any case, although the Argentina Works Programme revived prior experiences from the popular sectors and answered social demands to subsidise co-operatives, its launch represented an attempt at top-down restructuring (Natalucci, 2012) aimed at articulating territorial politics and channelling political and economic resources to municipal governments to the detriment of unemployed workers' organisations. Faced with this situation, these organisations did not react as one: some took part in the implementation of the Argentina Works Programme – not without tensions – while others turned to collective action as a means of demanding their insertion. In the following section, I describe the economic and political context in which the national government activated this top-down restructuring.

3   The Dual Logic of the Argentina Works Programme's Socio-genesis: Creating Jobs and Co-ordinating Local Politics

The socio-genesis of the Argentina Works Programme cannot be understood merely by reference to the field of social policy. In a context of slowing economic growth and political crisis for the national government during 2008 and 2009, the launch of the scheme had two objectives. On the one hand, the economic crisis and the slowing of economic growth provoked by the international crisis of 2008–09 created the need to design new tools with which to integrate excluded social sectors in the labour market.

On average during the 2003–08 period, annual growth of Gross Domestic Product (GDP) had been 7.9%. In 2009, this percentage shrank by around 6% (World Bank). Regarding labour market figures, the rate of unemployed between 2003 and 2008 had fallen steadily: whereas, for the third quarter of 2003, the rate of unemployment in all urban conurbations ran as high as 16.3%, by the same period in 2008, it stood at 7.8%. Against the background of the international crisis and its repercussions at national level, this process was interrupted in the third quarter of 2009, when unemployment rose to 9.1% (EPH-INDEC). This increase proved even more harmful for the population of the Buenos Aires Conurbation, since this region is used to seeing unemployment above the national average. The 2009 crisis raised unemployment to two digits: whereas, in the third quarter of 2008, it was 9.7%, by the same quarter in 2009, it had risen to 10.6% (EPH-INDEC). On balance, where the economy is concerned, I argue that the Argentina Works Programme sought to create jobs for sectors that had not been incorporated into the formal labour market, in a context of a clear economic decline.

On the other hand, regarding the political crisis, an adverse performance in the legislative elections of June 2009, at which the governing party lost its parliamentary majority, reflected seriously waning support. This cannot be grasped unless we take a retrospective look at the first semester of 2008 and the so-called *'conflicto del campo'* [agrarian strike].[6] Hegemonised by the most concentrated agri-business sectors, the prolonged conflict unified different social personifications in the sector with an alliance the national government was unable to break. What is more, it politicised, mobilised and polarised society like no other conflict since the general crisis of 2001–02 (Antón et al., 2011). The dispute ended in conclusive defeat for the government in the Senate of the National Congress, when the vice-president used his casting vote against President Kirchner's proposed bill to increase export duties on agricultural produce. The toll of the conflict was thus a united opposition and a divided and weakened government.

Then came the June 2009 legislative elections for seats in the chambers of Deputies and Senators. At the same time, elections were held for legislators in certain provinces and for municipal councillors in all districts of Buenos Aires Province. Pre-election dynamics had revolved around two issues: the elections as a plebiscite on the national government or as an opportunity to change direction (González, 2009). In the political jargon of the day, it is claimed that Buenos Aires Province is *'la madre de todas las batallas'* [the mother of all battles]. This is due, among other factors, to the size of its population: according to the INDEC's 2010 *Censo Nacional de Población, Hogares y Vivienda* [National Census of Population, Homes, and Housing] its population was 15,625,084 inhabitants, 39% of Argentina's total population. In the province, the districts comprising the Buenos Aires Conurbation, which represent just 2% of the provincial territory, take in 64% of its population.

As a consequence, the municipalities of the Buenos Aires Conurbation and the mayors that run them have historically held garnered weight in political and electoral dynamics. The aftermath of the 'agrarian strike' determined that the former president Néstor Kirchner and the then governor of Buenos Aires Province, Daniel Scioli, would head the province's list of national deputies. The weakness of the ruling government was demonstrated by the unfavourable results – mainly in Buenos Aires – with an attendant loss of their parliamentary majority. In the Buenos Aires Conurbation this process was also defined by *'corte de boleta'* [ballot cutting], which led to the governing party receiving

---

6   In March 2008 the Executive decided to establish a sliding scale for taxes on certain grains exports, raising levies and linking any variation in them to the evolution of international prices against a background of high returns on commodities. The main corporative bodies from the agricultural sector resisted the measure and resorted to road blocks with the aim of imposing a lock-out to block trade in grains.

more votes in the municipalities than their national legislative candidates. This demonstrated the pressing need to co-ordinate politics at the local level.

Subsequent to these events, the national government implemented various forward-thinking redistributive measures: the renationalisation of pension funds privatised in the 1990s, the promotion of a new audio-visual media law (which set the notion of the 'right to communication' against its conception as a tradeable good in an increasingly monopolistic market) and the launch of Universal Child Allowance. I contend that, by creating co-operatives to carry out works of public infrastructure in this context, the Argentina Works Programme not only pursued the goal of creating jobs as a form of 'social inclusion,' but also of co-ordinating and revitalising politics in the municipalities of the Buenos Aires Conurbation and contributing resources for infrastructure and employment.

In short, the Argentina Works Programme helped to consolidate the formation of co-operatives in the framework of a public policy that promoted the associational and self-managed work that had been under way since 2003. However, the evolution of these policies as the subject of an exhaustive investigation into the scheme's socio-genesis leaves plenty of room for exploration: the scheme's launch constituted a strategy to confront the economic slow-down and political crisis of 2008–09. In the following section, I suggest that it was this double logic that underpinned its conflictual character.

4   Induced Co-operatives? The Struggle of Unemployed Workers' Organisations

The launch of the Argentina Works Programme was announced on 14 August 2009. Little over a month later, on 22 September, the first protests by unemployed workers' organisations related to the scheme took place. At that time, around twenty organisations of unemployed workers carried out eighteen simultaneous road-blocks of access routes to the cities of Buenos Aires and La Plata (the provincial capital), as well as other road-blocks in another ten provinces around the country. Organisations were thus able to co-ordinate their resources, and simultaneously block roads and communication routes in a protest that covered vast areas. Organisations used these actions to critique the scheme's approach to management, denouncing the discretional selection of co-operative members and demanding their incorporation in the Argentina Works Programme, as well as the possibility of forming and running the co-operatives formed by this scheme. These criticisms, denunciations and demands were quickly amalgamated into the slogan '*Cooperativas*

Sin Punteros' [Co-operatives Without Brokers][7] and a campaign front that ran under the same slogan.

That said, let us rewind a few years to review the mobilising dynamics of unemployed workers' organisations prior to the implementation of the Argentina Works Programme. To do this, we shall revisit the work by Gustavo Antón, Jorge Castro, Julián Rebón and Rodrigo Salgado (2011) analysing the evolution of the struggles and organisations of unemployed workers during the period 2000–09. Over the early years of this century, unemployed workers' organisations had seen their demonstrations steadily increase, reaching a climax in 2002. By the following year, their mustering power had begun to wane, a trend that intensified through 2005 and culminated in 2007 with total demobilisation.

This was the result of a combination of changes in the political and economic spheres. In 2003, President Néstor Kirchner had changed tack over state action to protests by unemployed workers' organisations: from delegitimisation and repression, there was a shift to negotiation and dialogue, and repression of social protest was limited. The strategy involved providing resources for organisations – primarily those most closely aligned – and creating jobs to resolve the pressing problem of unemployment (Antón et al., 2011).

Both facets of the strategy were in fact effective. Economic growth and job creation undercut organisations' recruitment base and resulted in a loss of mobilising capacity. Furthermore, with the opening-up of new institutional channels, the central importance of protest actions began to fade. Additionally, the policies incentivising associational and self-managed work transformed the dynamics of organisations, which were increasingly oriented towards the running of productive ventures at the expense of contentious actions (Antón et al., 2011).

Nevertheless, if the organisations in 2007 barely mustered any demonstrations, their capacity for pugnacity from September 2009 experienced a new lease of life. In this vein, we ask ourselves why the launch of the Argentina Works Programme, which was establishing a new institutional channel and deepening policy to encourage productive ventures, was an incentive for collective action and opened up a new cycle of protest?

To answer this question, I borrow the concept of 'political opportunity structures' developed by Sidney Tarrow (1999). Tarrow proposes that, in the emergence of contentious action, a series of elements are amalgamated: increasing

---

7 In Argentina, the category of *'puntero político'* [political broker] is used to refer to people who, generally in working-class neighbourhoods, co-ordinate territorial politics with party leaders and state structures.

institutional access, instability of political alignments, conflicts among elites and the state diminished capacity for repression. These elements are usually combined with a generalised perception of the elevated costs of inaction. Let us now look at some of these issues for the case in hand.

First, the Argentina Works Programme was a social policy the organisations were familiar with. They had implemented part of their territorial political construction through the socio-productive ventures encouraged by social policies. Moreover, the Argentina Works Programme targeted their grass-roots and was geared to respond to unemployed workers' organisations' historical demand for work, albeit based on social plans. Therefore, the Argentina Works Programme's launch was a window on institutional access for organisations as a social policy that was familiar to them and which called on them to participate.

However, the dual logic of the Argentina Works Programme's objectives involved strengthening municipal governments. This had its correlation in the questioning of unemployed worker organisations' mediation in social policy. Organisations were effectively included only in the design and implementation of the Argentina Works Programme in a selective and limited way. Indeed, in some cases, the mere formation of co-operatives to bring their grass-roots support into the scheme was hindered by municipal governments.[8] This window of institutional access then, which could have been flung wide open, turned out to be a door half-open to contentious action.

Second, the Argentina Works Programme was launched in 2009 in the throes of the national government's political crisis. For this reason, unemployed workers' organisations found opportunities for action, as certain media groups opposed to the government found that broadcasting these actions could be a way to undermine its legitimacy. Last, these processes played out in a longer-term context of non-repression of social protest as express governmental policy. This, however, did not prevent repressive processes, primarily in the provincial and local arenas. Nor did it prevent prosecutions of social protest.

---

8 To define the target population for the Argentina Works Programme, and select districts and beneficiaries, the Ministry for Social Development established two types of criteria: focus and eligibility of the beneficiaries. Whereas the former defines vulnerable sectors as the potential beneficiary population, the latter limits which people within that population can become beneficiaries based on certain criteria. The Ministry did not stipulate any prioritising criteria to establish which individuals were actually included in the scheme. Therefore, the formation of co-operatives was left in the hands of executive bodies, namely municipal governments, who were given plenty of room for manoeuvre.

That said, we must turn our attention to the intensity and dynamics of contentious action, and to its principal demands. How did the Programme evolve and what was the impact of the struggle of unemployed workers' organisations? The input I use to answer these questions is taken from a catalogue of 307 collective actions featuring unemployed workers' organisations between September 2009 and June 2012.[9]

4.1 The Evolution of the Argentina Works Programme

The first period, which I term 'emergence,' lasted from the launch of the Argentina Works Programme until mid-2010. During this time-span, the scheme established its main features. In 2009, the aim was primarily to identify the target population, and to select the beneficiaries (60,000) and localities where it would be implemented (36 from the Buenos Aires Conurbation) (*Documento de Acceso a la Información Pública del Ministerio de Desarrollo Social*, 7 December 2010; *Ministerio de Economía y Finanzas Públicas de la Nación*, 2009). Co-operative formation training sessions and procedures were also carried out. In the first quarter of 2010, localities were incorporated from a further four provinces. Over the course of those months, promotional and registration campaigns were held, co-operatives were formed, agreements with the executor bodies were signed – mostly municipalities – and training schemes were run for Argentina Works beneficiaries (*Documento de Acceso a la Información Pública del Ministerio de Desarrollo Social*, 27 April 2010, 7 December 2010).

It was not until mid-2010 that most beneficiaries had been effectively incorporated and the worker co-operatives started up general productive activities. Around July that year began a second 'early implementation' period, lasting until November 2011. Registrations had now been made effective, and there

---

9   This was compiled from articles stored in the digital archive of the print edition of *Clarín* newspaper, published between 1 September 2009 and 30 June 2012. This newspaper was chosen because of its national scope and the quality and quantity of the records it provided. The time-period was chosen because by mid-2012 the characteristics of the scheme had already been defined and the largest number of beneficiaries had joined it. By mid-2012, after the early stages of expansion and implementation, the Argentina Works Programme began to decline: in an inflationary context, individual incomes stagnated and the possibility of incorporating new beneficiaries tended to diminish. The compilation of this database was a collective effort carried out within the research project of the National Scientific and Technical Research Council (CONICET) called *"Trabajo, redes territoriales y acción piquetera. El impacto del Plan Argentina Trabaja en un movimiento de trabajadores desocupados del Gran Buenos Aires"* [Work, Territorial Networks and Picketer Action. The Impact of the Argentina Works Programme on an Unemployed Workers' Movement in Greater Buenos Aires], coordinated by María Maneiro.

would be no further mass incorporations of beneficiaries: by the first semester of 2010, 157,089 people had been incorporated, whereas, more than a year later, by October 2011, data suggested there were 191,275 beneficiaries registered in the scheme (*Documento de Acceso a la Información Pública del Ministerio de Desarrollo Social*, 7 December 2010, 4 November 2011). This accounted for an increase of around 20%. Regarding its territorial scope, by the end of this second period, the scheme had extended to localities in six new provinces (*Documento de Acceso a la Información Pública del Ministerio de Desarrollo Social*, 4 November 2011).

The third period – which I term 'eroded continuity' – began in December 2011 with Cristina Fernández de Kirchner's second presidential term in office. The Argentina Works Programme had emerged from the crucible of a political crisis with the aim of organising local politics. Kirchner's victory at the polls in late 2011 cast doubt therefore on the scheme's continuity, but, in the end, the Argentina Works Programme survived, albeit much degraded.

First, the number of beneficiaries only rose by around 4% compared to the preceding period. Second, in terms of the scheme's territorial expansion, just one locality was incorporated towards the end of 2011, followed by localities from two new provinces over the course of 2012 (*Ministerio de Economía y Finanzas Públicas de la Nación*, 2012). Third, as Figure 4 shows, whereas the income received by co-operative members opened 2009 at around 90% of the legal minimum wage – in Argentina called the '*Salario Mínimo, Vital y Móvil*' [Minimum Living Adjustable Wage] – and remunerations for the lowest category of private household workers, by mid-2012 it had fallen to around 50%. This widened the wage-gap between co-operative members and workers registered in social security, even in the lowest and least collectivised categories, such as private household workers. It is worth noting that, at the start of the Argentina Works Programme, beneficiaries worked an eight-hour day. From 2012 on, the workday was divided between four hours' work and two hours' training workshops. Here we can see a link between the relative reduction in income and the workday.

There is no doubt that certain aspects of the Argentina Works Programme were not planned or that the process of struggle and bargaining with unemployed workers' organisations shaped it in unexpected ways. Next, based on an analysis of organisations' contentious actions, I examine their impact on the design and implementation of the scheme, that is, the definitions and changes triggered by these actions and interactions between organisations and the state. This analysis also allows us to understand the way in which the launch of the Argentina Works Programme was an institutional window of opportunity for collective action, permitting organisations to reinstate their demand

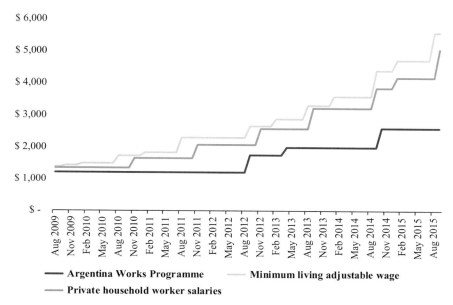

FIGURE 4   Nominal monthly evolution of Argentina Works Programme's individual subsidies, minimum living adjustable wage, and salaries for private household workers: Argentina, August 2009–September 2015
Note. Prepared by author based on *Programa Argentina Trabaja* documents; Resolutions nos. 2/09, 2/10, 2/11, 3/11, 2/12, 4/13, 3/14, 4/15 of the *Consejo Nacional del Empleo, la Productividad y el Salario Mínimo, Vital y Móvil* [National Council for Employment, Productivity and Minimum Living Adjustable Wage]; Resolutions nos. 1002/09, 1297/10, 1350/11, 958/12, 886/13, 1062/14 from the *Ministerio de Trabajo, Empleo y Seguridad Social de la Nación* [Ministry for Work, Employment and Social Security of the Nation]; and Resolution no. 1/15 from the *Comisión Nacional de Trabajo en Casas Particulares* [National Committee for Private Household Work].

for work and vie for the management of social policy. Specifically, I explore the organizational remainder of these struggles for unemployed workers' organizations.

4.2 *The Intensity and Dynamics of Contentious Action*

As Figure 5 shows, the first period is the most contentious: between September 2009 and June 2010, there was a monthly average of sixteen collective actions. This is related to the fact that many attributes of the scheme were yet to be specified: the number and form of incorporation of beneficiaries, the way of running the scheme and the co-operatives, and the tasks assigned to the productive ventures. This contrasts with the two subsequent years: the second period saw an average of four actions a month, while this average rose to ten in the third period.

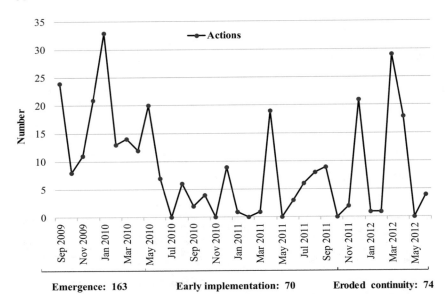

FIGURE 5 Number of collective actions by unemployed workers' organisations under Argentina Works Programme by month and period: Argentina, September 2009–June 2012

Note. Prepared by author based on catalogue of collective actions by unemployed workers' organisations under Argentina Works Programme. N: 307.

In May 2010, when the preparations got under way for the celebrations to mark the Bicentenary of Argentina's May Revolution to commemorate the first government independent of the Spanish crown, protests were on the rise, as were the government's unease about them. This accelerated negotiations and agreements between unemployed workers' organisations and state officials around the effectivisation of the incorporation of beneficiaries already registered and the incorporation of new ones. In June then, in the immediate wake of these agreements, incorporations of these beneficiaries into the scheme materialised and collective actions tailed off. By July, a new period characterised by low levels of conflict was on the horizon.

After that, the scheme was run by municipal governments and its dynamics tended to become localised. The recorded number of protests fell accordingly, which did not, however, imply the end of the dispute. Added to this, the national government had begun to recover from the political crisis, and the structure of opportunities for action consequently narrowed. The successful Bicentennial celebrations of May 2010, a watershed between the two periods, represented a turning point in that respect. Furthermore, the death in October

2010 of the former president, Néstor Kirchner, strengthened the image of the newly widowed president even further, and Cristina Fernández de Kirchner was eventually re-elected in October 2011.

Despite being a period low in conflicts, during the early implementation of the scheme, the dynamics of demonstration created significant positive organisational results: the creation of the *Asociación Gremial de Trabajadores Cooperativistas Autogestivos y Precarizados* [Union Association of Co-operative, Self-Managed and Precarised Workers] (AGTCAP) and the *Confederación de Trabajadores de la Economía Popular* [Confederation of Workers in the Popular Economy] (CTEP). The AGTCAP is a union organisation whose inception is linked directly to the emergence of the Argentina Works Programme:

> We're setting up a union, it's called the AGTCAP. The thing is to represent co-operative members. It isn't easy to put it together, it's pretty complicated. Even more so when you're just getting started, nobody gives you any recognition. One of our demands, one of the slogans we got is the nationalisation of the scheme [Argentina Works], that it isn't run by brokers, that it belongs to the social organisations. Then, recognition as AGTCAP, we want the Ministry for Labour to recognise us as AGTCAP, as a union of co-operative members. And then the issue of the rise, a rise to the level of the basic basket, to what it's worth today.
> CARLOS, member of an AGTCAP organisation, September 2011

The association states that the decision to unionise around 3,000 co-operative members from self-managed ventures working for the state, and mainly in conditions of precarisation, in the provinces of Buenos Aires, Córdoba, Chaco, Formosa, Tucumán, Santa Fe and Buenos Aires arose from a series of struggles summed up in the slogan 'Co-operatives Without Brokers' (AGTCAP, 29 September 2012; *ANRed*, 18 March 2011). This formalised the experience of the *Frente de Cooperativas sin Punteros* [Front for Co-operatives Without Brokers], formed in December 2009 in response to the implementation of the Argentina Works Programme. This organisation started from the diagnosis that, although, in recent years, the state had created work for thousands of unemployed people through public works and co-operatives, the forms taken by the labour relationship had kept these workers in a situation of insecurity and precarisation.

For its part, the CTEP not only incorporates Argentina Works Programme co-operative members, but also draws on other experiences of work within the so-called 'popular economy.' It brings together self-employed and self-managed workers, co-operative members, and workers from recuperated enterprises and social schemes. Similar to the AGTCAP, it is a union association that begins with the diagnosis that it is necessary to restore social and labour rights eroded by neoliberalism. It also posits that activism is fundamental in building unity and activating struggles in the popular economy, given workers' fragmentation and the absence of identifiable bosses (CTEP, n.d.; La Alameda, 19 August 2011; *Resumen Latinoamericano*, n.d.). Although its central organisation backed the Argentina Works Programme, the formation of the CTEP revealed the tensions and limitations of the scheme presented at the start of this chapter. In 2015, the CTEP secured the creation of a unionisation regime for workers in the popular economy and ensured that the Ministry for Labour, Employment and Social Security would grant it the right to represent the collective interests of these workers.

The third period opened with a marked rise in conflicts due to a relative decline in remunerations in a context of inflation. Moreover, historically speaking, December is a peak protest month in Argentina's culture of struggle. Accordingly, collective actions not only instated demands around remunerations but requested food from hypermarkets. Last, a rise in remunerations was announced in February for workers in the Argentina Works Programme,[10] but this was slow to be implemented. Faced with this uncertainty, March saw a rise in collective actions, which then tailed off towards the end of the month.

4.3   *The Demands and Forms of Contentious Action*

Organisations during the first period (Figure 6) focused on demanding incorporation to the scheme (78.5%), either through the demand to incorporate beneficiaries or through the nationwide extension of the Argentina Works Programme. In particular, they denounced discriminatory practices, claiming that municipal governments' running of the Argentina Works Programme was blocking the incorporation of beneficiaries proposed by organisations. The actions taken in this period were also geared to denouncing these types of practices in the running of the Argentina Works Programme and how co-operatives were formed (41.1%). Thus, they not only challenged the way the scheme was implemented regarding the inclusion of beneficiaries and localities but also demanded greater autonomy from local government bodies to form and run co-operatives. During this period, the watchword 'Co-operatives Without Brokers' caught on around twenty organisations in a front of the same

---

10   The same regulatory framework (Resolución del Ministerio de Desarrollo Social de la Nación N° 1499/12) that established the rise in income also stipulated a series of changes to co-operatives' structures. One of the most significant changes was the reduction of the original number of members: from 60 to 30.

name. Several of these ensured both the incorporation of beneficiaries and that these would join co-operatives formed entirely by organisations.

In terms of the format the actions took, most were roadblocks (55.8%) and demonstrations (21.5%). This is not surprising given that, in collective actions, actors draw on repertoires of performances, that is, learned and historically grounded routines for making claims specific to certain subjects in their interactions with particular targets and spatial-temporal co-ordinates (Tilly, 2008).

As well as the continued use of roadblocks or '*piquetes*' [pickets], the first period saw the emergence of a relatively innovative form of action: camps in public thoroughfares. The camps are roadblocks characterised by their long duration. In this respect, their content differs from traditional roadblocks: the long duration entails the transfer of daily life from the slums, shantytowns and settlements to the sites of the protests. Therein lies their novelty. Although precedents for this form of action can be found in the repertoire of struggle waged by unemployed workers' organisations, the novelty of the case analysed lies in the fact that this transfer of daily life was not to roads nearby as it was in 2001, but to the very heart of the capital (Maneiro, 2015).

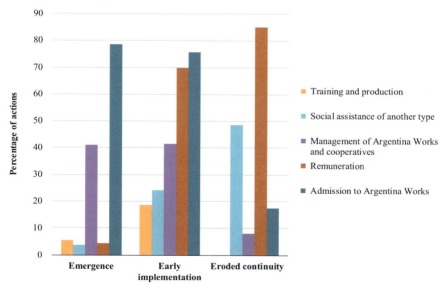

FIGURE 6   Claims made during collective actions by unemployed workers' organisations under Argentina Works Programme by period (in percentages): Argentina, September 2009 – June 2012
Note. Prepared by author based on catalogue of collective actions by unemployed workers' organisations. Multiple choice response. Total number of actions (n=307). Total number of claims (n=545).

The significance of this format to my analysis does not lie in its statistical weight but in the attention it stirs up in public opinion, the demonstration of resources it requires from organisations and the positive results it achieves regarding the demands being made. So, primarily through two camps occupying public thoroughfares outside the Ministry for Social Development in November and December 2009, results were obtained regarding the demands made by organisations. With the November camp lasting over 30 hours and the December one over 40, and 2,000 people participating in each, they became the condition of possibility for the main negotiations between the unemployed workers' organisations and governmental authorities to take place. Whereas, in the first period, 7.4% of actions took the form of camps, by mid-2012, the percentage had dropped to around 1%.

Widespread territorial actions like the roadblocks mentioned at the beginning of this section were also important in the early days. Unlike the camps, these demonstrations did not immediately force the government authorities into negotiations and concessions, but their territorial expansion did contribute to the effective inclusion of beneficiaries into the Argentina Works Programme. This expansion also helped to bed in the demand for the scheme's nationalisation and federalisation.

The second period was characterised by the dispersion and diversity of the demands. Those from the previous stage were upheld, albeit less forcefully, and demands over remunerations – for payment or increase – came to the fore. Demands like this were raised in 4.3% of the actions taken during the emergence of the Argentina Works Programme, whereas they were present in 70% of actions in the second period. During the early implementation of the scheme, the monitoring of presenteeism by municipal governments ahead of disbursements of remunerations led to administrative difficulties that caused errors in the disbursements and delays to wage payments, as well as deductions or direct cancellations of payment. As a result, the payment of income became an important claim in the set of demands over remunerations, along with the request for the incorporation of the complementary annual salary (a thirteenth salary divided in two instalments and a right of salaried employees in Argentina). However, the majority demand over remunerations was for the amount to be increased, having lagged behind the legal minimum wage and remunerations received by private household workers on the lowest rung (Figure 4). Furthermore, while they did not become serious requests, demands for training and production (assignment of tasks, delivery of materials, execution of works and so on) also rose in this second period, as did claims for other types of social assistance, such as the demand to end the incompatibility of Universal Child Allowance with other social schemes.

Last, in the third period, the claims for remunerations came to have a clear majority, primarily over the request for pay-rises. This request was granted on 28 February 2012, when it was announced that remunerations would increase as of April via two incentives: one for presenteeism, the other for productivity. However, these incentives only applied to the wages of 30,000 co-operative members in the Buenos Aires Conurbation, with a commitment to incorporate the rest in the next 180 days. The non-universality of the incentives and the uncertainty about when the pay-rises would materialise meant that contentious actions did not tail off after the announcement and that demands for increased wages continued to be made even after February. The request for food from hypermarkets was also incorporated. Regarding forms of action, during the second and third periods, roadblocks and demonstrations were even more predominant than in the first, and camps were only marginally deployed.

In conclusion, the approach focusing on contentious interactions between unemployed workers' organisations and the state allows us to examine the two-way impacts. On the one hand, the launch of the Argentina Works Programme represented an institutional window of opportunity for the collective action by unemployed workers, opening up a new cycle of protest, albeit at a level somewhat lower than at the start of the twenty-first century. In this context, two union organisations were formed, the AGTCAP and CTEP, which sought to put the beneficiaries of the Argentina Works Programme on the same footing as the classic demands of the salaried worker. This overall positive organisational result is thought-provoking because, although the organisations had previously been involved in social schemes with work requirement, it was only with the introduction of the Argentina Works Programme and the formation of co-operatives that they began to establish organisations linked to the field of work.

Running counter to these interactions, protest actions forced the scheme to reformulate, specifically the process of incorporating new beneficiaries and the nationalisation of the Argentina Works Programme during the periods of its emergence and early implementation, as well as the increase in remunerations during its degraded continuity. Consequently, although the scheme – and the 'co-operativisation' of social organisations – was not the result of struggle, the incorporation of beneficiaries from unemployed workers' organisations certainly was, as were the formation of certain co-operatives and even particular features acquired by the scheme.

Let us cast our minds back to the co-operative models outlined by Vuotto (2011): 'integrated' co-operatives, 'claims-based' co-operatives and co-operatives 'state-induced.' Integrated co-operatives refer to the experiences of traditional co-operativism, whereas claims-based co-operatives take in worker-recuperated enterprises. Co-operatives induced by public policies are formed by excluded subjects whose primary need is to obtain work. These co-operatives' difficulties lie in the hazards implied by a loss of autonomy, as well as the impact of a short-term view on their potential to develop shared norms, among other issues.

Juan Pablo Hudson (2016), for his part, focuses on co-operatives protected by state subsidies and classifies them under three types: 'non-state,' 'synthetic,' and 'amphibian.' While non-state co-operatives refer to recuperated enterprises, synthetic co-operatives emerge exclusively through state schemes and are characterised by being state providers with no connection to the market. Last, amphibian co-operatives combine elements of both: they are formed through an associational will that pre-exists any state intervention, but in a context of national government promoting associativism, which, in their early stages, implies the absence of struggle and state repression.

These categorisations and typologies are fertile ground for the analysis of concrete social forms, as they cast light on certain aspects of and trends in social processes, albeit not exhaustively. In the typologies mentioned above, the ways these experiences arise represent a key variable in their characterisation. The struggles, claims and interactions of cooperation and conflict with the state, primarily during the co-operatives' constitutive processes, are indicators that enable some types to be differentiated from others. For this reason, I believe that a deeper examination of the matrices from which co-operatives embedded in social policies emerge enables us to discern the hybridisations in concrete co-operative forms.

In this chapter, we have seen that, although state induction describes one aspect of the emergence of Argentina Works co-operatives, this categorisation tends to sidestep the contentious, claims-making dimension of the process. We have also seen that this claims-making referred not just to access to public resources but to a dispute over the forms the resulting co-operatives would ultimately take, or more specifically, over the degrees of autonomy they would be granted. Regardless of whether the state imposed the legal form, could the struggles studied here not give rise to co-operative forms embedded in public policies which cannot adequately be characterised merely by referring to 'state induction' or the 'synthetic' character of their formation?

Erik Olin Wright (2017) identifies several paths to setting up co-operatives, grouped in four kinds of formation: 'autonomous,' 'incubated,' 'guided by another co-operative' and those formed by the 'conversion of private enterprises.' I believe the concept of 'state incubation' to be the most suitable for characterising this type of co-operative in that it identifies the leading role of the state without eclipsing struggles or controversies. As in the case of recuperated enterprises, the contentious origins of these 'incubated' co-operatives and their anchoring in demands around work are hubs towards an analysis of their socio-productive character. I shall develop this line of investigation in the following chapters through case studies.

CHAPTER 3

Keeping and Having a Job

A Milestone in Constitutive Conflicts

Spanish has a popular saying that goes, *'para muestra, basta un botón'* [a button is as good a proof as any]. This nugget of wisdom reminds us of the issue of scale in social science research: totalities can be approached through case studies. Claudia Fonseca (1999) states that a well-constructed case study is not just a case study but references a system that goes beyond the singular. Qualitative approaches then have a great deal to contribute to the social sciences. From different epistemic frameworks, popular and academic knowledge alike rescue the small, which is frequently under-rated as a conduit to higher knowledge.

Whereas my focus has so far been on a macrosocial scale, from now on we shall be upping the gradation of our lens. I shall therefore be modifying the scale of analysis based on the multiple instrumental case study, which will allow us to go into the dynamics of conflicts in granular detail, as well as the characteristics of their social relations. In conversation with the first two chapters, I analyse the constitutive conflicts of the two co-operatives selected in order to chart their disputed origins and their links with demands aimed at guaranteeing social reproduction through work.

I first describe each conflict, focusing on the sequence and dynamics of the events, claims, forms of action and social identities at issue. I then compare the elements that give rise to the conflicts, their forms and the attributes of the adversaries, class antagonisms, types of co-operativism, characteristics of social organisations that participate in or promote them, as well as the scope and types of power the social groups comprising the organisations possess.

1 'Occupy, Resist, Produce' … and Have!

The recuperated enterprise I analyse in this section is a worker co-operative in the hospitality industry, located in the Balvanera district of Buenos Aires. It is important to note that its location with its high land prices has implications for the conflict we are about to analyse. In Balvanera, around the plot of land occupied by the hotel, there is growing pressure to develop real estate. This deepens the dispute over the property and sharpens the interest of the actors involved.

Opened in 1978, the hotel was built with funds provided by a loan from the *Banco Nacional de Desarrollo* [National Development Bank] (BANADE).[1] This loan was never repaid, and the hotel became the object of fraudulent purchase-and-sale dealings by its owners and administrators. In 1997, the hotel was sold to a Chilean business group for US$12 million, but the bill-of-sale was made out for just a third of its value. Upon default of the balance payment and with the hotel venture managed by the Chilean group in crisis, the original property owners rescinded the bill-of-sale and set up a 'ghost' corporation,[2] which they sold the hotel to in 2001. As a result of this mock sale the original owners underwrote their ownership of the property while simultaneously evading the transfer of debts and mortgages and lobbied for the bankruptcy of the Chilean enterprise to be declared, which, on losing ownership, would be unable to repay its debts. That year, the Chilean enterprise did indeed file for bankruptcy, and, on 28 December 2001, the hotel closed.

Over the course of what could have been straightforward bankruptcy proceedings and liquidation, a group of the hotel's former staff decided on recuperation as the only way to avoid losing their jobs. At the start of 2003, when the economy had not yet recovered, the evidence that the former boss was still using the hotel's premises[3] and the indifference of the bankruptcy receiver, coupled with the recuperated enterprise movement's public visibility all converged to promote ties between the workers and what was at the time the most important recuperated enterprise organisation.

> Me and a bunch of *compañeros* [work-mates] used to go along to the bankruptcy receiver cause we wanted to get paid the cash we were owed, cause they hadn't paid our holidays, all the money owed that we were entitled to, and they'd say: "No, you can't come in. And anyway, you've

---

1 This development bank operated in Argentina between 1970 and 1993, when it was liquidated. Its function was to finance private sector industrial investments with soft loans. However, the lack of clear accounts, the lack of orientation of its long-term loans to the industrial sector and the political manipulation of the bank led to it never fulfilling that function (Finchelstein, 2012). By the time of its closure, almost all its loans were irrecoverable, 50% of which were to around just twenty enterprises (López and Rougier, 2011).
2 A 'ghost' company is an organisation that is used to simulate business transactions and typically has no significant real assets. For a more complete description of the characteristic signs and evidence of the 'ghost' company formed in this case, see the article by Santiago O'Donnell in *Página 12*, 21 August 2007.
3 An apartment hotel belonging to the former owners and administrators continues to operate round the corner from the co-operative. The two were interconnected at the time, and the workers noticed that the apartment hotel was using some of the hotel's facilities, which they would later recuperate.

got to arrange a hearing. You can't show up here every day demanding something, it isn't right." [...] We'd tell them: "We don't want it dismantled cause we want to keep working at the hotel." Then a compañero told him we were going to call the media. It would never have crossed our minds to talk to the press, but she had this moment of revelation. That was when the only 300 pesos we all got paid came in. And that was when the compañeros we'd never seen since the hotel shut appeared. So, this one compañero came and said: "Listen, I know this bunch of people who can help you get your jobs back."

ANA, co-operative member, November 2014

∴

The hotel had been closed for ages. It was already dead. The thing was, we were famous at the time and [the country] was out of work. Remember, this was late 2002, early 2003, they [the staff] hadn't found any other graft. The hotel had been closed for a long time. It [the idea of recuperation] was about them spotting their chance, and again, we were famous.

MATÍAS, former leading figure in the recuperated
enterprises movement, April 2017

Amid resistance, scepticism and uncertainty, a series of meetings were held between a small group of former workers and leading figures from the recuperated enterprise organisation. In the early days of the conflict, the most prominent claims were around wages and were made with requests for meetings and attempts to engage with the judicial authorities. But the search for individual resolutions to wages owed and compensations proved inconclusive. The impossibility of reaching a solution through judicial channels, the confirmation of fraudulent dealings by the former boss and the connections with the recuperated enterprises organisation sparked direct action. Though not without misgivings and bitterness about the political dimension the conflict was acquiring, the act of recuperating the enterprise was set in motion as it gradually became clear it was the only way to protect jobs and reproduce the worker identity. Central to this process were the encouragement and support of the recuperated enterprises organisation, which contributed political entrepreneurs and leaders as well as organisational resources and accumulated knowledge.

We were out of it for a year till a few compañeros got in touch with the recuperated enterprise organisation. That was when we got down to the meetings to form a co-operative. So, we set up the co-operative feeling afraid and anxious cause I'm someone who'd never had any experience of activism in any political party or anything. [...] Not of us there who set up the co-operative had been an activist; only the guys in the recuperated enterprises organisation who helped us.

GRACIELA, co-operative member, August 2014

Eventually, one morning in March 2003, the hotel was occupied by 30 people, among them activists and leaders from the recuperated enterprise organisation, and other social and political organisations, members of neighbourhood assemblies, researchers and university lecturers, and a few former workers. This collective action fundamentally altered the property relations and expressed the formation of a social alliance around the recuperated enterprise movement. From the following interview excerpts, we can even see that the hotel's former workers were not the majority group driving the occupation at the very start:

On 21 March 2003, we arranged to enter this place at ten in the morning. One compañera already knew this was all set up. They'd met up before and, you know, gone to a few meetings held [...] We walked in like it was just another day, through the aparthotel, through the basement. The day we went in there were lots of people. There were actually seventeen of us compañeros as went in; then there were people who came in with us, I didn't know there were political people there. [...] That day there were militant *compañeros* [comrades] who came in with us; they helped us get our jobs back right there and then. When it opened – cause someone had made a hole there cause it was all walled off – everybody started pouring in.

ANA, co-operative member, November 2014

∴

There was a group of around 30 of us [...], it was early in the morning and there were only a few workers from the hotel: somewhere between three and five. We met up near the hotel and went in [...]. The leader of the recuperated enterprises organisation broke the padlock. I went along to show my support and entered with one of the workers, who later became president of the [recuperated] enterprise. When he went in, with tears in his eyes, he exclaimed "Back home again!" Over the course of the day, as we took over the hotel [...], as things started settling back to normal, other workers from the hotel who hadn't been there at the time of the occupation started trickling in.

IVÁN, academic researcher, February 2017

As I pointed out in Chapter 1, the adoption of the worker co-operative's form was in response to an adaptive strategy that gave legal backing to pursue the process:

> What the judge said was that, for us to stay here, we had to have a legal form. We debated which legal form to choose: we could have been a *sociedad anónima* [limited company] or a *sociedad de responsabilidad limitada* [private limited company], but cause we were all so worn-out by that whole business, the first idea put in front of us was the co-operative. In fact, we were already operating like a co-operative cause we took the decisions as a group and held assemblies. Mainly, the first thing we experienced about co-operatives was assemblies, but without being part of the co-operative. In other words, we started to meet and debate.
>
> DARÍO, co-operative member, August 2014

It was against this background that the co-operative was granted legal custody. While this did not officially grant the right of usufruct for the premises, it did enable the workers to remain in the hotel as responsible for protecting the assets. The infrastructure conditions, the lack of working capital and the time required to define the socio-economic and enterprise project meant that the early days of the co-operative entailed 'resisting,' in other words, keeping the occupation of the premises going. This meant standing guard, collecting money to fund strikes, applying for state subsidies and renting out some conference rooms. During the first few months, while the hotel was still in no condition to market its services, the co-operative spent its time developing non-market liaisons with other recuperated enterprises. These links involve cooperation interactions whose main feature is that they are unmediated by the market (Kasparian, 2013a).

> Actually, it didn't involve working; what we really did was receive organisations. [...] In the early days, we used to trade with provider co-operatives so they could hold their meetings, do the things they had to, so we used to trade paint. If they were construction co-operatives, we'd trade for building jobs. So, it was like this back-and-forth till 2004.
>
> DARÍO, co-operative member, August 2014

∴

there was also this ideological issue [...] There was this whole process of debate about what to do with the hotel, how to go about it. They thought we should go back to being the hotel they'd worked in. Despite the precarity in legal terms, they thought they were going to be the owners of a three- or four-star hotel. [...] I argued a lot with them then. I proposed setting up a sort of cultural hotel, putting four beds in each room, naming each floor after famous figures and revolutionaries from around the world, or artists, and building up the brand as the "biggest hostel in the world," the "recuperated hostel." We'd drawn up a business plan that really did work, it would expand the number of workers fast, the exchange rate really helped us, but they put up this mighty resistance cause they wanted to go back to being the hotel Menem had stayed at. In the middle of all that, we formed this cultural group and started throwing parties to raise some wonga [money] to support it, and we got shedloads of food from the Buenos Aires City Government. [...] They gave us workers a food parcel per family, we got up to five parcels per family a month. It helped a lot cause there was no hard cash. Then we started to get cash subsidies from the City Government and started to throw parties. What we did was rent out the conference rooms for parties.

>MATÍAS, former leading figure in the recuperated enterprises movement, April 2017)

The unsettled, embryonic character of the experience and the debates around "what to do with the hotel" during the first year of self-management and 'resistance' thus gave rise to two questions of relevance to my analysis. On the one hand, negotiations with the hotel's legal owners were developed over the course of the year. Only later on, faced with proof of the workers' determination to pursue their self-management project, did the legal owners of the property intensify the conflict over occupancy.

> We spoke to the legal owner of the property. [...] If we hadn't got stuck in, a year later they'd have been reopening the hotel, no doubt about it. They'd be back in business. [...] They'd have set it up again under a new company and opened it. We'd been negotiating that loads of times, pushed by the workers. [...] In our books, it was politically dead dodgy to do this: we needed a series of guarantees we didn't have. We were asking for a percentage share in the company for the co-operative. For it to be a company where the workers got a percentage through the co-operative, for them to earn a decent wage but have a share of the profits and some

control over it. Those guys weren't reliable, they didn't have the wonga either and, politically and publicly, it really was a bold move from us.
> MATÍAS, former leading figure in the recuperated
> enterprises movement, April 2017

On the other hand, the debate around "what to do with the hotel" also sparked tensions among the workers, which led to the departure of some of the members who had been leading the process over those few months and eventually to the co-operative being refounded in the summer of 2004. This case demonstrates that the political dimension acquired by recuperation processes generates tensions and conflicts among co-operative workers:

> They [the members who left] were quite reluctant to let politics interfere. I think they just got tired of it. It was a lot more heavier than what they thought it was going to be. Not for us, we knew, we'd been through a lot of these processes, we knew it wasn't easy to recuperate a company. At some point, I reckon, they thought they'd occupy the hotel, open it up, and it'd be theirs for good. But you know, political interference, various clashes with the police and that constant tension. [...] They couldn't hack [tolerate] the political dimension. [...] This whole political thing was too much for them. They saw red rags [left-wing insignia] hanging there, and they wanted a four-star hotel. [...] They thought it was just a matter of entering and setting up the company.
> MATÍAS, former leading figure in the recuperated
> enterprises movement, April 2017

The initial kick-start that made the hotel open its doors and start producing was an accommodation contract with the Venezuelan embassy in 2004. To this end, the Venezuelan government advanced the co-operative the sum for the accommodation so that it could refurbish various parts of the building. The opening made it necessary to bring new workers into the co-operative. This was done by calling on the hotel's former workers and, primarily, co-operative members' relatives. As a result, over the years following the reopening, the number of workers rose to around 130 by the close of our period of study.

The resumption of production ushered in a new phase: workers started receiving an income, new staff were incorporated, and a collective memory began to take shape around the early days of the recuperation. The perceptions and assessments around these first few years of constitutive conflict tend to construct a collective memory of the recuperation that retrieves its contentious character and the leading role of 'founder' members, namely those who participated in the occupation of the hotel and were part of the co-operative from its creation. These assessments of workers can be associated with concepts from the academic field that nominate the early days of the recuperation of an enterprise as the 'heroic period' (Lucita, 2009), beginning with the occupation of the premises, continuing with resistance and ending with the start of production and the accomplishment of expropriation. This collective memory can be glimpsed in the narrative of a 'founder' member describing a critical economic moment the co-operative would experience later on:

> That was terrible. We held a meeting, there were 132 of us compañeros, and we told the *cumpas* [compañeros] that we can't lie to them, we can't suspend them, cause when they come back after a fortnight, I don't know what's going to happen. So, then the younger ones said "We'll stay and resist. You all resisted; now it's our turn to resist. We're staying."
> MARIELA, co-operative member, August 2014

Meanwhile, concerned at the process of self-management taking shape and threatened by an expropriation bill in the Legislature of the Buenos Aires City Government in favour of the co-operative, the legal owners of the property lobbied support from a group of legislators and passed Act 1,914 on 6 December 2005. This stipulated the hotel's restoration to the legal owners of the property (under conditions to be established by a specially created legislative committee over the following 90 days), the maintenance of the jobs of the commercial company's salaried employees for at least three years and the granting of a subsidy for the refurbishment of the building.

During working hours that December 6, the co-operative members occupied the legislative chamber and succeeded in having the session adjourned; it was restarted after a few hours (*ANReD*, 25 February 2006; *Página 12*, 8 December 2005). Security forces were sent in to quash the occupation. Graciela, a member of the co-operative, describes it as follows: "When we went into the Legislature and got the session adjourned, they beat us; they dislocated my shoulder, it was mayhem" (August 2014). Despite this apparent defeat, the City Government's Executive did not enforce the law because, among other reasons, it would have involved the almost immediate implementation of budget allocations.

By mid-2007, the conflict looked as if it was heading for an outcome unfavourable to the co-operative. At that time, the National Court on Commercial Matters handling the Chilean enterprise's bankruptcy proceedings returned the property to the 'ghost' enterprise set up by the original owners and issued a 30-day eviction notice. This highlights an aspect of this case that implies an additional difficulty compared to other recuperated enterprises involved in bankruptcy proceedings, namely that the property is awarded to an enterprise other than the bankrupt one the workers maintained the labour relationship with. This situation hampered the judicial solution of the conflict over the hotel's premises and continued operation: the co-operative was unable to obtain any legal form to defend their continued presence in the hotel and, consequently, while the initial, most intense stages of the 'take' were a thing of the past, they remained in the premises de facto:

> That's the peculiar thing about the hotel: the bankrupt company not being the legal owner of the building. What many recuperated enterprises do is file to the judge for continued production, set up the co-operative quickly and the judge grants job continuity. In these cases, the reform of the [Competition and] Bankruptcy Act is important cause it guarantees that, just by submitting the paperwork for the co-operative's formation, the judge has to agree to the continuity of former workers. In this case, it was impossible cause the company wasn't the legal owner of the building.
> ALEJANDRO, co-operative member and leading figure in
> a worker co-operative organisation, August 2011

The co-operative responded to the Judiciary's ruling both by interposing measures in the judicial field itself and by taking collective actions: court hearings, extraordinary appeals, and applications for changes of jurisdiction were combined with cultural festivals and demonstrations. In response to the eviction notice, the co-operative lodged extraordinary appeals with the National Chamber of Appeals on Commercial Matters, which rejected them in May 2009. It then submitted complaints to Argentina's Supreme Court, which also rejected them in 2011. Both authorities upheld the Commercial Court's ruling. The hotel workers therefore embarked on an investigation to demonstrate the links between the hotel's original owners – namely, the first administration to apply for the BANADE loan – and the 'ghost' enterprise, whose right to ownership was recognised by the Judiciary. Along the way, they not only found evidence for these connections but also uncovered links between these enterprises and the last civil-military dictatorship. So, the co-operative sought to shed light on its adversary in the conflict, proving that the owner of the means of production and the former employer of the workers' collective was the same business group, while in turn revealing the fraudulent dealings the group had practised.

In October 2012, the co-operative succeeded in getting the commercial court judge to request the case file be referred to the Criminal Jurisdiction in order to investigate whether the original owners of the property had committed fraud against the state amounting to millions of pesos. The commercial court judge indicated a possible illicit association that might have implications in crimes against humanity perpetrated during the dictatorship. The deadlines of the eviction notice issued by the Commercial Jurisdiction were momentarily prorogued. However, in 2013, the Federal Court of Criminal and Correctional Matters ruled that the defendants be dismissed, and in March 2014, the co-operative was served with a fresh eviction order.

Throughout this whole period, the worker co-operative had to face several eviction orders. On all these occasions, the social legitimacy drummed up by the processes of enterprise recuperations, as well as the hotel's paradigmatic status within that universe, were central in the evasion and resistance of the evictions. Also significant were the leaders and organisational resources contributed by a federation of worker co-operatives formed after a split from the recuperated enterprise organisation that had been involved in the conflict from the early days.

The obvious difficulties posed by the occupancy of the hotel building gradually indicated to the co-operative's workers, and to the recuperated enterprise organisations and the many political spaces involved, that the judicial route was ineffective. Running parallel to the struggle in the juridical sphere, mechanisms were also activated to tackle the issue at the legislative level:

> The legal issue is coming to a close, which made us think for a long time too that everybody was banking on the idea there was a road to take and that, you know, floating the idea of expropriating the hotel, honestly, it's like opening a can of worms. It isn't a community canteen handing out glasses of milk in some neighbourhood in the city, tucked away, it's right in the city centre, it's very high-profile, and I reckon they must have been thinking, as long as there's a legal process, the co-operative can put up a fight, well, let's wait and see. That's come to an end now, cause the Court rejected the appeal, so the way out [resolution] of the conflict is the political solution, no doubt about it, and we have to twist the wills of those who are in a position to influence that.
>
> ALEJANDRO, co-operative member and leading figure in a worker co-operatives organisation, August 2011

Over the years several expropriation bills were submitted to the Argentinian Congress. The choice of the national arena instead of the Buenos Aires City Government Legislature was due to the workers and organisations involved considering that this was the most appropriate level, as it was the national state – via the BANADE – that was the creditor of the debt owed by the legal owners of the premises. The political strategy deployed by the co-operative involved a shift in the debate. The demand for the right to work as against the right of ownership expressed in the slogan that the hotel 'belongs to the/its workers' – linking work and appropriation – gave way to the watchword that the hotel 'belongs to all,' which entailed a debate around state-owned and public property. This did not involve dropping the first slogan, but rather foregrounding the latter. The configuration of this strategy took place against a background of revitalisation and growing legitimacy of the Argentinian state's intervention in the economy (Pérez and Rebón, 2016).

> The special thing about our co-operative is that it isn't just a debate about the right to [private] property against the right to work, which we uphold and discuss in every corner of the country with every case of recuperated companies. […] We're talking about referring legal issues over the conflict and ownership of the building [to the state], and then it [the state] should work with us to find a solution. From the moment the property's in the hands of the state, which is a debate we don't go anywhere near at the moment cause it's premature: it could be the transfer of the hotel, the mortgage and transfer through a 20–30-year mortgage loan, a concession, a commodatum ... there's endless ways, and it'll be debated later on how they'll be resolved, but the state has to have the deeds in its name and foreclose on the outstanding mortgages, needless to say. So, we duly submitted the expropriation bill regarding the special case of the hotel in the Chamber of Deputies.
> ALEJANDRO, co-operative member and leading figure in
> a worker co-operative organisation, August 2011

A correlate of this strategy was the fact that the hotel actively opened itself up to the community. On that basis, if there was a struggle over a public state property, non-market liaisons had to take pride of place. At the same time, these liaisons promoted wide-ranging support during the most critical moments of the conflict over occupancy of the hotel.

> Locals, unions, other co-operatives, the recuperated enterprise movement, workers' confederations, left to centre political parties, everybody was behind us. And we had this really open policy, you know, like that stuff about the hotel belonging to everybody. Cause the struggle's all about the building belonging to the state, so we boosted the campaign with concrete action. The building belongs to the Argentinian

state, to all of us [...] the co-operative runs it for the whole community. Everybody meets here, we offer rooms and conference rooms free as much as we can. So, they defend the hotel like it belongs to them, which is why by this stage we have such strong support. It's down to that, to not cutting ourselves off, to opening up to the working community, basically.

> ALEJANDRO, co-operative member and leading figure in
> a worker co-operative organisation, August 2016

Several years later, on 26 November 2015, in the Argentinian Chamber of Deputies' last session of the year, the bill proclaiming the hotel and all its amenities to be a public utility and subject to expropriation was passed unanimously.[4] The core of the bill passed was to realise the expropriation in exchange for the debt the legal owner of the property had with the state as a result of the loans issued by BANADE. It in turn stipulated the handover in commodatum of the movable and immovable property for the usufruct of the co-operative, which, in compensation, had to provide space for activities aimed at hospitality training in partnership with public universities and to promote cultural, educational, artistic and social activities. The legislation also specified that the co-operative should make at least 30% of the hotel's rooms available for social tourism and provide accommodation for patients from across the country with medical referrals from the *Instituto Nacional de Servicios Sociales para Jubilados y Pensionados* [National Institute of Social Services for Retirees and Pensioners]. Last, it required that the national Executive provide resources for the co-operative to restore and refurbish the hotel building. The legislation thus promoted a type of state ownership with social usufruct, meaning conditions of use that go beyond the co-operative's private and commercial ends and establish public uses of the space.

Although our period of study draws to a close in 2015 with certain breakthroughs in the legislative sphere, there subsequently occurred highly

---

4 Unlike the hotel, during the same legislative period, another emblematic co-operative succeeded in expropriating its premises through Act No. 27,224, on 25 November 2015. The success in the enactment of this law provides a powerful counterpoint to the case of the hotel and the characteristics of the adversary. In the case of the other company, the expropriated actor was the previous co-operative that managed the company. Consequently, there was no strong opposition. In the case of the hotel, the business group claiming ownership is a relevant actor that puts up resistance to the expropriation, not just by lobbying but by trying to influence public opinion through a website asserting "the truth" about the case. Also, the correlation of forces in the national Legislature and the different impacts of the political groups promoting each bill must also be considered.

significant events that are worth mentioning. During the last ordinary session of the Senate on 30 November 2016, the bill declaring the hotel to be a public utility and subject to expropriation became law. However, several weeks later, on 27 December, Argentina's president vetoed the law. Therefore, as well as the precarious situation the co-operative found itself in over the hotel's occupancy, having no form of usufruct rights, there was also the removal by the Executive of the political alternative to resolve the issue via the Legislature. For this reason, upon completion of this book, the co-operative remains in a situation of extreme precarity regarding the hotel's occupancy.

In short, several years on from the first recuperations, we are in a position to reconsider the closing stages of the constitutive conflicts and periodisations of these processes, which identify two main moments: first, a 'heroic period' of constitution of the experience, which would be followed by a 'market and competition period' grounded in legal, productive and economic stabilisation (Lucita, 2009). In contrast, as developed at a macro level in Chapter 1, the difficulties associated with carrying out the expropriations and thus obtaining ownership of the productive units have become apparent over the years. In addition, the analysis of the case brought insight into greater obstacles over obtaining the occupancy of the productive unit. I believe that the outright recuperation of an enterprise entails the beginnings of a solution to the issue of the property's occupancy, and, even more imperatively in our case, in that the service provided is inseparable from the building. I therefore contend that the issue's lack of resolution means that the conflict over the occupancy of the hotel, typically associated with the constitutive stage of recuperated enterprises, becomes recurrent: in other words, it remains unresolved even after the economic and productive stabilisation of the co-operative.

In conclusion, let us summarise some of the findings about this conflict. The crisis of the productive unit and the subsequent infringement of the wage relationship triggered the recuperation. This was perceived by the workers – in co-ordination with political entrepreneurs from the recuperated enterprise organisation – as the only alternative to keep their jobs, reproduce their identity as workers and guarantee their own reproduction. The act of recuperation involved the occupation of the work establishment where the infringed wage relationship played out and, after a brief attempt at negotiations, the hotel's legal owner – through the Judiciary – responded by issuing eviction notices. In response to this, the co-operative pursued both judicial and collective actions in the public arena, as well as attempts to resolve the situation through legislative channels. Upon completion of this book, while progress has been made along those lines, this was blocked by the Executive.

The struggle with the forces external to the productive unit of the Judiciary and political powers that be should not overshadow the fact that the co-operative's formation involves an intense judicialised conflict around control and occupancy of the productive unit between the group of workers and the enterprise that is the legal owner of the hotel. It is important to underline that, while this enterprise is not the immediate previous employer, it was so during the first administration. The juridical and political forces play mediating roles in this dispute, and at times even become the recipients of the claims. Some authors have pointed out that enterprise recuperation displaces the central conflict between capital and the labour force by the confrontation between the recuperated enterprise and the external institutional forces of the judicial and political powers that be, as well as the marketplace (Bialakowsky et al., 2004). I agree with this observation to an extent, insofar as the wage relationship tends not to predominate in these productive units. However, my analysis of the constitutive conflict in our case study allows us to refine this observation and highlight the dispute between the co-operative members and the hotel's legal owner – and former boss – over the control and possession of the property.

The co-operative's constitutive conflict, to wit, the recuperation of the enterprise in order to protect jobs, with the disruption of the relations of possession and appropriation of the fruits of labour that this entails, thus expresses a conflict with a class cleavage in that it rests on the antagonism between the owners of the means of production and the labour force. In this case, I use the concept of 'cleavage' (Lipset and Rokkan, 1967), as this allows us to distinguish the divides identified in this conflict from the more flexible, shifting ones analysed in the following chapters.

2 From 'Induction' to the 'Co-operative without Brokers'

In Chapter 2, I analysed the mobilising process triggered by the launch of the *Programa Argentina Trabaja* [Argentina Works Programme] (PAT) and how this gradually became interlinked with the scheme's design and implementation. I will now move away from the national scale to analyse the constitutive conflict of our second case study. The Argentina Works co-operative we will be looking at was created in 2010 under the umbrella of an unemployed workers' social organisation. It is a small productive venture located in a shantytown in the municipality of Esteban Echeverría,[5] whose main activity involves cleaning up the banks of the Matanza Riachuelo Basin.[6]

The processes of impoverishment, pauperisation and unemployment that had developed in the late twentieth century and early twenty-first had made the Buenos Aires Conurbation the main target for social policies, while social organisations embedded in local political networks underwent a process of consolidation. In Esteban Echeverría, parallel to the formation of various *Movimientos de Trabajadores Desocupados* [Unemployed Workers Movements] (MTDs) in the south of the Buenos Aires Conurbation between 1998 and 2001 (Svampa and Pereyra, 2004), unemployed workers' groups began to come together from different neighbourhoods and localities in the district to eventually form an MTD. Subsequently, in December 2003, in line with various general breakaways, splits and reconfigurations of blocs in MTDs (Svampa and Pereyra, 2004), the Esteban Echeverría grouping split in two.

The worker co-operative I analyse in this book belongs to one of these two splinter groups, which, when the Argentina Works Programme was launched, had a territorial presence in two shantytowns and formed part of a multi-sector front that brings together not just unemployed workers' organisations, but organisations of students, the employed, rural workers and other actors. At the time, each shantytown was running a community kitchen, and each was about twenty strong. Through the Argentina Works Programme, the organisation was able to form two co-operatives, one in each neighbourhood, and these became the central focus of their territorial action. Let us reconstruct the process of formation for the co-operative we are looking at.

The Argentina Works Programme had been launched in August 2009, and, by late September, the first contentious actions by the unemployed workers' organisations had already taken place. Their criticisms and demands had been merged under the banner 'Co-operatives Without Brokers' and a campaign front of the same name, with participation by the MTD to which our study's worker co-operative belongs. Against this background, at municipal level, on 20 November, a group of unemployed workers' organisations, including the MTD of our case study, mobilised between 300 and 500 people to protest outside

---

5   This district is located in the south of the Buenos Aires Conurbation and, according to the 2010 INDEC census, had a population of 300,959 inhabitants. The basic needs of 10.77% of households were not met, higher than the overall percentage for the Buenos Aires Conurbation (9.24%). Unemployment stood at 7.2%, whereas, in the Buenos Aires Conurbation, it stood at 6.3% (INDEC, 2010).

6   This river basin covers 2,200km², and crosses Buenos Aires and fourteen districts in Buenos Aires Province.

the Esteban Echeverría municipal building, in the centre of Monte Grande, to demand an audience with the local authorities[7] to address the issue of incorporating the organisations' members in the Argentina Works Programme. At the start of the month, this group had participated in the collective actions that had succeeded in securing a commitment from the Ministry for Social Development to distribute vacancies in the Argentina Works Programme among the social organisations. But the conflict did not go away; instead, its local dimension came to the fore. Having obtained this commitment, this group of organisations decided to switch to local negotiations with the communal authorities and carry out local collective actions to ensure the promise of incorporations was made good:

> We'd decided then, let's say, that nationally they wouldn't give us the time of day, nor in the municipality neither, so we said "Let's go here, to the district, but let's all go together," so like this was the first district where we said, "Let's check it out [see what happens]," whether, with all of us going together, they [the incorporations] would work out, and the first move [demonstration] we made, all going together, was right here in Echeverría.
>
> Group interview with MTD members, May 2010

The demonstration had the desired effect, and they secured a hearing: five representatives from the organisations were invited into the municipal building for a meeting with the Sub-Secretary for Social Development (*Clarín*, 21 November 2009). However, to the demonstrators' surprise, the police suddenly attacked the crowd waiting outside, arresting fifteen and injuring more than thirty with rubber bullets (*Agencia Universitaria de Noticias y Opinión de la Universidad Nacional de Lomas de Zamora*, 25 November 2009; *ANReD*, 20 November 2009).

> It were dead weird cause they'd already seen us in the town hall. Our compañeros had gone inside to negotiate, and we was all outside, more than delighted, singing, dancing, cheering them on up there, but no, when we wanted to find out what was going on, these "*cabezas de tortuga*" [tortoise heads: slang for local police] started coming out the woodwork. There was a bit of handbags, they pushed one compañero, tried to hit him, and

---

7 Between 2009 and 2015, the municipal Executive was in the hands of the same mayor, who won the elections in 2007 and was re-elected in 2011, aligned on both occasions with the national and provincial government in power, namely, the *Frente para la Victoria* [Front for Victory].

that's when it started, they tried to separate, they got stuck straight into the job of crushing us. With people sitting on the street, kids playing right up at the front there, where they [the kids] were, they didn't care and started to hitting, shooting, firing rubber bullets.

Group interview with MTD members, May 2010

After these events, the municipality distributed approximately 190 new vacancies in the scheme and set up operations to enrol beneficiaries. The co-operative analysed in this book also began to be formed around at this time. The events of 20 November were therefore perceived by members of the social organisations as the trigger for their incorporation in the Argentina Works Programme:

> They chased us, but with rubber bullets, they chased us, they hit us, they clobbered us. I think after that, a week later, we was told he [a local authority figure] wants to speak to us, and he gives us the co-operative just like that, cause first he lays into us and then he says "Fine, here you are."
>
> PAULA, MTD member, September 2011

This perception of the events is shared by municipal officials, who attribute to the 20 November conflict not just the incorporation of unemployed workers' organisations into the Argentina Works Programme, but also the specific features of the scheme's implementation in Esteban Echeverría.

> The mayor never made any space, room, opportunity, framework, on his electoral rolls for anybody he didn't want there exercising command and control when it came to putting their hands up. [...] They were all people who were in welfare work, but who were politically aligned with him but didn't have an organisation. The relationship, the dealings the municipality had with social organisations before the launch of the Argentina Works Programme were through the Secretariat for Social Development; the ones that had community kitchens were given welfare support with food. [...] First, the Ministry had already made the decision to allocate co-operative quotas to social organisations, so we had to organise the registration from state departments: how many people per organisation, cause they didn't always, or in some cases, have up to 60. All that I did with them [the organisations' members] and with the duo the Ministry'd sent us. The conflict in Esteban Echeverría had been so intense that they sent us the Minister for Social Development's right-hand woman. She

was one of those people the Minister sent to Esteban Echeverría to keep everybody in line.
> Esteban Echeverría Municipality official, June 2016

That said, the enrolment of beneficiaries through the operations mentioned by the municipal official was merely the beginning of the co-operative formation process. Although the first payments started to be made in March 2010 (Boix, Fernández and Marazzi, 2011; Reppeto, Boix and Fernández, 2011), the members of the co-operative in question, who had enrolled back in December, only started receiving their income in mid-2010. Moreover, they at first only took part in training activities organised by the municipality and engaged in no productive activities.

This partial incorporation in the Argentina Works Programme in December 2009 – given its workers started receiving their income from mid-2010 – shifted the relationship with the state over the ensuing months. The centrality of direct action – a notion encompassing forms of contentious action unmediated by the dominant institutionality (Rebón and Pérez, 2012) – led to a form of relationship with the state that had taken shape during the 1990s and been consolidated at the dawn of the twenty-first century. This form positions the state as the main interlocutor in the demand for work and combines direct actions with negotiation and dialogue, made possible by social organisation members' acquisition of skills and learning of mechanisms regarding the modi operandi of state bodies (Manzano, 2009).

> We enrolled in December and started getting paid in June. They were long months of seeing what we'd do and a lot of red tape too. Lots of paperwork, the compañeros had to draw up one list after another, cause something was always missing: a surname, a number, there was always some problem or another.
> PAULA, MTD member, September 2011

∴

And when Argentina Works comes down, as we were the ones as kicked up more of a fuss to be included in Argentina Works, they gave us the run-around, but they gave it us anyroads cause we kept turning up and banging on. Once we knew that people from the Ministry where there, we were the first to go and sit at the town hall entrance, and there was this official from the Ministry who told us: "But, when do you sleep?" We told

him: "We never sleep." We couldn't sleep [lose focus], cause if we slept ... And cause we kept insisting, we got the lot.
ADRIANA, co-operative member, January 2015

For the co-operative workers then, this protracted situation of partial inclusion in the scheme, on top of the 20 November repression, reinforced their appreciation for the co-operative as a right won through intense struggle. Belonging to a social organisation equipped the co-operative's members with interpretive frameworks that enabled them to legitimate their demand for inclusion in the scheme and ensuing collective action.

When I joined, everything was all already in the bag [set up], shall we say. I joined, and they'd already won the co-ops. But they told me they'd had all these demonstrations, suppression too in Monte Grande, that some compañeros had been hit by rubber bullets ... I mean, they put up a real fight. They didn't want to give it to them, cause they were from like this organisation, and they were sort of discriminated against cause it's like this organisation's against the government, why come here asking for subsidies? But the President decreed it was for everybody, I mean, it was his [the mayor's] duty to give it us anyway. But they just plain didn't want to, it really cost us. But then again, we won.
ANALÍA, co-operative member, November 2012

∴

The government wanted to leave us out of the Argentina Works plans, [...] they wanted to exclude the organisations as didn't belong to progressive Peronism. So, we decided that, like I told you before about the microventures, we was trying to find other solutions, we realised we needed to fight for worker co-operatives and our own autonomy. [...] I reckon, from my standpoint, a lot of resources are given to movements aligned with the government, and the movements that are more left-wing are kind of like excluded.
ARIEL, member of the other MTD co-operative, September 2011

The flip side of the perception by the co-operative members of the contentious character of inclusion in the Argentina Works Programme was that state officials reinforced the characterisation of the co-operatives belonging to social organisations as "conflictive" or "radicalised." In response to my question about why, in informal conversations among municipal officials, certain co-operatives were classified as "movement" co-operatives, one official remarked:

> What was really clear to us was the number of people with a quota for movements – social organisations. Just because of that, so we were clear about it. The others [other co-operatives] were run by leading figures, people more aligned to us; or from the job centre, who we didn't need to have them side-lined cause we knew more or less who we were dealing with, who we were talking about, how to handle them. That label may have been because they were in some way conflictive, in inverted commas. To be clear and avoid conflict. We'd sometimes believe any old thing, it was our *mambo* [problem] us thinking the relationship was always going to be a conflict, so having that identified properly, that's all.
> Esteban Echeverría Municipality official, June 2016

Last, in the Esteban Echeverría municipality, the first stage of the Argentina Works Programme's 'emergence' ended in August 2010, when the deadline stipulated in the first agreement signed between the Ministry for Social Development and the executive body, in this case the local government, expired (Boix, Fernández and Marazzi, 2011; Reppeto, Boix and Fernández, 2011). This stage saw the inclusion of the majority of the beneficiaries,[8] and the co-operative members began to receive their payments. In September 2010, the second stage of the scheme was officially launched in the municipality, and modifications to it brought tighter controls over the co-operatives, though also a degree of autonomy in line with the demands of the organisations. The first modification concerned the division of responsibilities between the municipality and the co-operatives: whereas, in the first stage, they shared certain responsibilities with the municipalities when it came to implementing public works and book-keeping, the responsibility for project management in the second stage was left to the municipality.

Second, there were modifications to the modus operandi for productive projects. In the first stage, the co-operatives were contracted by the municipality, and their internal division into work-teams meant that the co-operatives functioned simultaneously in more than one constructive module. In the second stage, the work-teams from a single co-operative were allocated specific

---

8 This first period saw the formation of 35 co-operatives in Esteban Echeverría, whereas the second period (September 2010–April 2011) saw just five. So, in mid-2011 the municipality had 40 co-operatives, with around 2,400 co-operative members (Boix, Fernández and Marazzi, 2011; Reppeto, Boix and Fernández, 2011).

tasks in the same project: in other words, the labour collectives from each co-operative began working together. Last, ways of monitoring were also altered: certification of works began to be carried out more frequently, accompanied by maximum and minimum performances (Boix, Fernández and Marazzi, 2011; Reppeto, Boix and Fernández 2011). We can see then that, while most of the changes tended to involve tighter controls over the co-operatives, one of the modifications tended towards conceding a certain level of autonomy to the worker collective: workers' groups could now work side-by-side on the same activity in the same space.

To round off this section, let us look back over some findings. As with the recuperated enterprise, the MTD co-operative had to undergo high levels of conflict in its formation. In contrast with the 'induced' character attributed to Argentina Works co-operatives, and like others also grouped under unemployed workers' organisations, our co-operative had to deal with the resistance at various levels of government. A brief digression is needed at this point. My fieldwork went beyond this particular case study and yielded insights into the experiences of social organisations which, albeit politically and ideologically wedded at a macro level to the national and municipal governments, also had to turn to collective action to successfully form their co-operatives.

Briefly, I contend that the co-operative studied is the product of a relational dynamic of confrontation and negotiation between social organisations and state apparatuses in the wake of the launch of the Argentina Works Programme. I would stress therefore that, while the scheme itself was not the result of the organisations' struggle, some co-operatives that came out of it were, and the co-operative in our study is a case in point. Unlike the recuperated enterprise, which takes the form of a judicialised conflict with some recourse to collective action, these actions play a more significant role in the conflict in the case of this co-operative. That said, alongside the clashes – and the suppression – there are instances of informal political negotiation with the state Executive.

As well as the disputed character of the co-operative's origins, I would underline that its formation does not spring from the workers' intention to set up a productive organisation inspired by a co-operativist vision. On the contrary, this co-operative presents us with a case of 'forced associativity' (Hopp, 2013b): a co-operative formed as a legal, operational requirement to access subsidies granted through public policies. It thus differs from the 'adaptive' co-operativism of the recuperated enterprise, which is formed in response to the judgment that this legal form is the best option to tackle unemployment and organise the workers' collective.

Last, the state constitutes the locus of the conflicts inasmuch as it is the object of the demands. The fact that it is the object of the actions taken by social organisations should not eclipse the fact that we are dealing with a work conflict. Workers facing difficulties to guarantee their social reproduction as a result, among other things, of the impossibility of selling their labour force, or pressed to do so under unstable and precarious conditions, demand the state provides access to the Argentina Works Programme and the formation of co-operatives through the social organisations.

It needs to be stressed that their designation as 'unemployed workers' organisations papers over the fact that they actually constitute forms of aggregation of unstable, precarious, pauperised workers, rather than strictly unemployed workers. Faced with this impossibility of selling their labour force and in the context of the scheme's launch, the demand for work – or its work requirement version of the social plan – was directed at the state, perceived as the main institution responsible for and capable of providing work. That said, our analysis enables us to surmise that the demand was not purely and simply for work, but rather for 'work without brokers.' In other words, it was as much about access to work as working conditions, which it was believed had to be independent of the state to avoid any form of subordination.

3   A Comparative Lens on Constitutive Conflicts

This final section develops a comparative analysis of the case studies and their constitutive conflicts based on the following focal points. I first examine its triggers, and the forms and characteristics of the opponents. Second, I specify the types of co-operativism that take shape. Third, I describe the social organisations together with the types of power possessed by their constituent social groups. Last, I analyse the class antagonisms evinced by the conflicts.

In spite of my statement that both co-operatives were formed contentiously, I now explore the particular elements that give rise to the conflicts in each. In the case of the recuperated enterprise, the crisis in the productive unit is the grievance that drives the recuperation but is not sufficient to trigger it. The failure to receive their outstanding wages and redundancy pay in a context that offers scant opportunities for reinsertion in the labour market, as well as their co-ordination with the recuperated enterprise organisation, are necessary factors contributing to the willingness to fight.

In contrast, in the case of the Argentina Works co-operative, the conflict cannot be properly understood by scrutinising the possible changes in the workers' situation – as is the case for the recuperated enterprise, where their jobs are under threat – but only by turning our attention to the political, economic and social policy context in Argentina. The workers forming the

Argentina Works co-operative represent sectors that have suffered long-term exclusion from the formal labour market, and the general political climate and creation of the Argentina Works Programme provide their organisations with a structure of opportunities that stimulate collective action. Nevertheless, the constitutive conflict does not arise until the state – at both national and local levels – limits the formation of co-operatives by social organisations and enables partial incorporations to the scheme.

Regarding the forms of the conflicts, whereas for the recuperated enterprise a predominantly judicialised confrontation between the workers and the hotel's legal owner plays out over the control and occupancy of the productive unit, in the case of the Argentina Works co-operative, we find contentious interactions alongside negotiations between the unemployed workers' organisation and the national and local state executive apparatuses over the formation and control of co-operatives.

In the constitutive conflicts, we can see there are two different adversaries: in our first case, the hotel's legal owner, with the mediation of the Judiciary; in our second case, the executive apparatuses of the state. Specifically, in the case of the recuperated enterprise, the state apparatuses adopt different positions: whereas the judicial authorities tend to privilege the private property rights of the legal owners, the Legislature and the Executive swing with the political climate, party membership and ideological affiliation. This apart, taking stock of the positioning of the state apparatuses upon completion of this book, we detected a degree of backing for the hotel's legal owners.

Regarding types of co-operativism, the creation of a worker co-operative to manage a recuperated enterprise can be considered an example of 'adaptive co-operativism' (Rebón, 2007), whereas the Argentina Works co-operative represents 'forced associativity' (Hopp, 2013b), in which there is no assessment by the workers about the benefits or potential drawbacks of this legal form. It should be noted that these characterisations refer to the co-operatives' inception, a starting point that contrasts with the voluntary character of the association put forward by the co-operativist vision. In no way, however, do they seek to advocate or value the development of a co-operative beyond its inception.

That said, the volitive gap between the 'adaptive' and the 'forced' in the formation of co-operatives should not conceal a fundamental similarity in the origins of both cases: both are forms of resistance to expropriation of labour insertion. In other words, they are a response to the dispossession of the workers, even of the possibility of guaranteeing their own social reproduction through the exchange of their labour force, or in Burawoy's terms (2008, 2015), the disappearance – or long-standing non-existence – of the guarantee of exploitation.

In this connection, I would like to examine the organisations constructed by these kinds of workers more closely. As a rule, the classic organisational form of the Argentinian working class, the trades union, excludes these sectors of the working classes, which constitutes an added similarity between our cases: the absence of union structures – or at least the most representative ones – from their constitutive conflicts. On the contrary, both struggles are embedded in social movements. It is relevant to insist that the 'movementist' character that certain social organisations' actions can acquire does not develop all suddenly and permanently, but refers to these organisations' capacity to make demands on the state authorities in a public, sustained and co-ordinated way based on a repertoire of actions (Tilly and Wood, 2010). In the initial stages, both recuperated enterprise organisations and unemployed workers organisations take on this character. On the contrary, during the later stages of retreat and fragmentation, when the organisations focus on their less public and contentious aspects, they cannot necessarily be analysed using this concept.

We should remember that the recuperation was pursued by a group of the hotel's former workers with the support of an organisation leading the recuperated enterprise movement at the time. However, the specific chronologies of each recuperation, and the need to sustain the occupation of the premises with a physical presence and concentrate on production in order to generate income hindered the organisations' capacity to mobilise and hence the continuity of the 'movementist' form of political articulation. This gave rise to a fragmentation into multiple social organisations, and these tended to act autonomously.

In the other case, we see that the unemployed workers' organisations assembled themselves into a social movement in that they carried out co-ordinated protest actions with the aim of being included in the Argentina Works Programme and forming co-operatives from their own organisations through the *Frente de Cooperativas sin Punteros* [Front for Co-operatives Without Brokers]. In contrast with the difficulties of sustaining mobilising capacity observed in the previous case, the income guaranteed by the state through public policy and the creation of productive units with similar activities generating similar needs and demands made it easier for unemployed workers' organisations to maintain their character as a social movement. However, albeit to a lesser degree, this 'movementist' character also petered out: the front formed to state demands and organise collective action tended to fragment when the co-operatives prioritised productive activity. Briefly, the Argentina Works co-operative's dependency on the state for income turns out to be an advantage here, compared to the recuperated enterprise's dependency on the market to sell their products and services as the financial costs of demonstration become more significant for the latter.

What kinds of power can the movements activate to get their demands across? To analyse this issue, I come back to Erik Olin Wright (2000) on the scope and forms of working-class power. Specifically, I take up the concepts of 'associational power' and 'structural power.' Associational power, which paradigmatically refers to institutionalised organisations, describes social groupings capacity to associate. This type of power is differentiated from structural power in that the latter derives from the location of groups within an economic or productive system. In this case, the bargaining capacity of social groups is related to the balance or imbalance of supply and demand in the labour market and with the strategic place occupied by a labour collective in the productive process of a key industry (Silver, 2005; Wright, 2000).

In the case of the recuperated enterprise, I contend that the capacity to carry out the recuperation lies in the workers' associational power. Specifically, in our case study, the trades union not only failed to support the recuperation but directly attempted to block it. The collective actor here was the recuperated enterprise organisations. Their organisational capacity differs from that attributed to the traditional working classes, whose associational power is institutional in that it tends to be embedded in stable legal frameworks, paradigmatic examples being unions and political parties. In contrast, the recuperated enterprise movement possesses a non-institutional associational power, whose composition rests on the symbolic potency of the recuperation processes. Through the concept of the 'moral economy of work,' we have already analysed the wide-ranging public repercussions and social legitimacy inspired by the process of recuperations. This is the source of the associational power achieved by the recuperated enterprise movement.

Albeit weaker than the power of workers organised in unions, this associational power sets up the possibility of occupying the productive establishment. This control over the space gives the workers a structural advantage and improves their capacity to bargain with the hotel's owners. This minor breakthrough in structural power allows them to continue existing and boosts their associational power.

In the case of the unemployed workers' movement, I also contend that the achievement of their goals is down to their associational power, sustained mainly by these organisations' mobilising and disruptive capacity through roadblocks or 'pickets' in certain social, political and economic contexts. Their lack of structural power is connected to their use of modular forms of protest (Tarrow, 2009) – like roadblocks and demonstrations – characterised by their adaptability to a wide range of settings. These types of actions differ from other formats that can only be performed by certain actors while stating particular demands, such as the strike, generally utilised by salaried workers.

While the social value of work equips the unemployed workers' organisations in building symbolic power, in a similar way to recuperated enterprises, this is relative: such a social value is not sufficient to counteract the stigmatisation these organisations are prone to. That is why only in certain contexts can the establishment of demands for work or social plans through protest action be legitimised or tolerated. I therefore believe that the central element underlying the associational power of unemployed workers' organisations revolves around the effectiveness of roadblocks when they attain high degrees of participation and co-ordination.

In short, compared with salaried workers, both struggles are sustained by 'resource-poor' social groupings: they lack structural power and possess a less institutionalised, relative associational power. As the conflicts played out, both struggles provide these social groups with minimal, precarious levels of structural power through the occupation of the productive establishment in the case of the recuperated enterprise and, in the case of the Argentina Works Programme, the inclusion in a co-operative under the auspices of a public policy. Although this power is minimal in either case, it enables these groupings' associational power to grow.

Last, I wish to go deeper into an analysis of the class relations in constitutive conflicts. The Marxist tradition defines social classes under capitalism mainly through the capital–labour relation and establishes a central link between class and exploitation: "classes are categories of social actors defined by the property relations which generate exploitation" (Wright, 1994: 45). The concept of class binds economic and political relations under one category in that class relations involve both exploitation and domination in the productive process.

Exploitation, the most traditional antagonistic social relation in the theory of social classes, is a form of antagonistic interdependency of material interests of the actors participating in economic relations (Wright, 1994). It involves not only excluding the exploited from access to and control over the means of production, which creates inequalities of welfare, but also the asymmetrical appropriation of the fruits of labour. In other words, the welfare of the exploiter depends on the efforts of the exploited, and not only on their exclusion from the property and control of the means of production. Exploitation thus operates on a relationship of 'doing and having' between two poles (Gómez, 2014).

Yet there are still other possible class antagonisms. Antagonistic relations can also take the form of non-exploitative oppression (Wright, 1994) or subordination, which establish varied combinations of 'doing-having' (Gómez, 2014). In these other forms of antagonistic relations, appropriation does not rest on the interdependency of the two poles: the dependency of the exploiter on the efforts of the exploited and their dependency on the former, in turn, for the sale of their labour power. In relations of oppression, the welfare of the appropriator lies in the mere exclusion of the oppressed from access to certain productive resources (Wright, 1994). In that the latter's efforts are not necessary – there is no dependency, that is – the oppressed could easily disappear. It thus operates on the relationship 'having and not having.' The antagonism is not grounded in the interdependency of poles with an internal relational connection, but on the correspondence of the poles which remain external to each other, on "the way in which the actions of each of the poles can affect the other" (Gómez, 2014: 148). This generates unequal capacities to condition the response of the other pole in preventing or imposing dispossession.

Last, according to Marcelo Gómez (2014), whereas exploitation configures an interdependent asymmetry, and oppression a non-interdependent, albeit corresponding asymmetry, subordination involves a relation of asymmetry tending to unilateral dependency on the dominant pole with a minimal capacity to condition action from the dominated pole. This is a relationship in which autonomy is obliterated through the relationship of 'having and not doing.' In this class-based relationship, there is no appropriation of the fruits of labour; instead, there is a transfer towards the subordinated pole in the form of social security benefits and conditional cash transfers.

In short, class struggles strive to alter or reproduce asymmetries, correspondences and dependencies around having and doing as they relate to the material conditions of life (Gómez, 2014). In this sense, I contend that the constitutive conflict of the recuperated enterprise dismantles the 'having-doing' pair entailed by the antagonistic relationship of exploitation, thus breaking the interdependency. One pole 'has,' albeit only formally, and consequently does not achieve appropriation: the other 'does.' The interdependency shatters because the workers' collective challenges and erodes private ownership of the means of production (the 'having' of capital) through their de facto possession.

The recuperated enterprise's constitutive conflict is proof of the displacements in the analysis of class conflict. The disruption of property and exploitation relations through enterprise recuperation leads to the conflict no longer being defined in terms of the internal relations of exploitation, but by the externals of the poles and their reciprocal constraints. The logic of antagonism in the conflict over the occupancy of the hotel gives rise to a correspondence in which the actions taken by one pole seek to condition the other. The workers' collective moves on the hotel and reverses the relations of exploitation and domination in response to their infringement by capital. Instead of buckling under their expulsion from the labour market, they find a way of 'doing' and

KEEPING AND HAVING A JOB 103

making headway in a precarious way of 'having': possession. Their 'doing' thus conditions the capital's capacity to 'have.'

That said, the obstacle in the workers' struggle lies in the mechanisms of oppression, and in their formal exclusion from the ownership of the hotel that is imposed by capital, and that conditions and restricts their actions. It is therefore necessary to unblock the relations of class oppression and exclusion from ownership that limit them in the development of their project. Though workers escape exploitation, the breakthroughs of the self-management process are constrained by failing to obtain formal occupancy of the productive unit. Not owning the property hinders their ability to make investments, both as a result of the difficulty of projecting any sort of foresight and as a result of the lack of guarantees with which to request bank loans. This is a variant of external oppression, different from that which operates during the capitalist productive process, which limits the worker collective's self-determination. For some time then, the hotel's legal owner's strategy was to wait for the co-operative's self-managed venture to fail as a result of these conditioning factors:

> At some stage, I think the old management – I wouldn't go so far as to say judge, but why not? – were banking on the co-operative's financial ruin, thinking "So, they've built up this protection of social legitimacy, how can I chuck them out? Let's wait till they go down under their own steam, let them fail and leave by themselves." So, then the struggle for management also became vital to the idea that this was building legitimacy, too. Just look what we achieved out of thin air, this was empty, they'd taken everything to the other hotel [...]. So, "Look what these people have accomplished, they've reopened the hotel, they've fixed it up as best they could – cause it's huge – and on top of that they don't go bankrupt. They make a living from it, there's more of them as time goes by, first there were twenty of them, then fifty, then eighty, and now there's more than a hundred." It's like torture for them. So, for us it was vital to start to understand legal issues, management, and how to train ourselves so we wouldn't have to give them back the keys.
>
> ALEJANDRO, co-operative member and leading figure in a
> worker co-operatives organisation, August 2016

This oppression by capital does not come to fruition because workers continue to enjoy the use of the means of production through their possession and the struggle sustaining it. Whereas workers confront this partial oppression, capital attempts to re-establish relations of exploitation by striving to exclude them from ownership. The dispute is politicised: state powers intervene in the conflict and, towards the end of the period studied, support the pole of capital. For all that the recuperation of the enterprise ushers in a stage of self-management – or self-determination for the workers' collective – the confrontation between the owners of the means of production and the labour force continues unabated in the struggle for ownership of the hotel, characterised by a non-dependent but corresponding antagonism. In this sense, property relations continue to structure a class cleavage in the dispute for occupancy of the hotel.

In the case of the Argentina Works co-operative, we return to relations of subordination. It could, in principle, be argued that the conflict expresses unemployed workers' organisations' struggle to evade the relation of subordination and unilateral dependency that public policy may potentially establish. However, what we actually observe is that the founding conflict is instead about entering into the potential relationship of subordination and, at the same time, limiting it by demanding the participation of unemployed workers' organisations in running the scheme and the co-operatives. Unemployed workers' organisations attempt to increase their capacity to condition the other pole by means of direct action and the disruption of the social order this produces. However, we lack the relevant elements to describe the relations between co-operatives and the state in terms of subordination given that here we analyse the constitutive stage of the co-operative and not the implementation stage of the programme.

To summarise, I have in this chapter investigated the origins of a recuperated enterprise and a co-operative formed under the auspices of the Argentina Works Programme while charting their disputed character. I have focused on the dynamics of events, demands, forms of action and social identities in play in the conflict. In a description of these elements, I have outlined similarities and differences between the cases regarding the characteristics of the conflicts and the types of co-operatives created, the social movements involved in each struggle, the scope and kinds of power brought into play, and their implications in terms of class antagonisms. What are the modes of organisation and work arising from the productive units that emerged from the conflicts analysed? Which social groups are formed in these settings?

CHAPTER 4

The Recuperated Enterprise and Social Power in Production

Recuperated enterprises are a controversial phenomenon. From the start, those who feel aligned to self-management and working-class struggles rewrote them in "that old story about the possibility of achieving change" (Klein and Lewis, 2007). On the contrary, their detractors considered them the "paradise of the bone-idle" (*La Razón*, 3 October 2002, cited in Rebón, 2007) or "acts of usurpation" that at most spawn "apparently unviable enterprises" (*La Nación*, 4 March 2004). Over time, faced with the reality of their persistence, not their dissolution, certain critical visions underlined the fact that recuperated enterprises are prone to "degenerating" in their social form, becoming capitalist enterprises due to both external and internal factors.

That said, a reliable way of getting to know enterprise recuperation processes in all their complexity, leaving aside romantic or stigmatising visions, is to look at their socio-productive nature as a set of social relations that orders a socio-productive process (Rebón, 2007; Salgado, 2012). I did not look into this process simply to provide a deeper description of social relations of production in recuperated enterprises. I am driven by a working hypothesis: I believe that the characteristics of the disputes developed in the co-operatives under review, once established, are linked not just to their contentious origins but to the socio-productive nature of co-operatives.

In this chapter, I focus on the hotel co-operative resulting from the recuperation of an enterprise. I reprise, as my primary reference, Erik Olin Wright's (1994, 2012, 2015) theoretical suggestions about the hybrid socio-productive forms, set out in the section on theory. I would remind the reader that Wright suggests four dimensions of analysis for social relations of production.

The first concerns property relations, insofar as ownership of the means of production constitutes a condition for their use and control, hence for the appropriation of the fruits of their utilisation. The second dimension analyses the logic of production in the sense of the criteria, principles and purposes that steer the allocation of resources and use of surpluses. The third tackles the political dimension of production relationships, namely, the ways power is organised during the productive process. In short, these dimensions allow us to analyse the forms of ownership of the means of production and the type of power that determines economic activities (the allocation and use of resources).

The fourth dimension explores the nature of the groups determined by production relations and sets out to understand the characteristics that stamp structural properties – listed above – on the formation of social groupings, on the main relations struck between them and on any potential disputes. With Wright, I assume that the different patterns of articulation and interpenetration of modes of production in productive units shapes frameworks that structure potential contradictions and confrontations.

The recuperation of the hotel brings a rare levelling-out of the co-operative's workers, but fresh inequalities too. What is more, while production here is consumption-oriented, it requires some degree of accumulation. Its members then are torn between keeping to strictly commercial activity or developing economic-political strategies. Last, recuperation opens up new experiences of self-management; over time, however, these deploy forms that involve delegation. Here are just a few of the paradoxes discussed in this chapter. Succinctly, the challenge is to find the emancipatory potential in the hybrid character of the hotel's recuperation. To put it in the political and chromatic terms commonly ascribed to left or right, neither red nor blue; a mottled rainbow web that only reveals its seams close-up.

1 Recuperators, Activists and the 'Born and Bred'

The worker co-operative studied is a medium-sized enterprise in the hotel and tourism sector. It offers room service, as well as a café-restaurant and function-room rental, with a wide variety of activities and tasks: administration, cleaning, catering, sales, laundry and others. It was founded in 2003 and had 30 members;[1] by the end of the period analysed it consisted of around 130.[2] Below, I describe the social composition of its workers based on two sources: a worker survey conducted in early 2011 as part of the project "La cultura de la recuperación de empresas. Representaciones y valoraciones de los trabajadores sobre el proceso" [Enterprise Recuperation Culture: Worker Representations

---

1 At the time of the failed enterprise's closure, the workforce consisted of about 70 employees. Most of the co-operative's 30 founder members were former hotel staff. After the recuperation, in the early years of self-management, around 30 new former salaried staff joined.
2 Although, at the extremes of the co-operative's operative period, we see more than 300% growth, the number of members in recent years has been declining: while the staff stood at 160 in 2011, by 2013 it had fallen to 142.

and Assessments of the Process]³ and semi-structured interviews with the co-operative's workers conducted throughout the field-work.

Based on a 2003 survey, Julian Rebón (2007) has described the archetypal profile of a 'recuperator.' He was a male, aged between 40 and 49, a wage worker from the small and medium-sized enterprises (SMEs) industry, registered in social security and having seniority in the enterprise, holding a position as a qualified operator, born far from the urban centre of the Buenos Aires Metropolitan Area (AMBA), who has not finished secondary school, resides in the Buenos Aires Conurbation and has some previous experience in struggles and claims.

A few years later, based on the 2011 survey mentioned earlier, Rodrigo Salgado (2012) differentiated two 'recuperated enterprise worker' archetypes and identified a key element in the development of these enterprises: the incorporation of new workers. On one hand, the 'recuperator,' with characteristics similar to those posited by Rebón (2007); on the other, the 'new' worker, a male with an average age of 30, not necessarily a member of the co-operative – as the 'recuperator' was – having a medium level of schooling and no experience in either collective struggles and claims, or participation in movements.

That said, let us turn the spotlight on our worker co-operative. Before describing profiles, I should make it clear that, unlike the 'archetypal recuperated enterprise worker' (Salgado, 2012), they are in this case men and women, the service sector, unlike the industrial sector, being characterised by a strong presence of women. What is more, there are no differences in the nature of the link between worker and co-operative: everyone in this enterprise enters as a member. Based on certain paradigmatic cases, I reconstruct below three archetypal worker profiles.

First, we met the 'recuperator' as described earlier, but in this case a woman. Rosa is a worker who has not finished secondary school and holds a post as a qualified operator. She resides in the Buenos Aires Conurbation and has worked at the enterprise since it opened in 1978. She has been in the same job ever since and, while over 70 years old, she has not yet retired. Rosa represents

---

3 The survey's sample was taken in quotas by gender and age. We interviewed 28 of the 160 workers in the recuperated hotel at the time. Although the sample was non-random, any potential bias over case selection was corrected, based on the parameters mentioned. It is not therefore possible to conduct a representative analysis of the workforce, although it is possible to make an exploratory approach. The research project was led by Julián Rebón and the field-work coordinated by Rodrigo Salgado. The triangulation of the survey with the semi-structured interviews conducted in the field-work has helped us to make the description more robust.

Argentina's stable working class: a full-time wage earner, with a long history in the enterprise and access to social protection through the wage relationship.

Second, we identified two types of 'new' workers in our co-operative. On the one hand, the 'activist,' who comes in during the co-operative's first upturn (2004–2006)[4] – that is, when it begins operations – via participation in the recuperated enterprise movement. It is usually a male, aged 33 on average, with medium-level school qualifications and slightly more experience in collective struggles and claims than the 'recuperator.' In this group, we pick up the case of Alejandro, who joined the co-operative in 2005 after participating in the recuperated enterprise movement. Aged thirty-six, not having completed university, he had previously worked in a family service venture and entered the hotel to work in the newly-created area of institutional relations, aimed at developing links with such external actors as politicians, civil servants and the media.

Unlike Rosa, Alejandro represents a type of worker socialised during the decline of the economic and social model that had enabled the socio-economic and symbolic integration of the stable working class. From a middle-class Buenos Aires family, his work was divided between the family venture and local neighbourhood party-political activism. Through his participation in popular assemblies, Alejandro entered a recuperated enterprise organisation and went on from there to the hotel, combining work and activism.

Third, we met the 'family co-operativist,' a 'new' worker who entered through a family member or friend during a second period of expansion of the co-operative's workers (2007–2011).[5] This last profile is a man or woman, aged 27 on average, with medium-level school qualifications and no experience in collective struggles and claims, nor any participation in movements. Gustavo, from the Buenos Aires Conurbation, entered in 2009, aged 19, together with a relative of his. With medium-level schooling, he had brief previous work experience in a tourism agency. In the early stages, he performed unqualified tasks, but thanks to the hotel's rotation policy, he gained experience in areas that required a qualified operative.

This third profile describes a young worker who joins the enterprise with little work experience and is trained in self-management and associated work. While this is not classic salaried employment, working in the co-operative is one of his first work experiences and provides him with stability and the

---

4 Many former hotel workers also came in during this period, as did workers' relatives.
5 After this period, the number of co-operative workers declined.

opportunity to gain qualifications. This profile represents the first generation of co-operativists in the enterprise, who are 'born and bred' in co-operativism.

Within this last profile, one group values the co-operative positively, both in terms of opportunities for personal growth and political training, and the change in working speeds and property relations.

> I only spent three or four months in the kitchens, and then the chance of getting promoted to one position or another cropped up, which I think this is what the co-operative gives you too: for us youngsters – I'm 23 – the possibility of growing professionally and personally in the issue of the character of ideas. Cause like I came in, all was fine with the co-operative, I got more and more steeped in the situation. Obviously, I choose the situation, having the work opportunity to go outside, but it helps me a lot in everyday life to too being here in the co-operative, being involved in the issue of the struggle. It's helped me to collaborate in situations in my neighbourhood, everyday situations. [...] So, the struggle here, or having ideas of my own, helped me use it outside too. Which is why I'm telling you, apart from being something work-related, it forms you as a person, your ideological thinking.
>
> GUSTAVO, co-operative member, August 2014

∴

> I didn't know it was co-op here. Later, the lady who's president now, explained what a co-operative was to me. I was gobsmacked, cause I'd never worked in a co-operative before. Gobsmacked I was: it was like I saw they was working without all that pressure you sometimes get in companies, where you've got the pressure of the manager, but with the same responsibility. [...] Then she explained they're all members, and everybody's got a voice and a vote. That's where I felt a bit like I owned the property, so like I took better care of it. I felt like it had a bit of me in it, let's say.
>
> JORGE, co-operative member, August 2014

Another group of 'family co-operativists' trains up and then get jobs in better-paid private sector hotels. What Rosa says about her granddaughter is illustrative in this respect:

> She was here nearly eight years. And, well, she had a pretty good experience, cause it was her first job, and sometimes she'd complain and say,

"Granny, you get paid peanuts here." And I was like, "If you wanna earn more, you're gonna have to find yourself another job, in other hotels." Cause she already had experience. That's almost always the reason in young people. We haven't got nowhere to go no more.
ROSA, co-operative member, August 2014

Ultimately, being 'born and bred' in co-operativism does not necessarily imply the configuration of an ingrained co-operative identity. Whereas among 'recuperators' we find some who see themselves as workers and others as co-operativists, 'newcomers' almost exclusively see themselves as workers. With the 'family co-operativist' category, we recognise an identity that is paradoxically built more on a 'family' than a 'co-operative' basis: along similar lines to those of a small family business, young people join in order to have their first work experiences and then, in some cases, obtain other work outside the world of co-operatives.

2 Property Relations: Social Possession and Differential Appropriation of the Fruits of Labour

The means of production in this recuperated enterprise are medium in scale. They include the hotel's facilities: the twenty-story building has 220 rooms with a capacity for up to 500 guests, function rooms and auditoria. In addition to the premises, the co-operative has over the years acquired means of production and invested in infrastructure with its own funds and with financing from various non-governmental organisations (NGOs) and state bodies. By 2012, the co-operative's investment in the hotel stood at AR$5,000,000.

The hotel's former proprietors and legal owners of these means of production have no effective capacity to determine their uses. While 'legal ownership' of the property grants them the right to transfer or destroy it, the co-operative's community of workers, through common 'possession' of the means of production, performs a social appropriation of the fruits of its utilisation. What does it mean for workers to form a community? I refer to the fact that all those entering the co-operative do so as members and therefore have equal rights regarding the ownership of the means of production and participation in decision-making.

However, this was not always the case. While existing worker co-operative legislation stipulates an associational – non-labour – link between workers and the co-operative, it also provides for a number of exceptions, according to which workers entry to the productive unit may be subject to a salaried employment relationship for a limited period of time. Recuperated enterprises have accordingly resorted to this practice.

In the case studied, in the early years of self-management, the hotel resorted to recruiting staff in order to cover seasonal increases in demand typical of the sector or as a trial period for aspiring members. However, as a result of labour fraud trials, in which efforts are made to demonstrate the existence of spurious elements in co-operatives' associational nature and non-compliance with labour regulations, it abandoned this form of recruitment a couple of years after the start of the experience and introduced membership for every worker from the moment of entry.

The case of a recuperated food enterprise in Rosario analysed by Victoria Deux Marzi (2014), whose only members are its fifteen founders, provides an interesting counterpoint. For the intake of new workers, this group decided to recruit ten through an outsourced enterprise, and 50 others by setting up a commercial company. Thus, the author postulates, the relations between the group of fifteen founders and the 60 new workers are salary-based and even harsher than under a boss, while the areas and forms of commodification of the labour force are expanded and deepened.

On the other hand, all the hotel's workers pool their labour force to produce a service and are equally entitled to participate in decision-making over assets and production. Work and ownership then are not divided in the co-operative; there is no place for the productive consumption of the labour force that characterises capitalist production. This joint ownership means the co-operative's possessions are not divisible among individuals but belong to the workers' collective, which imposes limits on private property. In a nutshell, there is a social ownership of the means of production.

The Co-operatives Act 20,337 aims in this direction. First, it states that co-operatives form their capital from shares comprising their members, while, in terms of participation in decision-making, the formula of 'one person, one vote' applies regardless of the number of shares subscribed. Second, if the co-operative's by-laws authorise the application of surpluses to any capital return, a limited interest is stipulated to social shares (not exceeding the Argentinian National Bank's discount transactions by more than one point). Third, in the event of a member's retirement or exclusion, or the dissolution of the co-operative, members are entitled only to reimbursement of the face value of their shares, with deduction of any losses, a proportion of which they have to bear. Fourth, surplus assets after the dissolution of a co-operative, should there be any, are allocated to the proper organisation for the promotion of co-operativism (*Instituto Nacional de Asociativismo y Economía Social* [National Institute of Associativism and Social Economy] [INAES]). Fifth, workers' incomes are calculated in proportion to how much work each actually performs, not the number of shares. Last, these shares can be transferred only between members and in accordance with the board. The practices developed in the hotel further deepen the measures stipulated by law because the amounts of shares involved are symbolic and a mere formality towards the formation of the co-operative.

That said, let us describe this social ownership more concretely in tension with its abstract conception. First, it is a low-depth form of social possession, not full ownership, as the co-operative only has de facto occupancy and has to fight off numerous eviction orders. The precarity of the possession is thus deeper than other enterprise recuperation experiences that have usufruct permits or expropriation laws in their favour. Moreover, its breadth is specific to the enterprise's facilities, a high-value fixed asset in terms of size and location (Image 1). For this reason, compared to other co-operative ventures, its relative breadth tends to grow. Last, inclusiveness refers to the scale of the range of people appropriating the means of production and the outcomes arising from their appropriation through productive use. In this case, the inclusiveness of society as a whole is limited because the community that performs the social appropriation is confined to the workers collective, given that, generally speaking, worker co-operatives are productive ventures that establish market exchanges with the rest of the social whole.

IMAGE 1   The co-operative's location
PHOTO BY DENISE KASPARIAN (SEPTEMBER 2020)

However, certain non-market liaisons counteract this form of relationship between co-operatives and the social whole. By 2011, about 70% of recuperated enterprises in Buenos Aires carried out liaison activities with society, including educational activities (*bachilleratos populares* [progressive secondary schools])[6] and other institutions), cultural activities (cultural centres, libraries and community radio) and economic activities (donations) (Kasparian, 2013a). In the hotel's case, these were mainly economic articulations, such as donating rooms for people with medical treatments residing outside the city and the hotel's spaces for use by other co-operatives, and various social, political and trades union organisations. Moreover, extenuating circumstances were established for market exchanges through a co-operative tariff for other recuperated enterprises.

Such linkages highlight the need to establish two fields of inclusiveness, one primary and one secondary. The first field covers the range of people carrying out the appropriation through the possession of the hotel. In this case, I refer to the primary group of the workers' community that instates a limited inclusiveness over the property when establishing market relations with the rest of the social whole. However, depending on a number of non-market liaisons, the spectrum of secondary inclusiveness enables an expanded use of the hotel's facilities. This radius of secondary inclusiveness is eminently corporate or sectoral in character, with relations usually being established with actors from co-operativism or the world of work in general.

Where appropriation of the fruits of labour is concerned, all the co-operative's workers being members, there is no labour force consumption. Work in the co-operatives is not remunerated via salaries. However, a description of the established way of distributing income allows us to nuance the basic equality among all workers that membership entails.

At the start of the recuperated enterprises' experiences, workers' wages are often egalitarian – that is, with no monetary differential – for two main reasons. On the one hand, because incomes tend to be low in that the need for working capital means that workers prioritise capitalising the co-operative at the expense of their immediate income; on the other, it is necessary in the early moments of the recuperations to unite the labour collective.

In this latter respect, it is important to consider the levels of conflict in the origins of each enterprise's recuperation. Salgado (2012) contends that the mode of distribution of what is produced acquires early on a more egalitarian

---

6   *Bachilleratos populares* are schools for young people and adults created in 2004 within the framework of social organisations and worker-recuperated enterprises in Argentina. They embrace popular education as their pedagogic and political approach.

character in enterprises where workers struggled together more intensely in the origins of the recuperation. However, this egalitarian social character is not necessarily kept up once the 'heroic period' (Lucita, 2009) or 'moment of conquest' (Meister, 1974, cited in Rosanvallon, 1979) is over. On the contrary, in some cases, this period forms a kind of corporation that tends to cause distributive imbalances against the new workers based on exploitation or opportunity hoarding mechanisms (Salgado, 2012). The founding conflict early on is then an instance of gestation, not just of self-management but of an embryonic corporation.

To explain this imbalance, Salgado (2012) picks up Charles Tilly (2000) and Wright (1994). Tilly (2000) outlines two mechanisms: exploitation and opportunity hoarding. Exploitation refers to people who have resources from which they extract profits by articulating others' efforts, whom they exclude from any resulting surplus value. Plainly put, exploitation involves living off other people's work based on the availability of certain resources. Opportunity hoarding operates when one group of people gains access to a resource that is valuable, renewable and subject to monopoly. Both mechanisms may act in parallel but refer to different processes.

In Wright (1994), exploitation is exclusion with appropriation of the fruits of labour. If this latter aspect is not met, 'non-exploitative oppression' may occur, in which the fruits of labour are not transferred from the oppressed to the oppressor, and the oppressor's well-being depends simply on excluding the oppressed from access to certain resources, but not on their work effort. This notion is associated with opportunity hoarding, namely, the control of resources subject to monopoly. For my research, Salgado's analysis (2012) of distributional relations in recuperated enterprises and the imbalance that underlies two categories of member – 'founders' and 'newcomers' – is food for thought.

This inequality underlies two ways of establishing differentiations in wages. On the one hand, differentiation in the co-operative is by seniority (Salgado, 2012), with the 'founders' or 'old' workers at the apex of the pyramid. This differentiation expresses the existence of exploitation and opportunity hoarding mechanisms not founded on control of alienable assets, as in the Rosario enterprise analysed by Deux Marzi (2014). On the contrary, exploitation and opportunity hoarding mechanisms are founded on control of organisational assets (Wright, 1994), namely, the planning and articulation of the division of labour. In this sense, control of these resources by the 'founder members' is the material basis for the exploitation of 'new' workers through the establishment of the seniority differential.

On the other hand, there is differentiation by professional category, a commonly used criterion in the labour market, but which in recuperated enterprises is minimised by setting caps or maximum differences on remuneration across the categories of the scale or by reducing the number of categories (Salgado, 2012). This criterion is not based on attributes of the relationship established between worker and enterprise, as it is with seniority, but on the characteristics of the task performed by the worker. Workers involved in the recuperation also control any 'organisational assets,' occupying the highest-rated positions – command and promotion – by hoarding the most profitable categories, thereby obtaining a differential appropriation of what is produced.

Salgado (2012) thus identifies that both types of remuneration differentiation reflect opportunity hoarding through control of organisational assets. These are jobs linked to the productive unit's function of management and monitoring roles, and co-operative governance or moral authority when it comes to establishing and legitimising criteria to differentiate wages. This kind of control is exercised by those who participated in the recuperation of the enterprise, commonly referred to as 'founder members'.

That said, how do 'founder members' manage to control organisational assets by excluding 'new' workers? Following Norbert Elias's (1996) schema of the "established and outsiders" when analysing the socio-dynamics of relations between groups, Salgado (2012) contends that, based on the characteristics of the link between workers – and, more specifically, its longevity – this group of 'established' members capitalises the trajectories of work and of the recuperation struggle they have shared, as well as the principles and values constructed.

This group of 'established' members achieves greater unity, identification, cohesion and integration – and therefore social organisation – than the other member groups. This enables the institution of power tips the scales in their favour, such as ownership of the productive unit[7] or control of organisational resources, reflected in the ability of the 'founder members' to establish differentiating criteria for remunerations in their favour.

This control can be reversed as long as the workers' collective is made up entirely of members. The association relationship provides a level playing field in decision-making that facilitates the reversal of the unequalising process. On the contrary, in labour collectives with hired workers, this becomes difficult in that such a condition excludes workers from the possibility of participating

---

7 In the recuperated enterprise in Rosario analysed by Deux Marzi (2014), the workers participating in the recovery are the sole members of the co-operative; the workers entering later on did not, however, join as members. Behind the categories of 'members' and 'non-members' then is the pair 'founding member–new worker'.

in decision-making. The dynamic of the relationship between the groups thus shapes potential conflicts. The greater the power inequality between the groups, the more likely the tensions and conflicts between them are to remain latent, and the less marked such an inequality is, the more likely the conflict is to become constant or manifest (Elias, 1996).

In the case analysed, the monthly income consists of a basic remuneration that establishes an egalitarian base, with bonuses for punctuality, presenteeism, seniority in the co-operative, founder member status and level of responsibility or minimized labour hierarchy. By 2014, no bonuses exceeded AR$500 pesos, so differences in income were minor. In addition to this, the hotel workers received the individual subsidy from Line 1 of the *Programa de Trabajo Autogestionado* [Self-Managed Work Programme] of the Ministry of Labour, Employment and Social Security of the Nation. Last, each member's *monotributo* [monotax] payment (a simplified tax regime for self-employed workers and small taxpayers) was paid by the co-operative and meals were provided by the hotel's dining room.

At the start of the experience, wages were differentiated by level of responsibility or minimized labour hierarchy. Whereas the collective labour agreement of the branch of activity proposes a scale of eight professional categories, the hotel sets a bonus by labour hierarchy, which is only received by those occupying positions of control and supervision of the co-operative's productive or governance process, namely, sector *responsables* [supervisors][8] or members of the board. So, in its early days, the worker co-operative resumed a classic criterion of salary differentiation, testing a simplified reproduction of the criteria for setting wages in enterprises under boss.

However, unlike traditional capitalist enterprises, such posts in the hotel are not occupied according to workers' educational and professional skills or credentials in keeping with the qualifications of the job but are primarily based on criteria of seniority and commitment to the co-operative:

> I changed cause someone was needed in the warehouse to administrate the merchandise … Someone older, to look after things. Cause we had a hard time keeping them, so I came to the warehouse. To make things a bit better and keep an eye open. Especially keep an eye open. Cause don't forget we have to create our own salary, and if there's nobody to keep an

---

8 '*Responsables*' literally means 'people responsible for something.' In worker-recuperated enterprises, this term is chosen to avoid the traditional word 'manager' and to differentiate from capitalist companies. In these worker co-operatives, such posts are embedded in democratic and horizontal relations among workers at all levels.

THE RECUPERATED ENTERPRISE AND SOCIAL POWER IN PRODUCTION 117

> eye open ... Young kids are young and still don't understand what it is ... We weren't used to working without a boss. Now we're more organised about keeping an eye on things.
>
> GRACIELA, co-operative member, August 2014

∴

> She had no knowledge, but I could see she really cared about things, about the co-operative [...] Loads of times I was in security, and she really got worked up [cared], her too, about everything, and I could see she had that feeling. Cause it's not like "I do the hokey-cokey and that's that, day over." So, you see, you sense the feeling she's got. And she wasn't this old compañera from years back. I worked with her on the shopfloor for a while, and then I was in security and I used to see her. We'd just have a bit of a chat, but we never chatted about her working with me in the board.
>
> ANA, co-operative member, November 2014

This is then a bonus that hybridises an emulation of the classic recognition of the figure of the salary for those workers performing functions of control and co-ordination of work, but it is also about a recognition typical of recuperated enterprises, where commitment to the co-operative, usually associated with seniority and thus with 'founder members,' is rewarded. Most of the co-operative's 'founder members' in the recuperated hotel hold positions as sector supervisors, area co-ordinators or board members whatever their position in the failed enterprise.

By 2006, when the co-operative was already up and running, and its labour force had quintupled, 10% of the basic income – the same as the percentage for minimised labour hierarchy – began to be added the basic remuneration of those who participated in the enterprise's recuperation and founded the co-operative. I infer that, in a context of workers' staff growth, the 'founder member' bonus was established in the enterprise to recognise and reward the struggle of members who had participated in the recuperation process.

> [There is a bonus] for being a founder member, [...] recognition for so many years. The sacrifice of spending nine months without getting paid a thing. Cause when we came in, we spent nine months without getting paid a thing: from 21 March to 24 December.
>
> GRACIELA, co-operative member, August 2014

Over time, other bonuses were introduced into the basic income. Equally distributed among members who meet the required conditions (tolerance of two late arrivals and no non-attendance per month), incentives for punctuality and attendance constitute mechanisms of self-regulation of work[9] geared to encouraging greater commitment. A further bonus for seniority was introduced in the co-operative around 2009.[10]

> There didn't use to be any seniority. There was a bit of extra cash, AR$200 pesos that founder members got paid cause they'd literally been starving for a year and a half till the hotel could open. So, they had like this general agreement in assembly for all the people in the co-operative at the time to collect a bit more dosh cause it was understood it was up to them whether everybody who'd come later could join. And that started going rotten as time went by, and the rest didn't see a red cent. So, when I came onto the board in 2009, we started arguing about being able to set seniority parameters, like they do in companies, and that's what we did. [...] We said "Let's not take that prize, the others' appreciation, away from the founder members, but let's add an item of seniority, the result of seniority in the co-operative" [...] The founder members and those who only arrived in March are about to turn thirteen. The founder member still has that prize. [...] The argument had started up about "He came in yesterday and earns the same as me, and I've been here for ten years"; the same old argument, which at the time was about that.
> ALEJANDRO, co-operative member and leading figure in a
> worker co-operative organisation, January 2016

In short, it is possible to establish links between the criteria for differentiating remunerations through minimised labour hierarchy, founder member status and seniority, and the different periods of new workers' entering the co-operative. In the early days of the experience, the wage gap of the enterprise under a boss was significantly narrowed through the minimising of differentiation by labour hierarchy. This was made easier because workers in positions requiring professional or technical qualifications in the failed enterprise, as in

---

9   Cecilia Calloway (2016) defines the concept of 'self-regulation of work' as the set of collective practices replacing the manufacturing discipline typical of vertical organisation in a self-managed organisation. I look at this issue more closely in Chapter 6.
10 In the hotel and catering sector, the percentage – ranging from 1% to 14% – increases with seniority. However, the percentage in the hotel is fixed: 2% of the basic wage is applied, and the amount is multiplied by the number of years in the co-operative.

most recuperated ones, left the productive unit. This not only facilitated the levelling-out of the labour collective but enabled unqualified workers to take up operational or technical positions. One example is the woman who was the co-operative's president at the time of the close of our fieldwork, who worked as a cleaner in the failed enterprise.

After the hotel's reopening and productive upturn between 2004 and 2006, the labour force grew exponentially, which was when a bonus was introduced for being a 'founder member.' In this way, all 'founder members' – even those who did not hold positions controlling or co-ordinating work – obtained an income differential from the bonus for their participation in the recuperation.

Last, the differences in seniority, closer to the typical form of salaried employment, emerged from the second wave of entries to the hotel, between 2008 and 2011. Several years had elapsed since the start of the experience, and the intake of a new batch of workers introduced the need to hierarchise those who, while not 'founder members,' had seniority within the co-operative. I therefore hypothesise that, in recuperated enterprises with longer track-records, 'old' workers are not confined just to 'founders,' making the groups' structure and socio-dynamics more complex.

These 'new' – yet 'old' – workers dispute the differentiation criteria for wages and succeed in introducing the seniority bonus. As the bonus for 'founder member' status is a form of differentiation of remunerations endogenous to recuperated enterprises, it has difficulty mustering legitimacy and sparks disputes over what is fair. As a result, a second wave of workers' entry to the hotel means that 'old' non-'founders' succeed in introducing a relatively favourable differentiation as compared to 'new' workers.

That said, this last way of differentiating remunerations reinforces the differences favourable to 'founder members,' since the category of members receives both the 'founder member' bonus and the maximum for seniority. For all that, those who participated in the process of recuperating and founding the co-operative have a power differential that becomes evident in opportunity hoarding. They often hold positions controlling the productive process and governance of the co-operative, while also being the most senior, and achieve a differentiated appropriation of the fruits of labour. Yet this does not happen without this differential being challenged by another social grouping: the co-operative's 'new' senior workers.

I should make it clear that I am referring to opportunity hoarding through the control of organisational resources, not to exploitation processes: for one thing, because the scale of the difference between wages is extremely low; for another, because the 'founder members' do not live from the other categories of workers' efforts. In other words, their well-being does not depend on the work of others, but they also perform daily tasks in the co-operative. The identity of the 'founder members' does not therefore constitute an exploitative identity.

Let me summarise what I have developed thus far concerning property relations. In the recuperated hotel, there is social possession of the means of production by the workers' collective. We can see a non-split between direct producers and means of production, since all workers enter the co-operative as members, which stipulates equal political and possession rights.

This social ownership is low level, with a specific extent and limited primary inclusiveness, although it is broadened through secondary inclusiveness with sectoral or corporate characteristics. Last, this social possession does not result in a radically egalitarian appropriation of the fruits of work. The opportunity hoarding evinced in the control of organisational resources by the 'founder members' allows them to operate a slight differentiation in remunerations compared to other members.

However, with the development of the co-operative, a category of non-founder workers with seniority in the venture succeeds in introducing a seniority differential, which does not, in any case, violate the differential obtained by the 'founders.' The possibility of creating bonuses that set out to reverse inequalities – or introduce new ones – is due to the form of the relationship between workers and the co-operative: the associational link makes it possible for everyone to participate in decision-making.

3   The Logic of Production and the Issue of Sustainability in Recuperated Enterprises

When it comes to the immediate destination of production, the enterprise does not depart from the general run of recuperation processes in that it produces exchange values to sell on the market. However, recuperated enterprises arise to defend jobs and this logic permeates production. The purpose of the co-operative is not therefore geared to accumulation with a view to maximising profits, but to the consumption of the workers and their families: in other words, the reproduction – simple or expanded – of life (Coraggio, 2008).

That said, a certain degree of accumulation, both economic and political, becomes necessary as a result of such consumption needs, which tend to take precedence. In economic terms, from its formation until 2015, the co-operative had invested AR$5,000,000 pesos in infrastructure. In terms of political accumulation, the hotel has established itself as a paradigmatic case of linkage with its social environment. This encourages public procurement, as well as the support of society and a wide range of organisations, particularly being faced with conflicts around the ownership of the property. Political accumulation thus has a hand in the sustainability of the venture oriented to hotel workers' reproduction: in other words, it is a means to reproduce life, not an end in itself. Since recuperated enterprises are not geared towards maximising profit, the appropriate yardstick is not profit-focused efficiency.

Related to this issue, a debate has opened up in studies of the social economy around how to conceptualise recuperated enterprises' sustainability in particular and the social economy's endeavours in general. The notion of 'sustainability' can be generically defined as a productive enterprise's ability to endure over time and produce its own income (Fernández Álvarez, 2012b). Faced with the criterion of 'strict' market economic sustainability, which involves evaluating ventures on their ability to generate a monetary economic surplus, some authors have outlined alternative notions. José Luis Coraggio (2008) proposes to analyse these ventures' sustainability using the notion of 'socio-economic sustainability,' in other words, depending on ventures' ability to reproduce the lives of their members, admitting commonly available state economic subsidies (like education) into the schema, as well as contributions and resources based on relations of reciprocity. Gonzalo Vázquez (2014) posits the notion of 'plural collective sustainability' to highlight the plurality of economic principles intervening in sustainability, and the political and cultural capacity needed to build power relations to promote public policies favourable to the sector's collective sustainability.

From this standpoint, we can understand that, even if there is no surplus after the work is remunerated, production for recuperated enterprises is sustainable if it preserves working conditions (Rebón, 2015). I refer specifically to income levels similar to the sector average (with bonuses and holidays), job stability and access to social security. To what extent is this situation reached in the case in question? Seen in terms of the reproduction of its members' lives, sustainability in the hotel is achieved with certain limitations and vulnerabilities.

First, the income received is below the activity branch average,[11] they have paid holidays and, given that the supplementary annual salary is not available in co-operatives, the hotel pays a similar amount through the distribution of surpluses in the middle and at the end of the year. Second, where job stability is concerned, the co-operative is in a vulnerable position due to the precarious

---

11   The individual income of a worker just joining the co-operative is at the level of the legal minimum wage and, while the individual subsidy of Self-Managed Work Programme's Line 1 is added, it still remains below the average salary for this branch of activity.

occupancy of the premises and the risk of eviction. However, in individual terms, each worker's member status provides greater job stability when compared to the failed enterprise. Third, in terms of social security, the recuperated enterprise pays the members monotax, given the lack of a regime for worker co-operatives.[12] The monotax includes contributions to the tax system, as well as retirement and health coverage contributions, which is why workers only gain access to two of the five social security components and are excluded from family allowances, unemployment insurance and occupational risk insurance. The members' coverage in the event of accident or illness at work is difficult, as the regulations stipulate the employers' obligation to hire an occupational risk insurance company. In the absence of a labour relation, co-operatives are legally obliged to take out personal life insurance. This has the disadvantage of covering a minimal share of the damages, without covering the wages of workers given accident or sick leave; the monotax also only allows access to the minimum retirement pension.

In short, the transition from wage labour in the failed enterprise to associational, self-managed work in the recuperated enterprise implies a relative precarisation in terms of labour rights. I am not, however, making an apology for wage labour here. On the contrary, I emphasise that the recuperation of the enterprise reverses the impoverishment that led to the capitalist withdrawal of production. As research into the subject shows, it expands workers' political and social participation and increases the margins of self-determination in the work sphere. Moreover, the hotel has a rotation policy in its posts, or 'high-end polyvalency': this favours training in labour and social activities.

That said, to go back to the debate about the sustainability of recuperated enterprises and social economy ventures, it is unavoidable that the market

---

12   Access to social security for members of worker co-operatives is regulated by *Administración Nacional de la Seguridad Social* [National Social Security Administration] (ANSES) Resolution No. 784/92, Article 1 of which states that, not being salaried employees, co-operative members are considered self-employed. Furthermore, Resolution No. 183/92 of the *Instituto Nacional de Acción Cooperativa* [National Institute for Co-operative Action] – an agency that would later become the INAES – states that worker co-operatives must guarantee access to social security and meet the necessary contributions for the welfare regime in the self-employed workers system (Deux Marzi and Hintze, 2014). In late 2013, the INAES issued Resolution No. 4664/13, replacing No. 183/92. This regulation introduced two changes concerning the social security of workers in worker-run co-operatives: (1) the option to make contributions to the *Monotributo* (Monotax) or to the salaried employment regime; (2) it urges *aseguradoras de riesgos del trabajo* [occupational risk insurers] (ART) to issue policies for co-operatives. On this last point, co-operatives face major difficulties, as the law regulating ARTs stipulates requirements that co-operatives find it impossible to meet.

and competition should impose their conditions. At some point, co-operatives have to maximise the productive process if they are to compete in costs and quality terms, thereby obtaining surpluses that make it possible to constitute working capital and reinvest in order to capitalise on the productive unit. They thus face the challenge of managing the tension between consumption and accumulation, which is observed precisely as being at the origin of certain work conflicts in the hotel.

Various researchers have shown that this tension can be tackled by limiting the market nature of the experiences through reciprocity relations with other actors and redistribution with the state (Deux Marxi, 2014; Fernández Álvarez, 2012a; Itzigsohn and Rebón, 2015) that help to generate different types of markets. I assert that sustainability tends to be achieved if co-operatives achieve increasing autonomy from the classic capitalist market. In doing so, recuperated enterprises can escape the fate of dissolution or capitalist normalisation, formulated early on by Rosa Luxembourg (1979), by adopting a criterion of efficiency that focuses on the combination of various economic principles tending towards the partial demarketisation of the experiences.

In this sense, the recuperated enterprise carries out activities not mediated by the market. These activities are considered by workers to be a kind of reward, giving back the support received in the recuperation of the enterprise. This is not to imply that social relations built on this logic of gift–countergift (Mauss, 2010) are lacking interest or sustained solely by generosity and gratuity. On the contrary, this link implies an expectation of reciprocity, of an obligation to give back, configuring networks of alliances, confidences and reciprocities. These liaisons even enable marketing strategies that allow the co-operative to become partially autonomous from capitalist market rules and recreate co-operative sector-specific rules. For example, the hotel has four differentiated rates: the highest is the 'over-the-counter' tariff; then, in descending order, the 'corporate' tariff for events or government agencies, the 'travel agency' tariff and last the 'co-operative' tariff.

The market principle in the experience analysed has not been limited just – or primarily – by the principle of reciprocity. Thanks to market exchange relations with the state, minimised by the principle of redistribution, the hotel has benefitted from the state purchase. While the government did not develop a formalised public policy of preferential procurement from worker co-operatives, it became a major client for recuperated enterprises. By 2008, 60% of the hotel's turnover came from services provided to the state. Over the years, the state gradually lost its central place in the client portfolio: in 2015, 75% of turnover came from services provided to the private sector.

That said, as I pointed out regarding differential tariffs, we find clients in the private sector who are at the same time part of the group of allies participating in reciprocity relations.

> The bulk of our clientele come in through politics and social organisations: about 80% of what comes in is from there. We're hired by ministries, we're hired by different NGOs, co-operatives, mutual associations. The bulk of what we invoice comes from that. And then we have a couple of travel agents that hire us.
> OMAR, co-operative member, May 2011

We can see then that the market principle in the co-operative is minimised by the principle of state redistribution and, to a lesser extent, reciprocity. Public procurement and procurement from other co-operatives and ventures in the social economy have been central to the co-operative's sustainability, helping to create other markets, distinct from the competitive, supposedly deregulated one. In this sense, although the price, characteristics and quality of the service can guide procurement by state entities, recruitment is without doubt ultimately determined by the history of struggle and the legitimacy that the enterprise recuperation process brings.[13]

> Mario went early and rang us from there, he told us the President [Cristina Fernández de Kirchner] was going. And we went and took her a letter and talked to her. We told her about our situation, and she said, "Don't worry, I know about you." "Yeah, but we need you to do something more than just know. There are 130 of us compañeros fighting, men and women fighting for our jobs." The letter said the same thing, but we told her personally. Alicia [Kirchner, Minister for Social Development] was there too, Alicia always came. We were staging a fashion show of self-managed textiles, it was getting organised. So, we see Alicia, and she says, "How's the show

---

13   Similar observations can be found in the work of María Inés Fernández Álvarez (2012b). There, the author points out that a recuperated enterprise winning a contract for the manufacture of *Aerolíneas Argentinas* staff uniforms – Argentina's national airline – does not primarily depend on the quality or price of the product, even if those factors are necessary preconditions for the contract. On the contrary, underlying this is "the social, political, collective nature that builds the public meaning of being a recuperated enterprise […] the fact that it has been carried out by workers who have fought and recuperated their 'sources of work'" (p. 12).

going?" "It's moving forward, Alicia." "Right, tomorrow I'll send you someone." When that someone turned up, so did all the ministries.
MARIELA, co-operative member, August 2014

In short, it could be argued that the efficiency centring on the reproduction of workers in social economy ventures involves the ability to connect up various economic principles. In Chapter 6, I develop the idea that several enterprise projects are configured in relation to the degrees and modes of this connecting-up of principles and practices. These are not just productive but also contain political projects to bolster the enterprise and, in that sense, they lie at the heart of conflicts over the running of the co-operative.

4 The Political Dimension: Between Self-management and Delegation

Geared towards the harmonisation of individual activities according to a plan, the function of management is inherent in any social co-operation process, including the collective labour process. In capitalist mode of production (Marx, 2011), in which the decisive objective is the valorisation of capital through production of surplus value, the function of management takes on particular characteristics. Its content is two-sided: it must not only co-ordinate bodies for the production of use values but also for the valorisation of capital and is, in this sense, personified by capital. In formal terms, it tends to be despotic, or co-active, as expressed in the verticality of command and in the hierarchical transmission of rules and regulations. It is, however, advisable to play down this observation: contemporary research like Michael Burawoy's (1983) demonstrate the existence of factory regimes built on hegemony rather than despotism.

In contrast, the recuperation of an enterprise democratises the function of management: recuperated enterprises often express forms of autonomous co-operation, where the rules and regulations governing labour processes are collectively constructed. In their early stages, recuperations display two central transformations in the function of management: this comes to be personified by the labour collective and the assembly takes hold for decision-making. The development of self-management, understood as the collective, autonomous exercise of productive management, stems from two elements: on the one hand, the co-operative legal framework that establishes the assembly as the supreme decision-making body, comprising all members (one-member-one-vote); on the other, in the case of the recuperated hotel and recuperated enterprises in general, the co-operation relations developed during the founding conflict forge new degrees of unity among workers and lessen asymmetries and hierarchies (Rebón, 2007).

The assembly is the highest self-management body, with all associated workers being entitled to vote. Co-operatives Act 20,337 establishes an obligatory annual ordinary assembly to approve the balance sheet, annual report and other documents. It also allows for the eventuality of extraordinary assemblies called by the board or the syndic or requested by a group of members.

Assemblies in recuperated enterprises are often periodic and, especially in the early days of recuperation, frequent. Later, when the fully productive stage is entered, they tend to tail off. This process is general to associational and self-managed work experiences. In *L'Âge de l'autogestion* [The Age of Self-Management], Pierre Rosanvallon (1979) picks up Albert Meister's developments (1974) around worker co-operatives and working communities. Meister proposes a periodisation based on the degrees of direct democracy observed. In the first period of constitution of the workers' collective or 'moment of conquest,' direct democracy is predominant. The conquest phase is attended by 'economic consolidation,' in which direct democracy focuses on extra-economic activities, giving way to delegated democracy taken up by a group of leaders and specialists. Then comes the moment for 'co-existence,' when delegated democracy succeeds in setting aside direct democracy. Last, comes the phase of the 'power of administrators,' in which power passes from the group or its direct representatives to the technicians and leaders who split from the workers' collective.

During 2015, approximately eighteen extraordinary assemblies and 'extended board meetings' were held at the hotel, also called 'informal meetings.' Whereas extraordinary meetings count as formal bodies, that is, reporting to the INAES and held under relevant regulations, 'extended board meetings' or 'informal meetings' have a different dynamic and offer greater flexibility. Attendance is not mandatory; indeed, the very name 'extended board meetings' reflects their optional nature: those who have to attend are the sector or area supervisors, whereas the participation of the other members is down to their personal discretion. Moreover, they do not have to report to the INAES for a fortnight, nor to adhere strictly to the regulations.

These assemblies are usually attended by 40% of members, a percentage that varies with the importance attached to the subject of the meeting. Once production has started up, moments of conflict revitalise the assembly space, in terms of both frequency and levels of participation. Assemblies in the recuperated hotel become accordingly more frequent at key moments of the conflict over the occupancy of the premises:

> The frequency of assemblies, it depends ... now, for example, with all the activities we've had on the issue of expropriation and eviction, they're much more often. There was a time we'd have two or three meetings a month. Cause every now and then we'd go and talk to so-and-so over there, to pass on news. I mean, the folk representing us came and pretty much made a fair copy of [summarised] what had been discussed, what the response was, what was put out there. A lot of the time they're informal, we may have been in the dining room, and then, about ten minutes to make a fair copy of the information.
> GUSTAVO, co-operative member, August 2014

The level of participation is also linked to the time factor. For example, some members from the reception sector argue that they can only attend for a limited time because of the nature of their work. In contrast, 'extended board meetings' seek to rectify this limitation because their informative nature – information is socialised through the board to the rest of the workers – enables formal assemblies to be reserved exclusively for final decision-making and, consequently, limits to be placed on their duration. The information that circulates in these meetings does not remain confined to such spaces; instead, attendees often convey the most important aspects to colleagues in their area or sector.

> [If you don't turn up to the assembly] I pass it [the information] on to you. You're my compañera, you've got the day off tomorrow and you pass it on to me. [...] Next day, my compañero tells me, "This, that or the other happened." When there's going to be a vote on something and what they're going to vote on matters to you, cause it involves you too, then you do turn cause you've got to vote, and at the vote you've got to sign and all. So you turn up cause it involves you.
> FERNANDO, co-operative member, September 2014

Assemblies are effectively intended for decision-making primarily around investments, the approval of balance sheets and requests for removal in the face of expulsions of members. As well as being more informative than formal assemblies, 'extended board meetings' are preparatory bodies that modulate tensions and conflicts. Decision-making then is more process than moment:

> We're on last year's annual report balance now. So, then we deal with it beforehand, so as we won't spend 500 hours arguing in an assembly. We do an expanded board, and then, the accountant comes, submits the

balance sheet, the annual report's submitted, to see if any points need changing, or discussed or whatever, so when we call an assembly, you just go straight in there and vote. [...] All members [participate] cause they have to know what's going to be discussed. [...] Cause if you just tell the co-ordinators, then they're taking decisions for the other compañeros, who might not agree. [...] This space is there so as not to take so long over an assembly. Cause it can take you five hours and the compañeros don't understand, and there's a pause as is left in between. But not this way. This way it's already been presented before the compañeros, there are some points that, if they aren't understood properly, you ask everything you need to ask, everything you have any worries about. So, when you take it [the annual report] to assembly, which is at two in the afternoon, by three in the afternoon you're all off back home. The extended board meeting is going to take a little longer, obvious it is.

ANA, co-operative member, November 2014

In short, while the assembly is more limited in frequency as a decision-making space, bodies develop in its place to socialise information that can enrich the assembly and provide solutions to the difficulties of collective decision-making already beginning to be seen in 2006:

> The foreman or maintenance supervisor had to be changed. We took it to assembly, cause there was this whole big fuss about it. [...] But again sometimes, the issues as are a bit beyond the scope of the board, calling an assembly about them is also taking the compañeros an issue that ... if you ain't got it straight, matey [compañero], then god help the rest. Sometimes you've got to be careful about that.
>
> MARIO, co-operative member, September 2006

For its part, the board of the co-operative analysed is responsible for most of the day-to-day running of the venture, as well as decision-making regarding disciplinary measures and the nomination of sector *encargados* [overseers].[14] Among board members, there are concerns about channelling certain routine issues through intermediate management and co-ordination bodies in order to focus efforts on designing marketing strategies, evaluating investments and seeking suppliers that keep costs down.

---

14   Closely akin to '*responsables,*' '*encargados*' literally means 'people in charge of something.' Again, the use of this term seeks to differentiate the hotel from capitalist companies.

"Ah, you know what, I need to change my day-off," they came banging on to the board, when the members' office is there and its overseer, its co-ordinator. So, we worked on that then, to try and lighten the workload a bit and look more at what's commercial, what we can do to sell more, see if we need to fix rooms up. In other words, to really think through the subject, beyond a change of day-off, right?
    ANA, co-operative member, November 2014

The rotation of board members in the recuperated hotel takes place every three years. Six boards were formed during the period studied in this book. These show how the function of management in the hotel has come to be specifically personified by its members. This process is consistent with the observations of Neusa Maria Dal Ri and Candido Giraldez Vieitez (2001), who note that delegation in recuperated enterprises tends over the years to become accentuated and supervision by cadres becomes especially relevant for the labour collective to take on the function of management. Given the medium scale of our enterprise, it is hard to apply other less delegative management alternatives, although this does not sidestep the fact that the assembly remains the body that makes the rules or audits the actions of the board members. We accordingly have records of decisions by the board to 'dismiss' members that were reversed in assemblies. Such cadres effectively serve as identities that express the labour force in its exercise of the function of management.

Nevertheless, there is a degree of circumspection among workers about the role of board members. Although they are expected to move the conflict over the occupancy of the premises forward, there is also a certain "suspicion" surrounding those who take on such responsibilities. A key informant close to the co-operative states that "there are very few people moving the conflict forward. It's a tacit delegation that also looks on those running it with suspicion" (Adrián, key informant, October 2014). A member who joined the co-operative via a recuperated enterprise organisation – and sat on the board – thinks along similar lines:

There's a few as grasp the need to ask for help quicker, and others aren't so quick, and others who accept it cause they've no alternative. Some think outsiders are made of wood [have no say in it], and they say as much [...] I've been just another co-operative member for a long time, and that's how my compañeros see it. But I've also got this label that's like "He's the one with the politics, ask him, or ask him to see to it," the ones as appreciate it. And those as don't will say, "Christ knows what shit this guy's up to." That's inevitable.
    ALEJANDRO, co-operative member and leading figure in a
    worker co-operative organisation, January 2016

On the subject of rotation in posts on the board, the first four boards varied their make-up completely. This was not due to a lack of interest among those in leadership posts or to clear policies of rotation of the posts. On the contrary, many board members stood for re-election but failed to win. Then a fifth board was formed, with members who had held different posts on previous boards, and the last one, voted in at the end of 2015, completely re-elected its predecessor. It is thought-provoking that four of the six boards have been chaired by 'founder members.' We can see then that 'founder members' hold key posts in the enterprise, be they governance posts or posts of work supervision and control.

That said, both statutory worker co-operative bodies have their limitations. The assembly as the main organ of direct democracy raises difficulties regarding the maintenance of all workers' participation and involvement, and also regarding the time needed for decision-making and the differences in the members' weight and ability to develop, convey and establish their views. The size of the hotel also complexifies its operating capacity: the holding of assemblies with all members may experience greater difficulties than smaller enterprises. For its part, delegation in the board displays tensions typical of representative democracy: the risk of representatives' autonomisation (Dal Ri and Vieitez, 2001) and the tendency for the relationship between representatives and represented to become a relationship between leaders and led (Rosanvallon, 1979). To summarise, the risks lie in the distance and difference between representatives and represented (Schnapper, 2004). For these reasons, in addition to statutory bodies, the recuperated hotel has developed intermediate bodies and mechanisms – between the workers' assembly and the board – for decision-making and organisation of the work process. The figures of area or sector 'supervisor' or 'overseer,' and 'area co-ordinator,' were established accordingly.

The hotel is organised into thirteen areas (press, administration, reception, bookings, sales, security, food and beverages, general machine maintenance, member office, public areas, laundry, flooring and linen), plus the board and the syndic. Each area is in turn made up of sectors, each of which has one or two 'supervisors' or 'overseers.' These people perform co-ordinating and supervising tasks, which involve making day-to-day decisions on areas related to the organisation and regulation of work. Relations between sectors are channelled through their supervisors, unless there is some additional difficulty or conflict, in which event the inter-area or intersectoral relationship is managed by the co-ordinator. Moreover, informally, the sector supervisors have the function of providing guidance around the implications of working in a co-operative and of communicating the history of the hotel and the co-operative that manages it. Last, they are also in charge of training workers to operate in the productive process. In this context, board meetings are held with sector overseers, primarily to socialise information.

Supervisors are appointed by the board according to criteria such as knowledge of the sector's tasks, seniority in the co-operative and degree of perceived responsibility. One member points out that, while supervisors are appointed by the board, "There's a kind of consensus about the person who's going to that sector being cause they want to do things better or cause they know" (Fernando, co-operative member, September 2014). Furthermore, the board's decision can be questioned by workers in the sector and even amended. Regarding the rotation of these posts, there is no policy to keep them dynamic. On the contrary, they are only modified if required by the sector or the board deems it necessary. It should be noted that, while not all supervisors are 'founder members,' almost all of them hold some position of responsibility, often because these posts are avoided by other workers because of the responsibilities that come with them:

> I'm not a fan of this system of co-operativism for catering. Cause it's very hard to be in charge and be properly in charge, know what I mean? [...] The difficult thing is we're all members, so there's people who toe the line and there's people who don't. And the people who don't toe the line still go on being members; so, it's hard going. That's why I never wanted to take up any post. Since I know a lot about catering and I know how you work in catering, you've got to have lots of discipline and lots of common sense, cause even when you're feeling tired out, you have to look after people just the same. So, this liberal direction the co-operative has, I find it hard going. I'm not saying you can't, but to me, personally speaking, coming from a different kind of catering, the private kind, which was pretty despotic, but they got things right, so I find it hard going. [For example], I can't say, "Will you give me five hundred pesos? I've found a stand-in chef in Burzaco, and I'm paying for him to come in a taxi." Oh no, nobody's up for it cause we're all members [and colleagues believe that all decisions must be collective]. On the other hand, in a [private] thing, there's always a general manager to take the decision. That's why I'm insisting to you about not wanting to take some things on, cause when you have to take a decision, they throw it back in your face, and I don't appreciate that.
>
> FERNANDO, co-operative member, September 2014

In addition to the figure of sector 'supervisor,' during the board's administration between 2009 and 2012, a change of by-laws was approved. On the one hand, the board members were expanded from five – president, treasurer, secretary, chief spokesperson and deputy spokesperson – to eight, with the introduction of 'vice-president,' 'assistant treasurer' and 'assistant secretary.' On the other, the two spokespeople began to take responsibility for co-ordinating areas and sectors. Their function is to intervene in specific inter-sectoral difficulties to improve labour processes and ensure the circulation of information between the board and other sectors.

> We approved the change of by-laws. We did this flow-chart and said, "The new flow-chart has to be accompanied by a change of by-laws that incorporates the new line of responsibilities in the flow-chart into the board." In other words, the board and some co-ordinators lower down, but for the co-ordinators to be part of the board so you have the whole hotel at the board meeting, all the sectors represented.
> ALEJANDRO, co-operative member and leading figure in a worker co-operative organisation, January 2016

The tasks assigned to the spokespeople and the introduction of the figures of 'vice-president,' 'assistant treasurer' and 'assistant secretary' point to the development of a training policy and the establishment of a reservoir of cadres. While there is no explicit policy in the recuperated hotel for rotation of workers in leadership posts, the extension of the board and the co-ordination tasks assigned to the spokespersons – who had no previous responsibility of this kind – imply a socialisation of governance technique.

> There were a lot of passive sitting on the board, cause when you vote, you vote for president, treasurer, secretary and syndic. There are four of them, and they have to have a stand-in for reasons of force majeure, in case anything happens to you or whatever. So, that's four more people who are always out of it, unless the other one gets ill. So, we said, "Why? People elected them to answer, to be co-ordinators and for that person to pull their weight as well. To be on the same footing as the board and pass on information to the board. Don't let them be passive till someone gets ill." Sometimes the president or the secretary would get ill too, and the stand-in had to come in and didn't have the foggiest what they had to do. [...] And now these people are co-ordinators [...] and what they do is handle information and make sure it gets to the right place.
> DARÍO, co-operative member, August 2014

In short, the amendments to the by-laws have multiple purposes: to divide the work among the members of the board, to improve the work and productive process through the intervention of the co-ordinators, and to establish – primarily informative – mediation mechanisms between the board and the workers' collective. Moreover, even when the frequency of and participation in the assemblies' decline, these intermediate bodies make it possible for the important decisions to be the result of a collective decision-making process. This shows that assemblies in medium-sized recuperated enterprises may not be the sole body of collective decision-making and legitimisation. Although the mechanisms and bodies designed keep their place in the field of representation, we could claim that they tend to establish a more participatory representative democracy.

In this instance, it is worth gauging the tension between self-management and delegation in recuperated enterprises. As I have suggested, the frequency of and participation in assemblies tends to tail off once production starts, in line with different periodisations of worker self-management processes (Lucita, 2009; Meister, 1974, cited in Rosanvallon, 1979). However, such periodisations have their limitations: the case of the recuperated hotel illustrates that times of increased conflict around the hotel's occupancy breathe new life into direct democracy.

I therefore find the developments of Ana María Fernández and Sandra Borakievich (2007) more productive. They believe that self-management in recuperated enterprises is a moment on the way and not a static mode or state which is accessed, and in which one remains. The time of self-management becomes one of the poles in the productive tensions that shape and drive these experiences; the other is delegation. Fernández and Borakievich argue that the beginnings of enterprise recuperation processes are moments of closure of the representation, in which the logic of self-management overflows the logic of representation, and delegation is suspended rather than suppressed. Similarly, bearing in mind the tension between the poles of self-management and delegation, the development of the experiences may mark the closure of self-management in the deployment of delegation (Salgado, Kasparian, Hernández, Diaz, Ferramondo, 2012).

The richness of this last schema is that it allows for the tension between the two poles. While we see a drop in the frequency of and participation in assemblies with the start-up and development of production, this is countered by their revitalisation at certain moments. Moreover, the co-operative has such designed strategies as 'informal meetings' and co-ordination bodies to ensure the function of management continues to be embodied by the workers' collective. Last, we must not forget that the assembly remains a body for decision-making and legitimisation, and even a space to roll back decisions made by the board.

To sum up, we find in the recuperated hotel a form of autonomous co-operation, even given the tensions between self-management and delegation. Juan Pablo Hudson (2011) has suggested that recuperated enterprises are free from capital domination within the productive unit but encounter new systems of control and discipline. On the one hand, the market imposes goals that recuperated enterprises cannot meet because of their financial and technological precarity. On the other, the only financing alternative they have comes from state schemes targeting the sector. So, says Hudson, recuperated enterprises are behoven to a dual dependency: the need to respond to market demands while invariably depending on state funding. I believe this point is important, although I choose to refer to conditioning – rather than dual dependency – to ensure the autonomous co-operation characteristic of this recuperated hotel is not eclipsed.

5   Social Groupings and Potential Antagonisms: Opportunity Hoarding, Enterprise Projects and Work Generations

Looking back over the three dimensions analysed so far, I contend that the hotel embodies a form of workers' self-managed production (Wright, 1994) that is a hybrid socio-productive form, interpenetrated by elements of socialist and capitalist modes of production, with a predominance of social power in production. This comes out primarily in two elements: one, the power emanating from the collective of workers joining of their own volition determines the allocation and use of resources; and two, the fact that there are no exploitation relations. However, although it is, in the absence of exploitation, collective in character, as a private venture in relation to the social whole it is a hybrid form. In other words, collective self-appropriation does not include the working class but only direct producers.

First, where property relations are concerned, we can see social possession of the means of production by the community of workers. Nevertheless, the secondary mode of inclusiveness deployed by the enterprise extends usufruct limits to other social identities linked to co-operativism and the world of work. The form of ownership accordingly becomes hybrid, with a predominance of social power.

Second, the co-operative is geared to the production of exchange values in order to ensure the reproduction of the lives of workers and their families. Accumulation is a necessary instance in the same direction and not the criterion guiding production. Following Salgado (2012) then, I diverge from Wright's (1994) model, who posits that accumulation in workers self-managed production becomes the parameter on the basis of which surpluses are utilised. The schema of hybridisation outlined here implies that the production of exchange goods is oriented to consumption by workers for the reproduction of life. I would also add to Wright's schema the consideration that not just a certain degree of economic but of political accumulation is needed to achieve sustainability in the recuperated enterprise.

Last, as far as the political dimension of production relations goes, we can see that the function of management is exercised on the basis of autonomous co-operation from the workers' collective. Nevertheless, opportunity hoarding – based on the control of key posts – by the 'founder members' is also present. I also detected a crystallisation of this group distinction in a small bonus to the monthly wage of this group of members.

In this light, the socio-productive ordering structures and de-structures social groupings within the enterprise. In my analysis of the constitutive conflict, I observed that recuperation de-structures the class antagonism in production. The class cleavage, however, continues to operate through property relations. The co-operative's member collective and the hotel's legal owner vie economically for ownership of the premises. That said, the dispute goes beyond the economic level towards a political and institutional dimension in the search for the passing of a law of expropriation of the hotel. The co-operative's workers and the hotel's legal owners form antagonistic social groups, giving rise to an open conflict external to the co-operative geared to acquiring occupancy of the hotel.

As a counterpoint to the existence of this cleavage within our co-operative, let us recall the Rosario case analysed by Deux Marzi (2014). In that recuperated enterprise, where new workers join the co-operative as salaried employees, it can be argued that the class antagonism in production is not de-structured, there being a tendency to personify capital among the founder members. This relationship is not found in our case study, where labour force recruitment was abandoned early.

However, Salgado's (2012) research warns that the possibility of one social group exploiting another in recuperated enterprises not only depends on the control of such alienable resources as property. It can also be founded on organisational resource control, when a group succeeds in hoarding management or governance positions. His research suggests that, as a result of the longevity of their relationship, resulting in increasing levels of cohesion and unity, the 'founder members' succeed in occupying key positions in the organisation, as well as capitalising the relationships and values built up during the recuperation process.

'New' members do not achieve the same levels of organisation and cohesion as 'founder members,' and inequality mechanisms are established. This crystallises in the installation of differential remunerations. Thus, the dynamic of relations between the groups configures potential antagonisms between 'founder members' and 'new' members. In a similar sense, albeit focusing on the notion of identity rather than the groups' socio-dynamics, Alberto Bialakowsky, Guillermo Robledo, José Manuel Grima, Ernestina Rosendo and María Ignacia Costa (2004) highlight the existence of new forms of symbolic capital appropriation through identity accumulation by the 'founder' workers of recuperated enterprises. These new forms give rise to the groupings of 'founders' and 'new workers.'

In short, while work and ownership are not split in the worker co-operative investigated and we cannot identify an exploitation relation as a product of differential income, we can see the formation of organisational divides between 'founder members' and 'new' members around the hoarding of organisational resources. 'Founder members' control key positions in the co-operative (governance posts, and posts controlling and supervising the labour process), which allow them to effect a slightly differentiated appropriation through the establishment of supplements to basic income. Following Salgado (2012), I hypothesise that unequal groups are formed in the co-operative that are not founded on a split between producers and means of production, but on the hoarding of organisational resources obtained by groups with greater degrees of social cohesion.

That said, it is important to note that, in the absence of the category of workers who are not members of the co-operative or 'hired' (Hudson, 2011), participation in decision-making and the reversal of these differentiation processes are always an option. In worker co-operatives, income without member status implies not only exclusion from ownership but from the citizenship granted by it, whereby control of the productive unit is exercised. The faculty for all workers to participate in decision-making is central in preventing this divide from establishing itself as a cleavage, and groups are thus configured that are more horizontal, variable and multiple in character. In this sense, the seniority bonus explains the emergence of a grouping – senior non-founder workers – that manages to introduce a favourable differentiation in wages compared to new workers, and questions participation in the recuperation as the sole unequalising criterion. We note then that inequalities between 'new' workers are established not just with 'founder members' but also with senior non-founder members.

Similarly, Fernando Balbi (1998) reminds us of the centrality of the mode of incorporating members in co-operatives in his analysis of workers' positioning in conflicts. The author notes that the web of personal relationships at the base of member recruitment to some extent defines the pattern of alignment in conflicts. This observation should be taken on board when analysing the formation of groupings: the incorporation of workers in the recuperated hotel has primarily been resolved through the intake of members' relatives.

Positioning ourselves in the dimension of the logic of production, we note that the orientation to consumption and the consequent need for accumulation – not just economic to make investments, but also political – combined with the non-closure of the conflict over occupancy of the hotel, can form groupings based on different conceptions of sustainability and, therefore, on different enterprise projects. In Chapter 6, we will see that one of these only makes room for the economic and market dimension and gives importance only to the development of market activity, disregarding the hotel's other activities, with a degree of suspicion for the political dimension of the enterprise's recuperation process. At the other extreme, we find a project that recognises the importance of political accumulation in these experiences, both through reciprocity and redistribution relations. These groupings could therefore also be linked to another axis of fracture: activism – or the absence of it – in the co-operative movement among the enterprise's members.

Where the function of management is concerned, the formation of the last two boards might be structuring an organisational differentiation and distance between 'leaders' and 'led.' The fifth board contained several members who had already held positions in that body. At the close of our fieldwork, this board was re-elected in toto. The identities occupying the positions on the board tend to become fixed. In addition, 'overseers' and 'supervisors' do not usually rotate, and there is no periodic replacement.

Nevertheless, at the level of non-supervisor workers, primarily among youngsters, occupational identity or hierarchy is minimised by the history of the co-operative and by the possibility of rotation.

> There are very few of us old caterers. The others are kids who maybe work three or four months and don't feel they're caterers. They're here today, there tomorrow, and they aren't bothered. Not like us.
> FERNANDO, co-operative member, September 2014

This excerpt also enables us to introduce the question of generational groupings, which have been tackled by other authors in terms of the existence of different imaginaries around work, the result of divergent employment paths of seniors and youngsters (Hudson, 2011). This sparks tensions between *'pibes'* [kids] and *'laburantes'* [grafters] primarily around labour regulations. While I agree with these observations, I note that several of the hotel's young workers gain their very first experience of work there, so there is no prior concrete experience. The excerpt below then allows us to discern that the category 'young' sometimes conceals the category 'new,' and that generations therefore are less to do with age groups than work generations in the co-operative: in other words, with the various cohorts of intake.

> There are many who share my way of thinking that the co-operative should be a source, shall we say, that it can give us a salary, a decent wage to live on, so our children can go to school or have decent clothes or medicine or be taken on holiday; but not so as we end up being … Cause that's the other side of the story, there's lots of young kids here as have jumped on the wagon and have never lived it, and we don't have the capacity, we've never given ourselves time to ask this compañero if they know anything about this story, cause come the end of the month, there's no brass. They come in, kick your door and view me as a boss. Cause here, when it comes to arguing the toss, they're all owners.
>
> MARIO, co-operative member, September 2006

We can see from the above analysis that the socio-productive form configured in the recuperated hotel democratises production, leading to more worker participation compared to workers locked in wage relations. With its horizontal and egalitarian aspects, this participation, shaped by the hybrid socio-productive form, results in the emergence of divides in the formation of groupings, which, though they may be present in other socio-productive forms, yet fail to emerge or express themselves in them. Moreover, the flexible, mobile character of groupings, due not only to the characteristics of participation but to the central importance of interpersonal relationships, generates divides that tend not to become stable, lasting cleavages.

Last, we see a certain gradient between the dividing axes of groupings in terms of how they specifically relate to the co-operative form of work. Whereas the 'founder'–'new' members pair is the most endogenous, at an intermediate level there are divides between work cohorts, the different enterprise projects and the 'leaders'–'led' groupings. In turn, the differences between the generations in terms of age are exogenous to the socio-productive unit. In Chapter 6, we will see to what extent these elements that form fractures or social groupings are activated in work conflicts, and ultimately, the ways in which the seams shatter that mottled rainbow seen from afar.

CHAPTER 5

The Argentina Works Co-operative and State Power in Production

The Riachuelo – literally, the 'Little River' – is, in topographical terms, the last stretch of a more than 60-kilometre watercourse that runs through Buenos Aires Province and flows into the River Plate. Also, in sociological terms, it is the signifier in which multiple historical, socio-political and cultural representations of Argentina flow together. From among all the postcards of the Riachuelo's long history, I have picked three that condense its meanings.

The first postcard might be entitled "Black Smoke from Factory Chimneys." On 17 October 1945, thousands of workers marched to the Plaza de Mayo in the centre of Buenos Aires to demand the release of Juan Domingo Perón, ushering in a core political movement of Argentinian society. Among those workers, a sizeable group from the south of the Buenos Aires Conurbation had to swim or raft across the Riachuelo, whose bridges connecting to Buenos Aires had been raised. Forming a natural boundary between province and city, this political icon also marks a limit between social classes: on its banks on one side, factories and *cabecitas negras* (literally, 'little black heads,' a derogatory name for the working classes); on the other, 'with its back to' the river, the middle and upper classes.

In her story "*Bajo el agua negra*" [Under the Black Water], Mariana Enríquez (2016) takes us for another swim in the Riachuelo: this time, a ghost swimmer who plunges into the great dustbin of Buenos Aires; my second chosen postcard. It is no coincidence that this is a horror story about the poverty, inequality and institutional violence that thrive on the banks of a foetid, rotten, toxic, dead Riachuelo. In the 1990s, the Riachuelo became synonymous with pollution and corruption: although several million dollars were earmarked to clean it up, the passing of time has demonstrated the increasing environmental degradation and acts of corruption surrounding the management of the Matanza Riachuelo Basin, which includes the Riachuelo itself.

The title of the third postcard is "Of Cabecitas Negras and *Planeros* [Social-Planners]." In the twenty-first century, Argentina's Supreme Court ordered the three governments involved in the basin – the Buenos Aires City Government, the Buenos Aires Province Government and the National Government – to implement a comprehensive clean-up plan. After lead, benzene and toluene contamination had been shown among the inhabitants of the neighbourhood '*Villa Inflamable*' (Inflammable Town), in a paragon of local industry,

Avellaneda, this order sparked the creation of the *Autoridad Cuenca Matanza Riachuelo* [Matanza Riachuelo Basin Authority] (ACUMAR), an autonomous, autarkic, inter-jurisdictional body (Nation, Buenos Aires Province and Buenos Aires City), whose objective is to clean up and reclaim the basin.

In this framework, ACUMAR set up the River-Bank Clean-Up Programme in 2009 as a component of its comprehensive recovery plan, with the aim of reclaiming and preserving the river banks and water mirror of the main channel and tributaries of the Matanza Riachuelo Basin. In this scheme, ACUMAR works with municipalities in the basin and co-operatives from the *Programa Argentina Trabaja* [Argentina Works Programme] (ACUMAR, 2015a).[1] In a mutual redemption of sorts, instead of 'cabecitas Negras,' and divested of access to decent work, it was hoped the clean-up of the also neglected Riachuelo would restore dignity to those now called 'planeros,' a stigmatisation of the impoverished working classes who depend on social plans for the reproduction of their lives.

In this chapter, I analyse the socio-productive nature of the worker co-operative under the Argentina Works Programme. To this effect, I make use primarily of the analytical framework presented in the previous chapter. Set up in 2010 by an unemployed workers organisation, the co-operative is a small-scale productive venture in the service sector. Its main activity is to clean up the river banks of the Matanza Riachuelo Basin in the framework of the ACUMAR scheme. It is therefore simultaneously part of two separate schemes: the Argentina Works Programme and the River-Bank Clean-Up Programme.[2] Specifically, the co-operative's job is to clean up a watercourse in the Basin outside the co-operative's headquarters in the premises of the *Movimiento de Trabajadores Desocupados* [Unemployed Workers Movement] (MTD). This activity usually consists of grass-cutting, raking, sweeping and collecting piles of refuse. However, like the territory it occupies, the co-operative is also burdened with logics, purposes and practices that go beyond these tasks.

1 **The Labour and Socio-spatial Precarity of Argentina Works Programme Workers**

The co-operative is located in the town of Nueve de Abril in the north of Esteban Echeverría, which borders the districts of La Matanza, Lomas de Zamora and

---

1 By the first half of 2015, 24 agreements between ACUMAR and municipal governments were in place, including a total of 53 co-operatives responsible for cleaning up the Riachuelo's banks. Of these agreements, five covered Esteban Echeverría and accommodated 199 co-operative members from ten co-operatives (ACUMAR, 2015b).
2 In 2012, the co-operative joined the River-Bank Clean-Up Programme, whereby co-operative members are given an additional income to the one provided by the Argentina Works Programme. The co-operative had previously participated in programmes of *Agua y Saneamientos Argentinos S.A.* [Water and Sanitation Argentina plc] (AySA).

Ezeiza. Specifically, it is located in a neighbourhood approximately twenty-five kilometres from the city of Buenos Aires and about 50 blocks from the centre of Monte Grande, the district's main town, on the edge of the urban sprawl, and in front of a tributary that forms part of the Matanza Riachuelo Basin. Recently created, the neighbourhood emerged from a process of informal self-urbanisation as the result of a land-take in 2002. So, it is characteristic of a particular kind of urbanisation: it is the result of a collective process, located in a peripheral area of low environmental quality, being close to a river, and presents a planned subdivision of land with expectations of regularisation.

The dwellings tell of a process of self-construction characteristic of the settlement of the Conurbation's periphery by the working classes precariously inserted in the labour market during the 1980s and '90s (Farías, 2014). The neighbourhood has few power lines, little drinking water and no sewer network or gas mains. As the Image 2 below shows, dirt streets predominate, with just a few paved major arteries. Ownership of the land by its inhabitants is de facto, as there has been no land-title regularisation.

IMAGE 2   The co-operative's neighbourhood
PHOTO BY DENISE KASPARIAN (JULY 2016)

Formed between late 2009 and early 2010, the co-operative initially had 30 members; by late 2015, this number had fallen to fifteen. This decline is down to a number of reasons, including obtaining employment and transferring some members to other co-operatives. The characteristics of these workers differ from members of recuperated enterprises in that they are mainly women with similar work backgrounds characterised by the precarity of their employment.

From a sociodemographic survey conducted in the co-operative,[3] we can see that the group is made up of women workers combining different jobs cut off from social protection: childcare, cleaning private homes and businesses, self-employed resale, *cirujeo* (collection, sorting and transport of waste for recycling), with periods of unemployment or inactivity in the labour market and dedication to homecare. They also have a track record of receiving social plans: more than 75% were beneficiaries of other social plans prior to the Argentina Works Programme. In addition to working in the co-operative, about 70% perform other work activities to earn a living, primarily self-employed. So, given the spatial, social and labour precarities of the neighbourhood's inhabitants, the launch of the Argentina Works Programme was central to them.

2   Property Relations: Social Possession and Autonomy

The co-operative's means of production are extremely small-scale. They consist of premises with a storeroom, a van and low-cost tools and machinery (rakes, shovels, machetes, forks, wheel-barrows, waste bags, edgers, strimmers and weeders). The premises where the tools and machinery are stored is under the collective possession of the social organisation, established in the neighbourhood in 2006 after the purchase of a plot land. However, as there has been no land-title regularisation in the neighbourhood as yet, occupancy is only de facto and therefore precarious. The co-operative's van was acquired with resources from ACUMAR and the social organisation but was put in the name of a member. Used to transport tools and machinery, and workers when the channel cleaning is done some distance away from the premises, it is driven by a local resident who is paid a salary by the co-operative with funds from ACUMAR.

---

3   I gave eleven workers from the co-operative a short semi-structured questionnaire to gather information on the following: socio-demographic data, work backgrounds and receipt of social plans, political participation and assessments of the Argentina Works Programme.

Where tools and machinery are concerned, the official Argentina Works documentation states that each working module established through agreement between the Ministry for Social Development and the implementing agencies is to allocate 70% of funding to co-operative members' income (transferred to personal bank accounts) and the remaining 30% to the financing of materials, supplies and tools (Ministry for Social Development, 2010). The channels for granting co-operatives these tools, however, is not specified. In the productive venture analysed, the municipal government purchases the most important and expensive machinery and tools, as well as work clothes and personal protective gear. These are then delivered to the co-operative with documentation certifying delivery, archived by the co-operative as proof of ownership. The co-operative is also responsible for managing and safeguarding the tools and machinery, and for maintaining them: in other words, they are freely available to it.

These forms of possession have meant that the machinery, tools and the van can be used not just for channel cleaning. The co-operative also uses them in the construction and maintenance of its premises, and they are even loaned out to members of the co-operative, the social organisation or local residents for individual use at home. That said, it is important to stress that such full disposal of the means of production is framed by low levels of formalised possession.

The mediation of ACUMAR is key to understanding the social appropriation generated in the co-operative. The productive venture receives funds from ACUMAR in a current account under the co-operative's name. Some of these funds – as stipulated by ACUMAR – are earmarked for members, who thus receive a bonus to income from the Argentina Works Programme. Another portion is used in the maintenance of machinery, the payment of a mandatory medical emergency service and a salary for the driver of the van as haulage, and the purchase of petrol for machinery, food and beverages for mid-morning refreshments, as well as simple tools, among other expenses that have to be paid upon submission of invoices and reports.

In the early days of participation in the ACUMAR scheme, the co-operative was able to allocate some of these resources to the construction of the organisation's premises and the storeroom to keep the tools in, and subsequently the social organisation's other premises in a different neighbourhood. Over the years, these funds lost value owing to progressive widespread price rises without the relevant increase in funding. Consequently, the margin of autonomy provided by the management of funds from ACUMAR also fell.

I would therefore argue that there is social ownership in the co-operative, as the appropriation is in the hands of a collectivity. We are dealing with a small group of workers who have not split from the means of production: they pool their labour force for the production of a service, having at their disposal and making use of the productive unit within the limits indicated. In principle, they also have an equal right to participate in collective decisions. So, like the recuperated enterprise, work and property are not split for two reasons. On the one hand, the co-operative's legal form favours and guarantees this situation. On the other hand, we can see that certain means of production are held by the social organisation, not the co-operative. The element promoting the non-split of work and ownership is therefore not only the legal form but also the characteristics of the social organisation in which the co-operative is inserted. The multi-sectoral front uniting the MTD that contains the co-operative defines itself as an anti-capitalist organisation whose objective is the construction of popular power and socialism, as foreshadowed in its actual political practices. This organisational definition also contributes to the tendency towards the non-split of work and property found in the co-operative, because it seeks to shape a productive organisation in which the allocation and use of the means of production are guided by the social power of organised collectives.

That said, it is worth noting the low levels of formalisation and intensity of this kind of social ownership: this is not full ownership by the co-operative, but rather limited forms of possession or use. First, the machinery and tools are procured by the municipality but transferred to the co-operative along with supporting documentation. This is closer to the notion of 'commodatum' than ownership. Second, the van was purchased by the social organisation with its own funds and funds from ACUMAR but put in the name of a member and placed at the co-operative's disposal. Last, the premises appear as being under de facto occupancy by the social organisation but is also placed at the disposal of the co-operative for its use. Also, leaving aside the potential use of the means of production, the ownership is in hybrid character, combining elements of private ownership (the van) with social ownership (the organisation's premises) and state ownership (the machinery and tools).

Another issue is that possession by the workers' collective has a specific breadth or scope which, compared to the recuperated enterprise, is narrower. As the co-operative is a small-scale venture located in a shantytown in the Buenos Aires Conurbation, social possession is limited to low-value goods, in other words, to means of production on an extremely small scale. This counteracts the risks of informality, as there is less likelihood of precarious possessions being questioned or challenged.

Last, this is a kind of social possession that has limited primary inclusiveness. Marginal as the situation is, the co-operative excludes the van-driver from this associational relationship: he does his job in a wage relationship outside the workers' collective, not just in formal terms – in that he does not belong to the co-operative – but also, as one member points out, in terms of the 'we' configured around the productive process: "It [the van] was bought by the movement with all the ACUMAR funding and, cause none of *us* know how to drive, it's driven by this *other* guy" (Luz, co-operative member, September 2014). There is also another small group of two workers who are only paid the bonus from ACUMAR, but who are not part of the Argentina Works Programme, as it proved impossible to take in new beneficiaries after the first opening of vacancies. To offset the income gap, the co-operative stipulated that these workers be present just three days a week. Like the driver, they are thus also formally excluded from the co-operative, but not from the workers' collective, which has access to collective appropriation of the assets. I believe that this non-exclusion is due to the workers' collective being woven around membership of the social organisation and, first and foremost, around receipt of an income from public policy, rather than taking part in the co-operative.

As we can see in Image 3, taken on the co-operative's premises, and from our field observations, I realised that the grouping of the *'cuadrilla'* (or 'crew,' the workers' name for the co-operative) consists of *'cumpas'* (or *'compañeros,'* a name usually used in spaces of social and political militancy) who obtain some kind of *'recurso'* [resource] or income from public policy as part of the crew. I also noted that, even if they are few in number, each member is expected to perform a *'tarea solidaria'* [solidarity task] or *'tarea de la organización'* [organisation task]. Social plans thus become organisational resources not so much for the co-operative but for the social organisation.

Although the above situations strain the non-split of work and property, this is not the principal exclusion we encounter. I contend that social possession is of limited primary inclusiveness, being limited to the workers' collective and social organisation, which implies an exclusion from the use of that property by the rest of the social whole. Nevertheless, compared to the recuperated enterprise, I believe the secondary inclusiveness of social possession is greater.

What elements of the experiences of the recuperated enterprise and the Argentina Works co-operative link these differences to the types of expansion of secondary inclusiveness? It is pertinent here to mention María Victoria Deux Marzi's (2014) thoughts about conditions that favour the community

IMAGE 3   Composition of the co-operative by 'cumpas' and 'recursos'
PHOTO BY DENISE KASPARIAN (JULY 2016)

principle in her case study.[4] First, Deux Marzi points out that one condition favouring the principle of community is the co-operative signing waste management contracts with a concessionary mixed venture providing environmental clean-up services. These contracts are therefore 'armour-plating' protecting the co-operative from market mechanisms, a situation that helps workers to plan and build a more comprehensive project than landfill activities that extends to the community at large. In our terms, this 'armour-plating'

---

4 This is a waste management company formed after the enterprise employing the co-operative's founding workers abandoned its activities, and the mixed enterprise responsible for the integrated management of solid urban waste, which had contracted the employer company, decided to close the site where the activity was being carried out. Composed of its former workers, the co-operative succeeded in signing a series of contracts with the concessionary joint enterprise to provide the waste management services previously performed by the company that employed them. It also performs activities related to the production and maintenance of green areas, and encourages various projects and activities to promote community development in its local neighbourhood.

entails an autonomisation of the co-operative when it comes to the pressures and uncertainties of competition, while at the same time keeping control of the productive process and working speeds in the workers' hands. We can see then that the recuperated waste management enterprise more closely resembles the Argentina Works co-operative analysed here, which has the stable income provided by the scheme, and less closely the recuperated hotel, a venture operating in a highly competitive market that concentrates on large trans-nationals.

Second, Deux Marzi indicates the central importance of the venture's activities as a service that directly affects local residents' quality of life. It is thus the activity itself that links the co-operative to the surrounding community. Moreover, its workers reside in the same area. Here, we again see that this recuperated enterprise's activities have similarities with the Argentina Works co-operative, which also performs services aimed at the surrounding community and is made up of inhabitants from the neighbourhood in which it is located. So, in both cases, the links with the community are, from the outset, determined by the activity and reinforced by the overlapping of 'worker' and 'neighbour' identities. On the other hand, the hotel's services, mainly oriented to 'outsiders,' and its location in a central area minimise neighbourhood bonds.

Last, Deux Marzi (2014) considers the track record of local neighbourhood militancy by trades-union delegates who promoted the recuperation of the enterprise and early intervention by a trades-union organisation in the process. This background is important when it comes to understanding workers' identification with the neighbourhood they live and work in. So, this recuperated enterprise once again more closely resembles the Argentina Works co-operative, which takes part in a movement of unemployed workers and steers its political activity towards local neighbourhood militancy. On the other hand, while support from a wide range of social identities was important in the recuperated hotel, more important was the participation of a specific recuperated enterprise organisation.

The Argentina Works co-operative is part of a social organisation whose political designs have a strong territorial dimension, and it therefore tends to impress on the co-operative a logic regarding the use of goods that is aimed at improving the local neighbourhood's living conditions. This contrasts with the sectoral logic of the recuperated enterprise and expands the boundaries of secondary inclusiveness. We may then hypothesise that the type of secondary inclusiveness developed by co-operatives tends to be related to the characteristics of the market and the degree of autonomisation from the competition, the characteristics of their activity and the surrounding neighbourhood, and the type of social organisation involved in the co-operatives' formation and subsequent development.

These elements of social possession, with the limitations described, and of the tendency not to separate workers from the means of production allow them some degree of autonomy even when performing the tasks assigned by the Argentina Works Programme. This becomes even clearer when it is contrasted with another case. Through our fieldwork, we came to know a co-operative from a municipality bordering Esteban Echeverría, whose main activity is cleaning and sweeping the streets. The locus of the co-operative's work can change from month to month, entailing the transport of its members from their own headquarters to the headquarters of the relevant municipal delegation, where their work tools are stored under the care of the municipal authorities. We can see then how the collective possession of machinery and tools, and of a place to store them and from which to operate, increases the chances of social appropriation by the workers' collective.

Despite being a co-operative formed under a public policy then, we find no prevalence of state ownership in the forms of possession analysed. On the contrary, in the co-operative, we find a hybrid form where social ownership predominates, albeit not formalised and limited to a small set of workers. We identify private and state ownership which combine with elements of social ownership both of the cooperative and of the social organisation. This could set up tensions between these two where the use of goods is concerned. However, this linkage between the co-operative and the social organisation, among other aspects, makes it possible to expand secondary inclusiveness of social ownership.

3 The Logic of Production: Between Subsistence and Political Accumulation

The notions of 'socio-productive policy' (Hopp, 2012) and 'socio-labour policy' (Grassi, 2012) stand at the inter-section of social, economic and labour policy. Socio-productive policy refers to the field of social interventions by the state aimed at reproduction of the lives of individuals and societies through economic and labour policies that, by means of economic benefits, are involved in the primary distribution of income by stimulating production for the market. Traditionally, social policy is described as intervening in secondary income distribution (Danani, 2009). For this reason, faced with the multiplication of policies aimed at promoting social economy ventures, Malena Hopp (2012) introduces this concept of socio-productive policy to explain social policies directly involved in production and, hence, in the primary distribution of income.

Estela Grassi (2012), for her part, defines 'socio-labour policy' as the set of interventions whose object is work but which, strictly speaking, go beyond labour policy. This concept allows us to grasp work-oriented policies beyond their labour-wage form, such as self-employment or associational and self-managed work. Both definitions account, in different ways, for the existence of social policies targeting work and production, though not necessarily by redistributing income, nor considering just wage labour. How do all these elements and considerations combine in the Argentina Works Programme?

The Argentina Works Programme starts from a profiling diagnosis that characterises the scheme's beneficiaries as vulnerable or, in other words, unemployable. In response to this, on the one hand, by meeting the needs of vulnerable sectors outside the labour market with public funding, it operates a secondary distribution of income that indirectly regulates the labour-capital relation. On the other hand, this policy stipulates a work requirement implemented through the creation of co-operatives to carry out local infrastructure works. By creating jobs in co-operatives, it intervenes directly in the world of work and the primary distribution of income, though not in the predominant (labour–capital) employment relationship, but rather in a different way of organising production. Furthermore, the production of these co-operatives is not in principle market-oriented but is instead geared to meeting social needs of sanitation and local infrastructure, among other activities. It should be remembered that the scheme's regulations do not stop co-operatives gearing their production to the capitalist market as well.

In short, the Argentina Works Programme is a work-targeted social policy involved in some way in primary income distribution, forming co-operatives that participate – or have the potential to participate – in the field of production, while not necessarily inserting their products in the capitalist market. The Argentina Works Programme thus involves a combination of state intervention in primary and secondary income distribution and creates two analytically differentiated social spaces.

The first space is organised around the mechanism of redistribution – or secondary distribution – established by the subsidy granted by the scheme with the aim of alleviating inequalities created by the market economy. The second space is that of the co-operatives themselves: this is where the productive process of goods or services takes place. The subsidy thus triggers the configuration of a productive space – the co-operative – which, while related to welfare policy, has logics of its own.

In analytical terms, these two spaces refer to two different units of analysis and scales: the state and public policy, on the one hand, and co-operatives, on the other. In actual fact, we encounter an overlapping configuration of the productive unit, in which various logics are linked together. In addition, reference to the scale of the state and public policy requires further specification: although the Argentina Works Programme is a national scheme, it is mainly implemented at the local level by municipal governments. In this way, referring to the logic of production in our case study requires consideration of both analytical spaces and the multiple actors intervening in them.

In terms of the immediate destination of production, the exchange value is not predominant. The priority is the use value; in other words, the service is oriented to meeting needs and its production is tied to these criteria. However, the channel clean-up is not defined as a need that deserves to be met exclusively – or primarily – by the co-operative. On the contrary, the definition of the activity is the product of a complex co-ordination by the Ministry for Social Development, the municipal government, ACUMAR and the co-operative, in which the latter tends to become subordinate. Constructive modules are defined in agreements between the Ministry for Social Development and the municipal government, in which ACUMAR is included through the River-Bank Clean-Up Programme. As I analyse in the next chapter, the definition of the productive activity is an object of dispute between the co-operative and the municipal government.

But apart from meeting the need to clean up the urban space, production of the service is a mechanism of non-market exchange or circulation between the co-operative and the state, guided by the public policy's principle of redistribution.[5] More than a need to clean up the channel, the logic behind the production of the service is linked to the schema of social policy with work requirement. In other words, the service's use value aside, the work requirement itself is important. Indeed, doubt is cast on the importance of the criterion of use when Luz, a worker we interviewed, questions the intermittent frequency with which the service provision is completed:

5 The essential logic of the statist mode of production during the existence of the USSR as conceptualised by Erik Olin Wright (1994) is that the state directly organises the entire system of production and appropriation through central planning. Given that the state varies with time and place, when I refer here to statist elements, I am not necessarily referring to central planning of the economy by the state. In this case, the elements of the statist mode of production identified in the social form of the worker co-operative do not refer to a state that intervenes on the basis of central technical plans but to a state whose logic of intervention in the case of the Argentina Works Programme is to redistribute in accordance with the development of policies that target vulnerable sectors.

> Sometimes we stay a bit longer cause *sometimes* they send trucks. There's no point cleaning up if the trucks don't cart it [the refuse] away. You collect, and then it's all dumped again.
>
> LUZ, co-operative member, September 2014; interviewee's emphasis

And indeed, if the trucks do not enter the neighbourhood, the members do not bag the refuse but simply pile it in mounds, because, in the event of rain, the bags obstruct the normal flow of the channel far more than the loose refuse. So, much as the co-operative's productive logic is determined by the production of use values, it is inadequate to analyse the provision of the clean-up service from that perspective alone. From the logic of public policy, the value is the work requirement itself, whether or not it is useful in meeting the need at which it is aimed, a key element of the exchange between the state and the co-operatives.

Since government agencies require a four-hour workday (8:00–12:00),[6] co-operatives can allocate a half-day to other activities, using the resources, machinery and tools furnished by the scheme. The co-operative has not, however, undertaken any market exchange-oriented production. What it has undertaken are other activities with no market sense, such as cleaning up gardens and schools in the local neighbourhood and building the premises for the social organisation from which the co-operative operates, a community snack-bar and a *murga* [street-band] workshop.

Underlying these relations established with the neighbourhood is the principle of reciprocity, linked to the social organisations' logics of political construction, formed during the transition from a popular politicity focused on the world of work to one focused on territorial activism (Merklen, 2005). So, while the co-operative's main activity is based on the co-ordination of its own and the government's criteria, involving a degree of subordination of the co-operative, we can see that the social possession of the means of production is

---

6   According to the scheme's information pack (National Ministry of Social Development, 2010), workers had a 40-hour working week, five of which were earmarked for training. After the passing of the Ministry of Social Development's Resolution No. 1499/12, the workday changed to four hours in situ and two hours' training workshops. Yet, as one official from the Esteban Echeverría Municipality remarks, this was never clearly stipulated: "It might never have been written down anywhere in any documents, but we presumed it was eight hours, then [the Ministry] changed it to six a day, then four a day. A year later, they encourage everyone to join the FinEs [an education completion scheme]. So, in the last stage, I think those who went straight to the FinEs weren't going in to work, no worries. Look at the transformation the scheme went through [...] completing your education was like this priority for the scheme." (Esteban Echeverría Municipality official, June 2016).

the element that allows it to carry out other activities under the principle of reciprocity.

As for the purpose of production, it is guided by workers' consumption in the framework of a multi-activity strategy implemented by working-class sectors to secure their subsistence in contexts marked by instability. When their income from work is insufficient or non-existent, the local neighbourhood becomes the main provider of support for survival. It provides a stabilising principle in the experience by structuring local solidarity and collective demonstrations to access the necessary resources in the form of decentralised, focused, time-limited social policies (Merklen, 2005).

For this reason, under this territorial logic of securing the means of subsistence, the income received by co-operative members is not only intended for individual consumption but, as we have seen, for collective consumption in a particular territory. To build the premises then, the co-operative had to relinquish funds that could have boosted individual incomes. In Chapter 6, we look at how this became a source of work conflicts:

> We made these whole premises with the work of the co-operative. Cause there are funds we kept putting by and, instead of spreading it around all the *compañeros*, we bought the things to make the shed. [...] We break for snacks, and the break costs $6,000 or $7,000 pesos. We find it really tough going to build up all this awareness and say we actually want our physical space to grow. So, we all get together and talk, and, instead of buying the $6,000 pesos' worth of refreshments, we buy $4,000, and there's $2,000 left over to spend.
> ADRIANA, co-operative member, January 2015

The purpose of production is to protect the subsistence income from public policy. In this sense, just the way I asked how recuperated enterprise enables the reproduction of its members' lives, it is worth asking here about the scheme's contributions to the subsistence of workers and their families.

The scheme establishes certain changes compared to previous plans, both from the co-operative members' viewpoints and the design of the scheme, which bring it closer to the socially recognised idea of work. Half of those previously receiving social plans suggest that the difference between the Argentina Works Programme and other plans is that Argentina Works is a "job," as opposed to previous schemes that were merely a "help." The perception of the scheme as a job has to do with the timetables to be respected, the control they undergo in the daily experience and the level of wages. By 2015, the co-operative members' income stood at AR$2,600 pesos[7] per month, and 40% of interviewees stress that this is higher than in previous schemes. Moreover, 20% of interviewees say that another difference in the Argentina Works Programme is that it provides access to social protection, that is, healthcare, state-provided social security contributions and occupational risk insurance.

That said, the appraisal of this scheme as a job in socially recognised terms is shaped in the link of the experience in the co-operative with partnership in a social organisation. To the question "What elements of the scheme would you change?," one co-operative member replied:

> Make it a job. Don't let them treat us like it's a plan. I don't see it as a plan anymore, anyway. It's a plan but ... I see it as my household's source of income. And I have to look after it. [...] And I see it as a job.
> ANALÍA, co-operative member, November 2012

What is more, it is precisely its perception as a job that allows questions to be raised about the type and conditions of the work. Along these lines, one member proposed the following:

> Thinking like the government says, it's the same social plan as before. But we're thinking of it in a different way. That we've like got it, we want to believe it as a job. A lot depends on the attitude of each co-operative, each movement how they handle it. Cause the government, they pass it off as just a social plan; they give us enough, so we don't go out anymore [to protest]. They want to get us off the streets, so they chuck all this our way. [...] It needs to come from us ourselves, for us to value it like a job and fight for it like it's a job. [...] And us, to our thinking, we see it like it isn't manna from heaven, it's us as pulls out the stops [we struggle and commit ourselves] and, one way or another, we make it feel like it's a job. Outsourced, badly-paid, but it's a job.
> DANIEL, co-operative member, October 2012

---

7   In 2009, when the scheme was launched, the beneficiaries' income was set at AR$1,200 pesos. In February 2012, a significant increase was announced: to the initial AR$1,200 was added AR$300 for social productivity and AR$250 for presenteeism. This increase was only received by all co-operative members by around September. Then, in April 2013, an increase of AR$250 was announced – AR$100 for presenteeism and AR$150 for social productivity – taking the wage to AR$2,000 pesos. The final increase came in October 2014, when it rose from AR$2,000 to AR$2,600 (AR$1,400 basic income and AR$1,200 for social productivity and presenteeism).

Daniel's words invite a brief review of the ruptures established by the Argentina Works Programme in terms of design compared to other plans with work requirement. To what extent are we looking at a redistributive policy and not at precarised state employment? Is this a question of productive consumption of wage labour force by the state through labour fraud? I do not claim to close out this question, but rather to provide certain elements to analyse it.

Generally speaking, the co-operative members in the scheme have received training and education about co-operativism, reflecting the state's willingness to promote the formation of autonomous socio-productive units with the potential to develop beyond public policy. Although the amount of the subsidy fell steadily short of the legal minimum wage, the workday was also shortened. In the case of the co-operative analysed, the members engage in the service of cleaning up the channel for half a workday, so the co-operative could supplement their income through other activities. Last, after consulting the municipal authorities over the differences between municipal employees' salaries and co-operative members' wages, we obtained the following response:

> In the first stage, the income [of the co-operative members] was $2,000 pesos, and, depending on the category of the employee, in the municipality we still had some who weren't making $1,500 or who were getting paid $1,500.
>
> Esteban Echeverría Municipality official, June 2016

Nevertheless, despite having a higher income in the early days of the scheme than municipal employees, co-operative members do not access the same degree of social protection. In any event, I contend that work under the scheme to them stands as a progression regarding effective access to certain rights compared with their previous employment situation. Not only do they gain access to social protection, but they also get paid leave for maternity, sickness and holidays. While these three rights are not stated formally in the scheme, with the agreement of the authorities, our co-operative stipulates its own dynamics for leave and holidays. My analyses therefore differ from Hopp's (2013b), who contends that the socio-productive policies that encourage the formation of co-operatives promote labour precarisation due to their low remunerations and the persistence of inequalities in social protection between self-managed and salaried employees.

In contrast, about 80% of the co-operative members I interviewed first gained access to work-related social protection after joining the scheme. In the experience of this venture's workers, their participation in the co-operative signifies the opposite of a precarisation of their working conditions. I contend that, by establishing the work requirement, the Argentina Works Programme constitutes an intermediate state between an unemployment subsidy and the performance of jobs in exchange for remuneration paid by the state, or in other words, state employment. However, this hypothetical employment relationship occurs in a relatively autonomous way as the result of the co-operative legal form and of the social possession and collective control of the means of production.

That said, even when the logic of consumption predominates, production is also guided by accumulation criteria, albeit non-economic accumulation. If we position ourselves in the state's viewpoint, together with the dominant logic of consumption, we identify a logic of non-capitalist accumulation. In the context of the existence of experiences of real socialism, statist accumulation was defined by Wright (1994) as an accumulation of use values – unlike capitalist accumulation, which accumulates exchange values – in order to increase productive capacity and hence the political power of different segments of the state and bureaucratic apparatus.

In our case study, I identified an accumulation of power by different factions of public officials, who may also be leading political figures or party leaders, rather than by the state bureaucracy. This accumulation is based not only on the services provided by co-operatives and their foregrounding in the public space, but also on the influences and loyalties reaped in relations between officials and co-operatives in the framework of local politics. Let us not forget that the launch of the Argentina Works Programme sought to contain and knit together local politics, and this original logic therefore structures the production.

I also found another type of political accumulation linked to social organisations or co-operatives as political actors in the territory. In the case I analysed, besides seeking workers' subsistence, the social organisation is also geared to building more of a presence in the local neighbourhood, as well as means to motivate political participation by co-operative members. In short, from the perspective of the social organisation and the state, we can see that the logic focuses not only on workers' reproduction but also on political accumulation. Considering the interpenetration of modes of production allows us to explore the richness of the liaison of different logics of production and exchange. Thus, whereas sustainability in the recuperated enterprise relates to the ability to bring together a multiplicity of economic principles, not just the principle of market exchange, in the case of the Argentina Works co-operative sustainability is first and foremost linked to logics of political accumulation.

In sum, whereas the immediate purpose of production is a service provision that acts as a work requirement within the framework of a public policy while satisfying a social need in the vulnerable population, production is not only geared to workers' consumption but to political accumulation by the state – and its officials – and, secondarily, by the social organisation. The nature of accumulation in these experiences is a central structural element in approaching work conflict. The political and statist accumulation, and that of the social organisation described above tend to politicise struggles, blurring the line between economic and political struggle. The economic struggles over the definition of productive activities, the rise in wages, the requests for tools and machinery, and so on, immediately become a political conflict because production policies directly involve the state.

We must remember that, unlike the analysis of forms of ownership, the analysis of the logic of production allows us to focus on the strong presence of the state in the socio-productive unit. Whereas possession of the means of production by the co-operative and the social organisation tipped the balance of power in favour of civil society, the co-operative's productive logics are marked mainly by the predominance of the state at its different levels and agencies.

4   The Political Dimension: State Power and Co-management

In terms of the degrees of the co-operative's autonomy from external powers, we see a dependency on the state apparatus. The municipal government and ACUMAR deforce the management and supervision of the productive process. In a co-ordinated way between the two bodies, attendance is monitored daily, and the progress of works is managed and supervised.

While management is performed by government agencies, ACUMAR holds meetings – called 'assemblies' by the workers – with all three co-operatives in the neighbourhood running the channel clean-up module in order to pool work plans and organise and divide the work among them. Together, the three are made up of 50 workers. Co-operative members in these 'assembly'-like bodies even raise issues around working conditions. Apart from their eminently informative nature, 'assemblies' are a fertile space for raising concerns and discussing the work plan and the division of areas in the module among the co-operatives.

Based on this management and supervision structure, the co-operative retains a relative margin of self-determination in terms of the day-to-day co-ordination of work. In particular, it defines who carries out what activity and how, though in a way subordinate to state structures.

A certain amount of metres have to be done before the end of the month […] and we complete them. You're working, but some of us go off and sort out administrative stuff for the movement. But it doesn't get that complicated cause you talk; you find common ground. As long as we do the work, it doesn't matter.

      VERÓNICA, co-operative member, October 2012

∴

We know the machinists are the ones who do the part about cutting the grass. We co-ordinate with the machinists, and as they're finishing, we start with the rake.

      ADRIANA, co-operative member, January 2015

∴

The municipality co-ordinator who comes to inspect us, we've like already clocked where she's coming from, and she leaves us a bit longer [refreshment break].

      ANALÍA, co-operative member, November 2012

∴

We've got this compañera who organises the work. The thing is, that compañera may be here, but the one in charge is the assistant [from the municipality]. We can get organised, but if the assistant comes along and says "No, tomorrow we've got to do the other stuff," then what our compañera says doesn't stand.

      CRISTINA, co-operative member, January 2015

From the channel clean-up's component tasks to the social organisation's activities, times and dynamics are negotiated with state officials who, while granting freedom in the daily run of things, establish and can amend objectives and work plans. Whereas management and supervision of the work is undertaken by the municipality and ACUMAR, on a day-to-day basis, we encounter a structure typical of the co-operative's legal figure.

In line with Act 20,337, this co-operative has a board made up of president, secretary and treasurer, elected by the members. Notable among the elected authorities is the figure of the president, who is also a leading figure in the organisation, so her responsibilities go beyond the co-operative. Despite sometimes performing the same work as the others, she is more focused on administrative and scheme management tasks. However, not all administrative tasks fall on her or the other board members. In addition to this board, the co-operative designed and implemented an area-based *responsables* [supervisors][8] structure founded on a division of tasks. There are supervisors for administration, machinery, work and attendance, and refreshment breaks, with more than one supervisor per area. In this respect, almost all workers are guaranteed some function of responsibility. Short as the period of responsibility stipulated is (three months), it can be limited or extended depending on the willingness of the holder, as long as the other members agree.

Whereas administrative supervisors are central to keeping the co-operative within the lines of the scheme and worker co-operatives' regulations, it is the figure of the work and attendance co-ordinator that stands out in the day-to-day running of the co-operative. It is interesting that the people occupying both positions are characterised by their proximity to the state authorities and their oral abilities. One field-recording caught the following exchange:

CRISTINA: I look after attendance. And every five minutes I have a barny with the assistant. I hand the attendance register to the assistant. On top of that, I do the work he ought to be doing. [...] We have this notebook, a minute book like, where I write down everything we do every day, and he reads and signs it.

INTERVIEWER: In terms of how you all do the work and divide yourselves up, have you always organised yourselves the same or has it changed?

CRISTINA: We have been changing in as we've got supervisors. [It's] us girls as manage how many blocks we do, what we don't do. Whether we do this whole block and we're done, whether we go on with the next or leave half of it.

INTERVIEWER: And the lady co-ordinating that is the general supervisor?

CRISTINA: All of us. Almost all of them. We all stop at a corner, under the shade and see what we do. Every day we do that.

---

[8] As in the recuperated enterprise (Chapter 4), '*responsables*' literally means 'people responsible for something.' Again, this term is chosen to avoid the traditional word 'manager' and differentiate from capitalist companies. Moreover, as this worker co-operative takes part in a social organisation, its practices become infused with the terminology of politics: 'responsables' is a term commonly used in Argentinian political organisations rather than one typical of the workplace.

INTERVIEWER:	Isn't there a way to know how the whole week's going to pan out?
CRISTINA:	The one as knows the places is me, cause I talk a lot to the bloke who's the supervisor, the assistant. He tells me what we've got on. And I pass on the info about what we have to do to the compañeros. He tells me the place. I tell them what we have to do, from here to here. We have to do this place, and then we get organised to get it together.
INTERVIEWER:	Is that co-ordinated by two of you?
CRISTINA:	We co-ordinate, those of us who've pretty much got the contacts with the officials, and the assistant. And afterwards, we all debate what it is we're up to for a bit, and we get organised and work. We always try not to make heads [avoid hierarchies], but to get organised among ourselves. The information comes to me cause I'm the assistant's assistant [laughter], but I divvy out [share] the info, and they're the ones as pretty much …
INTERVIEWER:	How are these people chosen?
CRISTINA:	By assembly.
ELENA:	The most responsible one. We see them, someone as can talk.

Group interview with co-operative members, January 2015

Aside from any indications given by the supervisors during the workday and in the same area as channel clean-up, as is clear from the interview, these issues are discussed by the workers as a body both in assemblies and before the start of the workday. This relative margin of self-determination defended by the co-operative is usually the result of negotiations and arrangements with the state authorities and is made possible by the fact the co-operative belongs to a social organisation:

> We've got this municipal inspector as comes to check on us, and if you stayed inside [the premises], he'd ask, "Where's so-and-so? And what are they doing?" Now he's got to know us, and he knows we have meetings, that we're an organisation, that we ain't just some bunch of people. He's got to know us now, he knows what the politics being implemented are. They don't want us, but then, what can you do.
>
> ANALÍA, co-operative member, November 2012

The assignment of individual workers to the co-operative was also defined in negotiations between the municipal government and the social organisation. Again, we see how the margins of autonomy from the state relate to the co-operative's inclusion in the organisation and its ability to negotiate and run the scheme. Unlike our case study, in another co-operative I visited, which has weaker links to a social organisation, workers were assigned on a bureaucratic basis.

Regarding internal democracy, we see a combination of direct democracy (in assemblies) and representative democracy (based on the formation of the board) as part of the social organisation's dynamics. The co-operative's assembly is therefore subsumed in the social organisation's weekly assembly, where the matter of the co-operative is moved to the top of the agenda. These assemblies also discuss aspects related to demonstrations, the community snack-bar and a textile venture in the organisation. All its participants thus have full voting rights in the co-operative whether they work there or not. So, we see an overlap in the functions of the co-operative and the social organisation.

ADRIANA: Our movement's assembly is on Wednesdays. So, there's a time we just talk about the co-operative, a status report's read and the problems that are happening, and then we get on with all the business to do with the organisation.

INTERVIEWER: And those who aren't in the co-operative express their opinions or just you lot?

ADRIANA: Everyone usually weighs in. Everyone here weighs in. It's an everyday thing.

INTERVIEWER: And how many of you are there in these assemblies of the movement?

ADRIANA: Thirty, thirty-two, thirty-five, it depends. About half of us are from the co-operative.

ADRIANA, co-operative member, January 2015

In short, we observe that there is a prevalence of state domination with elements of self-determination made possible through moments of negotiation. These margins of self-determination are broader than experiences not embedded in a social organisation. For example, in the case of other co-operatives in the scheme, members have to work in spaces established by the municipal authorities, who stipulate clocking-on and clocking-off times, and manage and control the work performed by the co-operative. They do so to such an extent that the possibility of taking short breaks from the physical exertion required by the activity has become a recurring claim among the co-operative's members.

In this instance, in analysing the distribution and exercise of power in the co-operative, the theoretical developments of P.K. Edwards (1978) around the evolution of types of control in production are of relevance, as are those of Michael Burawoy (1989) regarding the production of consent in hegemonic modes of the organisation of work. The co-operative combines such simple control mechanisms as the presence of an assistant in the workplace and such bureaucratic control mechanisms as taking attendance and carrying out administrative procedures by the co-operative required by the municipality and ACUMAR – such as book-keeping and balance-taking – with moments of negotiation between the co-operative as part of the social organisation and the state authorities. The result of this is a degree of consent among workers (Burawoy, 1989), rather than coercion of the state apparatuses plain and simple.

That said, unlike Burawoy's concept, consent here is not geared towards garnering surplus value, but towards statist political accumulation first and of the social organisation second. The degree of bureaucratisation in an organisation – in other words, the degree of institutionalisation and depersonalisation of power – is conceived as a relevant variable in labour conflict (Hodson and Roscigno, 2004). Indeed, in Argentina Works co-operatives, it is central in avoiding open conflicts. The scheme's organisational structure, involving the formation of co-operatives with the consequent need to manage and run multiple aspects, enables the social organisation to build spaces of self-determination, on the one hand, and the state to exercise a mechanism of bureaucratic control over them, on the other. In the words of one member: "It's like 'We're keeping them busy with all that bureaucratic stuff.' They don't give us time to make any demands" (Verónica, co-operative member, October 2012). This structure and the political negotiations tend to defuse conflict between the co-operative and the municipal government or ACUMAR.

To summarise, two central aspects of the total labour process are defined within state bodies. This shows the predominance of state domination in the work process of this productive form: I refer to the definition of the co-operative's activity, and the direction and supervision of the productive process. However, other aspects are defined in the co-operative, often through the social organisation: I refer to worker assignments to the co-operative, the election of authorities and supervisors, as well as other subsidiary activities and the daily co-ordination of work through the configuration of spaces of self-determination. We could then talk about this case in terms similar to those of a co-management rather than a self-management schema.

5 Social Groupings and Potential Antagonisms: State Officials, Co-operative Members and Activists

The analysis so far makes it possible to draw some conclusions about the socio-productive character of the co-operative. I contend that it is a non-market hybrid social form with the predominance of state power, which subordinates the workers' self-managed production. The predominance of the state is evident in the power it exercises in defining the logic of production, and in the productive process. Workers' self-management emanates from the spaces of self-determination and free availability of the means of production, which make collective appropriation possible. Based on this characterisation, I would venture certain hypotheses about the groupings or fractures structured by this socio-productive order.

In principle, the co-operative is a productive unit oriented to the consumption of workers belonging to sectors long excluded from the labour market. This purpose is not achieved by the sale of exchange goods, but by maintaining the income from public policy. In this way, the state logic establishes the general conditions of production: it is informed by the principle of redistribution and an orientation towards politico-statist accumulation. This means that potential confrontations occur between co-operative workers and state officials, and that these are eminently political and not merely economic struggles.

I contend that, in this case, an analysis of surplus appropriation is not necessarily fruitful. Bearing in mind that this productive space is organised by the logic of redistribution and political accumulation rather than the pursuit of maximum profits, the antagonism among the personifications of the last paragraph is structured around the contradictory interests surrounding the domination and control of the productive process in a given social territory. Accordingly, each social grouping seeks to bring its own logic of political accumulation to bear.

However, conflicts between these groupings may not occur if we consider the forms of control established in the Argentina Works Programme and the River-Bank Clean-Up Programme, a combination of direct, classic and bureaucratic forms. The latter give rise to an operational dynamic that fluctuates between administrative requirements and negotiations. In other words, as well as exercising control over the workers' collective through mechanisms perceived as objective and depersonalised, it ultimately paves the way to negotiation between the co-operative and the state authorities. Only after these moments of negotiation are exhausted is there likely to be an open conflict between these social personifications. The worker co-operative legal form is thus a 'bifunctional' factor: it facilitates the establishment of controls that may discourage conflict, while providing a relative margin of autonomy for the labour collective and promoting the production of demands.

Alongside such formation of social groupings, I identified ways workers get involved with the co-operative that might lead to a divide related to opportunity hoarding. I refer to the case of wage labourers and workers not formally associated with the co-operative. While, in some cases, they are able to participate in decision-making, none of them serve in the positions of responsibility that I have described, nor can they sit on the board. I therefore suggest a tendency towards inequality between members and non-members.

Regarding the organisation and co-ordination of work, as mentioned earlier, a division is made by area, and supervisors are collectively elected for each. The area of administration comprises a member and the president, a woman like so many others in the co-operative. Whereas the former is responsible for the administration of the co-operative as such, and thence linked to both schemes, the chairwoman takes part in these tasks too, while also dealing with the more political negotiations and arrangements in response to government bodies.

The group of maintenance overseers and machine operators is made up of the co-operative's male members. The tool supervisor keeps a record of any loans and runs a weekly check on the storeroom. Refreshment supervisors are two members who buy and organise food and beverages for breaks during the workday. Last, the presenteeism supervisor and work keeps records of members' attendance, while both she and the chairwoman maintain relations with the assistant and the works progress supervisor, who oversee the work.

While rotation schedules and the collegiate character of these structures are taken into account, the same people have remained in administration and machinery since the co-operative started up, and it has always had the president. Machine operators and maintenance overseers have not been rotated, as they argue that the job requires physical strength and may injure women. In administration, the work requires a certain technical knowledge, as well as oral abilities, which is a barrier to other members' wanting or being able to become involved. Furthermore, while not a rule generally applied to co-operatives, members of the same family cannot sit on the board. This reduces board nominations, as co-operative members are recruited not just from the local neighbourhood, but from family and comradeship. Leadership positions have thus tended to be fixed, creating an organisational divide between 'leaders' and 'led.' However, this division by area does not exempt the supervisors from the riverbank clean-up work, even when sometimes they have to be absent, and this reduces the chances of a divide between manual and non-manual workers.

Last, the co-operative's inclusion in the social organisation allows the deployment of several elements of the workers' self-managed production. These include the social possession of the means of production, the performance of other activities geared to worker and local neighbourhood consumption, and the existence of spaces for self-determination or autonomous co-operation. There is no underlying principle of market exchange in these activities, but rather reciprocity based on a logic of political accumulation by the social organisation. Here, I hypothesise work conflicts arise as a result of the coupling of the co-operative and the social organisation.

In this sense, I observe organisational divides but in terms of participation in social organisation rather than work. Being a member does not necessarily involve active participation in the organisation, although this is desirable. This organisational coupling informs two groups: those who join in with the activism and those who do not. This in turn shapes attitudinal or cultural groupings around perceptions about work and attitudes towards it. As in the recuperated enterprise, the socio-productive form enables a democratisation of participation that gives significance to workers' conceptions and perceptions and leads to them being expressed. From this perspective, we can understand such tensions between different conceptions of work and political participation. Nevertheless, as I point out that this socio-productive form is marked by state domination, it should be stressed that it has lower levels of democratisation than are seen in the recuperated enterprise.

In a gradient ordering the divides of groupings from most to least endogenous to the socio-productive form, I propose the following characterisation. The most endogenous is the cleavage between workers and state representatives, followed by member–non-member organisational groupings. Among the least endogenous are the divides between leaders and led, and attitudinal groupings around various conceptions of work and politics.

May 2013 saw the unveiling of the "*Coloso de Avellaneda*" [Avellaneda Colossus], a monumental iron sculpture, fifteen meters high and weighing more than ten tons. On the south bank of the Riachuelo, the figure of a worker holding a portrait of Evita commemorates the popular demonstration of 17 October 1945. Its productive process is also a homage to collective work: funded by factories in the area, the Colossus was erected thanks to the collaboration of sculptor Alejandro Marmo and workers from the space "*Arte en las Fábricas*" [Art in the Factories]. Created by Marmo in the 1990s and inspired by recuperated enterprises, the project was born on the premise of salvaging the vestiges of closed factories in the Buenos Aires Conurbation, turning them into sculptures and taking the art co-produced with unemployed and excluded workers to workplaces, mainly recuperated and self-managed enterprises.

The postcards that open this chapter take us back to a military state trying to quell popular mobilisation and, several years later, to a corrupt, ghost state. Our third postcard, however, plays out with a state that adopts a different stance: for all its limitations and tensions, it promotes self-management and associativism as a way of gaining access to economic, social, territorial and environmental rights. Even so, the Colossus still stands on the Riachuelo's south bank, striding forth, perhaps in challenge to the other shore.

CHAPTER 6

The Production of Co-operative Conflict

The case studies are underpinned by deep immersion in the analytical universes. Regularity and methodological systematicity are the tools and the source of hope that the research questions will find answers in the fieldwork. In my case, I had spent months – even years – visiting, interviewing and observing. Yet the conflicts in the now established co-operatives did not become apparent either in events or discourses. An in-depth knowledge of the socio-productive character of the cases and their constitutive conflicts allowed me to hypothesise tensions and axes of potential conflicts. But why and how did these co-operative workers without bosses fight once their co-operatives were under way?

On one of my visits to the recuperated hotel, during an interview in which I set out to understand the enterprise's regulations and disciplinary measures, my interviewee mentioned that several '*socios fundidores*' – '*founderer* members'! – had left the co-operative. He had to repeat the term for me. I was not sure whether I had heard the word '*fundadores*' [founders] – a category in the world of recuperated enterprises to denote those who start the co-operative – or the word '*fundidores*' ['*founderers*'], in the sense of people who scupper something or cause it to founder or, in this case, go bankrupt.

The history of the recuperated enterprise, with its origin in the *fundición* – 'foundering,' scuppering or bankruptcy – of the failed enterprise and the subsequent *fundación* – foundation – of a co-operative, provides a glimpse of a parallel drawn between former bosses and this group of '*founderer*' members. The parallel could refer to a number of dimensions open to comparison between the two: the managerial, that is to say, authoritarian attitudes of these '*founderer* members,' their practices tending to bankrupt the business again, or the perception that, like the old bosses, these members were working in unproductive tasks. All these dimensions were clearly present in the way the work conflicts I analyse in this chapter play out.

That said, my research sought to tackle together two universes – recuperated enterprises and co-operatives in social schemes – that, while paradigmatic of new worker co-operativism, tended not to be approached comparatively. The co-operative of the *Programa Argentina Trabaja* [Argentina Works Programme] seemed to target a single object for its demands: the state. But, while attending a meeting between state authorities and co-operatives that shared the working module, including the co-operative analysed, I took the following field-notes.

> The president of the other co-operative claimed people were going around saying she was taking co-operative members away from the others, but she mentioned the fact that people were joining of their own accord. She also said, "Her arms were open wide to welcome anyone who wanted to change to her co-operative." The president of the co-operative I'm analysing told her she'd never said that. When the meeting was over, the co-operatives went their separate ways, the president of the other co-operative approached the group, asked Sonia if she was coming with them and what she finally intended to do. Sonia said yes and just upped and walked off with the group from the other co-operative.
> Field-notes, June 2015

At that moment, I was staggered as it dawned on me that, in that single act, Sonia was leaving the co-operative I was researching and moving to another also operating in the local neighbourhood. There was a knot here that I absolutely had to unravel. If remunerations and work were defined in state bodies, what conflict could underlie Sonia's departure for another co-operative belonging to the same scheme? Coming back to comparative analysis, which identities in each co-operative were entering into dispute and how were they linked to its socio-productive characteristics? In the foundry of diverse elements involved in setting up a labour collective, what logics, relations, practices or values lay behind the clashes?

In this chapter, I deal with work conflicts in both socio-productive units once they have been established, in other words, once production has started or at least a work regime has been laid down. I draw connections between these conflicts and the constitutive disputes discussed in Chapter 3. I also analyse the associations between the co-operatives' conflicts and socio-productive characterisations, paying special attention to the divides, cleavages and oppositions that are activated in the disputes. Last, I periodise each co-operative's development process to identify landmarks in institutional innovation and change due to the conflicts, for example, in the modes of decision-making, the expansion of the members' participation, the forms of work control and others.

In expository terms, I look first at two work conflicts in the recuperated enterprise: around the running of the co-operative on the one hand and work regulations on the other. Second, I look at two conflicts in the Argentina Works co-operative: one, around the definition of the task and, the other, over the purpose of the production. Last, I analyse conflicts from a comparative perspective to make conflicts in the predominant forms of twenty-first-century worker co-operativism more intelligible.

1   Board Removals: Conflicts over the Running and Expansion of the Productive Process

The recuperation of the enterprise under analysis gives rise to autonomous co-operation in the workers' collective. This democratising character of enterprise recuperation makes the function of management an aspect potentially open to discussion (Rebón, 2015). Its orientation and form apart – which vary with the characteristics of the mode of production – the function of management is to do with the distribution and exercise of power in an organisation, and with the ability to govern and run the enterprise: in other words, with the political dimension of a socio-productive process.

This recuperated enterprise dismantles the classic mode of organising power in capitalist enterprises, based on a top-down system of control (Edwards, 1978). The function of management is thus politicised, in the sense posited by Chantal Mouffe (2007) that it exposes its antagonistic dimension. Mouffe differentiates 'the political' from 'politics': 'the political' refers to the constitutive dimension of antagonism in human societies; 'politics' encompasses the set of practices and institutions whereby a certain order is created to organise societies in the context of the conflicts inherent in the political. In this instance, when I refer to the politicisation of the function of management, I am adopting Mouffe's definition of 'the political.'

Just as despotic co-operation and consent in traditional private-capital enterprises are not built and rebuilt without labour disputes, the constitution and maintenance of autonomous co-operation in the recuperated enterprise analysed here raise disputes around the running of the co-operative. It is no longer the unlimited commodification of the labour force, nor its exploitation during production that mobilises the struggles of the labour force, but the will to take increasing control of the productive process and the different perceptions and considerations about how it should be organised.

Although the function of management is personified by the labour force, I pointed out in Chapter 4 that, in our case study and in other recuperated enterprises, this function is taken on specifically by the board members and secondarily by the sector and area *responsables* [supervisors] – proposed by the board members. The board then becomes the privileged sphere where the function of management is exercised and hence the locus of conflict over the running of the co-operative.

That said, what observables indicate the politicisation of the function of management, or in other words, the disputed character of the running of the co-operative? In the experience under study here, I highlight the rotation of board positions, the holding of competitive elections (the existence of real options and the possibility of altering its composition), the modifications implemented in the systems for electing representatives, the results marking a polarisation of the labour collective, the resignations of presidents and the removals of board members. In this section, I look at the removal of one board and the call for early elections to form a new board. This dispute is an open conflict, whereas the other indicators listed refer instead to tensions around the running of the co-operative.

From 2003 to 2015, there was a succession of six boards. The first, in the early days of the experience, was chosen by consensus and common agreement among members. This was made easier for a number of reasons: the co-operative was newly formed, there were few workers, and most were also former employees of the hotel and therefore former co-workers.

This first board tackled the process of recuperating and developing the infrastructure. The first activities revolved around the rental or barter of function rooms, while the possibility and modalities of opening the tower (the rooms) was being debated. This only came about in 2004, thanks to a loan from the Venezuelan state allowing production to be resumed on a permanent basis. This board's administration is characterised by members as a stage "focused on the conflict, so the main concern wasn't to balance the books" (Alejandro, co-operative member and leading figure in a worker co-operative organisation, January 2016), and as a period marked by "disorganisation":

> It was a complete shambles. The pay was lousy, it wasn't very organised, shall we say. [...] Back then, the economic situation was better than now, to my mind. [...] Back then, a lot of things hadn't gone up; you could make ends meet. [...] It was more an issue of organisation.
> VIOLETA, co-operative member, August 2014

By 2006, when it came to renewing the board's representatives, the board members expressed a will to remain in their posts. There were consequently failed attempts to draw up a single unity list with other members also interested in running the co-operative and thereby maintaining consensus as an election mode:

> I said to the *compañero* on the Purple List, "Right, let's find some unity here. Let's talk to people, get them to throw in some names and go to a *previa* [Monday briefing]. So let's get behind them then: the one as comes top comes top." So, we went on Monday, 77 compañeros declare my re-election. So this group of kids, the young ones … I get there in the morning and find the hotel completely papered with compañeros: the president, the treasurer, *vocal* [speaker] one, vocal two! I sign in, check and say, "What's this?" Purple List, I start seeing the lads in the photos. We'd talked about unity, about having to stick together, and now they come and tell me they're here and want to talk to me. You can't want to talk when you've already drawn up a list.
>
> MARIO, co-operative member and Yellow List candidate, September 2006

In the end, the consensus failed to hold, and three lists faced off in the election: the Yellow List, unsuccessfully seeking re-election; the Blue list, led by a member who would only succeed in winning the presidency in the 2012 election; and the Purple List that won the day. Despite consisting primarily of 'founder members,' the Purple List was led by a presidential candidate who was not one of the members that had participated in the co-operative's recuperation and formation. In addition to this, the group embodying the Purple List was singled out as 'young' group: one key informant interviewee pointed out that "It was the first attempt by a younger generation" (Adrián, key informant, October 2014). What is more, this grouping differed from the others in that it submitted a written project for the running of the co-operative, a project that focused on its economic and financial administration:

> We were the youngest group we had at the time. [...] I wasn't 40 at the time, I was thirty-six. So, we were all 40 or under. [...] Meetings [were held] cause the compañeros wanted to know what plans we had for the co-operative. It was a plan of youngsters the one we had. [...] What we wanted to do with the hotel, how improvements could be made. And, kind of like the other compañeros were forced as well, cause suddenly we'd submitted this plan and all they did was talk; so as to get something down in writing. [...] On the side of investment and costs, what we can reduce and how we can boost compañeros' wages. That kind of thing, I really liked the idea cause I could see something structured, something good, and serious, that could be implemented. [...] Us, when we started out, we voted for the sake of voting. We had no idea at all what a co-operative was. [...] Cause there were the compañeros who'd been voted in, but we didn't have the faintest idea what they had to carry out. You

could see what could be improved as well based on another compañero's mistake. So, actually, on that basis, maybe at the time the books weren't up to scratch, so first and foremost we had to bring the administration up to date. On the administrative side, improving all those points. [...] It [the result] was 40 to 70 [votes]; we'd won. I do remember that perfectly, cause they said, "Well, you almost doubled the other list's votes."

ANA, co-operative member and Purple List candidate, November 2014

So, the Purple List's victory meant that, in 2006, it took over a more "technical" board (Adrián, key informant, October 2014). The president did not last a year in office, however. Accused of stealing money from a subsidy, the elected authority decided to stand aside from the presidency and then resign from the co-operative. The out-going president had failed to channel the objectives of administrative ordering proposed during the elections, and it was this situation that threw his presidency into crisis:

They ended up accusing the president of stealing money from a subsidy, but there really was no way to prove it, it was part of the chaos in administration. Cause Mario's first board was the occupation, so there were no books, the company was set up like a corner shop. I think some papers were missing that vouched for the documentation of the dosh attributed to this lad, and the *pibe* [kid] had a hard time. At the assembly they practically wanted to lynch him and the pibe quietly said he wouldn't let them accuse him of something they couldn't prove, but that he was leaving the presidency, stepping aside, and that the secretary took over as president.

ALEJANDRO, co-operative member and leading figure in a worker co-operative organisation, January 2016

In response to the situation, a members' assembly decided not to call elections and for the president's place to be taken by the secretary of the board. The new president received support from members active in recuperated enterprise organisations and thus successfully completed her term. The difficulties of running the co-operative, coupled with the internal repercussions of the 2008 international economic and financial crisis and the 2009 swine flu pandemic – which hit the influx of tourists – created a fragile economic situation in the enterprise, which had a knock-on effect on workers' remunerations. Indeed, some members received no income for a couple of months. This administration thus came to be associated with a period of economic down-turn.

It was 2009 and elections to fill the positions on the third board were coming up. The first elections held by simple majority, with the submission of closed lists, had been riddled with '*chicanas*' [dirty tricks], rumours and mutual smear campaigns. Interpersonal relationships had suffered, leading workers to alter the type of election: nominations became individual, and the way of electing representatives was changed.

> In one assembly, we all put candidates forward. So, we already knocked it down from 160 to twenty or 25 people. You could put yourself forward. Those twenty or 25 of us put together a voting form with the posts on it, so we set up our board out of those twenty-five. Who would win? Not the one as collected most votes across all categories, but the one as had most votes for president, most votes for secretary, most votes for treasurer.
>
> ALEJANDRO, co-operative member and leading figure in a worker co-operative organisation, January 2016

From the workers' perspective, the abolition of closed lists would avoid the formation of groups and the polarisation of the labour collective of previous elections. Nevertheless, this way of nominating and selecting representatives culminated in arguments delegitimising the eventual winners. On that occasion, a member of the kind described in Chapter 4 as a 'new activist worker'[1] was elected to the position of president. He had joined formally after the start of production in late 2004, and his distinguishing trait was as a political cadre from the recuperated enterprises movement. The elected secretary and treasurer were also members who had joined after the recuperation, both aged under 30. Both president and treasurer having obtained a significant share of votes, the questions were put to the secretary. This woman member had received fewer votes overall than the former president, who had submitted her individual candidacy and had won none of the posts. The questions over the secretary arose not merely from the degree of legitimacy attributed to her victory in contrast with the former president's defeat but were also linked to interpersonal relationships: the young member was the daughter of a 'founder member' who was not appreciated by a significant number of members.

The beginning of the board's administration was thus marked by questions over its electoral legitimacy and also by certain disgruntled sectors seeking to remove it, or at least force a resignation. Some members presented the *Instituto Nacional de Asociativismo y Economía Social* [National Institute of Associativism and Social Economy] (INAES) a petition questioning how the

---

1 Let us bear in mind that this expression does not constitute a native category but arises from the development of archetypal profiles.

THE PRODUCTION OF CO-OPERATIVE CONFLICT

board had been formed. This petition was then rejected by the INAES, which ratified the co-operative's autonomy to define its model for electing authorities. While electoral arguments were invoked to delegitimise the board, this questioning also accounted for the resistance of certain sectors in the enterprise to the explicit incursion of 'politics' into the board through 'new activist workers.' After this experience, the following elections saw a return to the list system.

But let us backtrack for a moment. What elements can we associate the victory of a 'new activist worker' and the absence of 'founder members' with on the third board? As described in Chapter 3, the Judiciary had granted legal ownership of the property in 2007 to those who had been the hotel's original owners and administrators and had ordered the co-operative's eviction. In response to this judicial measure, the co-operative had implemented a series of co-ordinated actions with the worker co-operative federation to which it belongs: the presentation of extraordinary resources to the Judiciary, the drafting and submission of expropriation bills, the organisation of festivals and public demonstrations, and so forth. The persistence of the conflict over the occupancy of the premises demonstrated the importance of developing not only a productive and administrative plan, but a political plan containing a strategy with a view to securing some degree of occupancy of the premises, a key element towards ensuring the co-operative's continuity. I would therefore contend that the needs created by the struggle with actors outside the co-operative over the occupancy of the premises and the personal traits of the candidate for president (his track record as an activist and his knowledge of co-operativism) attracted votes in his favour. That said, it should be noted that this tipped the scales but did not stop the questions coming.

After these challenges, the board stabilised and even managed to design and approve a change of by-laws, a remarkable landmark in the co-operative's institutionalisation, which I go into in more depth in the following section. Notwithstanding these changes, the presidency continued to be opposed: "How come someone who'd joined later – quite a lot longer after the start – was going to be the president while all the founder members were going to be left out?" noted one key informant (Adrián, October 2014). In the electoral contest, I saw tensions between these founder members and the new generations. So, in opposition to this board, a grouping gathered strength headed by a 'founder member' who was against 'politics' in the hotel. He had already stood in the 2006 elections and would win the elections in 2012.

Let us look at the specific features of the 2012 election. Two lists were submitted on that occasion: on the one hand, the one mentioned above, headed by the 'founder member'; on the other, the one headed by the 'founder member,' who as secretary had taken over the presidency after the early departure of the president-elect in 2006 and who had won a significant volume of votes at the 2009 elections. Last, the members of the out-going board had decided not to run. The hallmark of the 2012 election was that the winning list garnered only ten votes more than the loser. This result set the model that, at least regarding preferences towards the board, the workers' collective was split in two almost equal parts, a state of political polarisation unprecedented in the hotel.

The winning list represented the sectors against *"los free"* [freebies] or *"amiguismos"* [cronyism] from the start of the co-operative: namely, non-market liaisons and reciprocity relations. On the other hand, for other sectors of the hotel, these represent ways of establishing alliances and solidarities in the framework of a political strategy for the venture's sustainability that, as the interviewee points out below, goes beyond the fact of "earning another salary":

> Sometimes when you loan out a space ... The kids who are in sales or administration say "This is an expense," "Stop all the freebie spaces and those kinds of things." There are compañeros at Zanón who've ended up on the street cause the guy from reception didn't want to give them a room, the other day the president of Pigüé Textiles turned up and they didn't want to give him a room. [...] The compañero can't get his head around the fact that the closer we are to the social body, the more solidarity we're going to have. Cause what I see every time we need a hand is that it's in the social body or in small groups and organisations that there's an immediate, constant response. So, the compañero's wrong, the thing is the member's up to something else, earning another salary [sic].[2]
>
> MARIO, co-operative member, September 2006

From some workers' perspectives, the list won the election because some of the earlier boards were thought not to have soundly managed the enterprise, resulting in a drop in monthly pay. In response, the list promised sound running of the enterprise based on the idea that "we come in to work, not to play politics" and that the "freebies" had to be stopped (Adrián, key informant, October 2014). Although all of this may have been viewed positively at the time of the election, it was also considered to have been one of the reasons for its later removal:

---

2 Two emblematic recuperated enterprises in Argentina are the co-operatives FaSinPat (called Zanón in their administration by bosses) and Pigüé Textiles. FaSinPat is a ceramic tile factory located in Neuquén Province, recuperated in 2001. Pigüé is a textile company recuperated in 2004 and located in Buenos Aires Province.

He was a man who wouldn't ask for anything; ask in the sense of political matters. [...] We need everything, we've got to realise that, if we don't have support from outside, all this goes to pot. [...] We don't wear anyone's t-shirt, but we're aware that without the politicians we're nothing.
GRACIELA, co-operative member, August 2014

What "political matters" is the member specifically referring to? I recorded two milestones in the fourth board (2012–2013), both related to the conflict over the occupancy of the premises. On the one hand, the fourth board's administration saw the tenth anniversary of the recuperated enterprise, a fitting moment to hold an event to demonstrate the reach of the co-operative's social and political support. As opposed as the board's president was to it, the activity was eventually held. This undermined the board's authority. Furthermore, the record of the commercial suit for bankruptcy had been forwarded in October 2012 to the Federal Criminal jurisdiction to investigate whether the legal owners of the premises had committed fraud towards the state in complicity with the civil-military dictatorship. The federal criminal suit expired in 2013, complicating the co-operative's judicial affairs. This fact was attributed to the board's refusal to appear as the plaintiff in the case.

From the above, we can establish linkages between the confrontation over the occupancy of the premises – the conflict geared towards actors outside the productive unit – and internal conflicts – specifically here around the running of the co-operative. Just as I qualified the idea in Chapter 3 that the conflict between capital and labour force loses momentum in recuperated enterprises, I here contend that such a confrontation with external forces has contentious implications among workers in the productive unit. In the co-operative itself, different stances form around the conflict against external actors over the occupancy of the productive unit. These stances generate – and are also being contained by – various political and productive enterprise projects which harbour different notions of sustainability. The lack of resolution of the property issue is central to understanding the two projects, which tend to become polarised.

One project envisages a notion of sustainability based on two fundamental tenets: on the one hand, multiple principles of relations, tending to gain the co-operative more autonomy from the capitalist market through public procurement and exchange with other co-operatives; on the other, a political strategy based on strengthening links with numerous social and political actors through the co-operative federation under to which the hotel belongs. The politicisation of the experience is adopted as the reproductive form.

The second project sets out to make production more efficient under a strictly market criterion of economic sustainability. From this perspective, the productive process is restricted to its market dimension, without taking into consideration elements previously undertaken by the boss, lobbying by businesspeople, for example. In this sense, it implies a view restricted to the place once occupied by workers in the enterprise under a boss. A rigid disciplinary regime is therefore implemented and non-market liaisons and socio-political relations with actors outside the productive unit are abandoned. The project also considers that the resolution of the hotel's occupancy involves negotiations with the legal owner of the premises with no prior consultation with the workers.[3]

These projects, it should be remembered, are not explicitly proposed or unequivocally supported by the members. The labour force is not unanimously divided between these projects; rather these are usually embodied in personal leaderships and can be variously supported by the other members. This variability is linked to the weight of interpersonal relationships in the worker co-operative. Indeed, it is a medium-sized enterprise in which family ties are hierarchised as a criterion for incorporating new workers and some of the members are extremely senior. Preferences during elections are therefore usually not informed exclusively on the basis of the political and productive projects embodied in the candidates, but by interpersonal relationships and perceptions around earlier boards' administrations.

The worsening of the conflict over the hotel's occupancy makes the need for 'politics' unavoidable. What is the point of guaranteeing and increasing incomes if the co-operative can be evicted from one day to the next? To what extent is the income guaranteed without resorting to reciprocity and redistribution relations with the state? The moments of external bitterness over the property tend to tip the scales in favour of the first project. These moments are proof of the need for political liaisons and to adopt a comprehensive criterion of sustainability. This is central to understanding the pronounced conflict that played out in the co-operative, leading to the removal of the board. This board side-lined the "political matters" at a critical time in the conflict over the hotel's occupancy, when the workers' collective united behind the defence of the hotel and its co-operative nature. Its legitimacy was thus undermined: the workers were aggrieved at the board's failure to protect the co-operative and the consequent threat to its continued existence. As Lewis Coser's (1961) sociology of social conflict points out, external confrontations have connective

---

3   In the next section, I look more closely at an attempted negotiation with the legal owner of the premises.

effects on the group in that they establish its boundaries, reaffirm its values, increase internal cohesion and reinforce participation:

> [I remember] one of the last [assemblies]. The eviction issue was pretty firm. There was lots of new compañeros, the old ones had left by then but the really old ones had stayed on, and the ones like me who'd been in the co-operative for four or five years. [...] People who've been there since 2003, between 2003 and 2007, the generation that was there obviously experienced this problem more often than we did. I joined in 2009, and the situation was, generally speaking, a bit steadier, a bit quieter by then. [...] By the time we came, the conflict was pretty low-key, the situation looked stable by then, we weren't a nuisance, and the Judiciary weren't screwing [bother] us either. So, it was like something new. Seeing the newcomers, or myself ... It was a nice meeting cause the president of the board came, stood up and said, "What do *you* want to do? I'm not going to stick my neck out for 120 compañeros when 40 or 50 people want to leave or arrange it so as we leave." Then people who'd never said a word and never spoken up in an assembly said, "I want to carry on cause of this, that, the other." [...] So at that meeting, one compañero who's the same age as me and has two daughters got up to speak and said, "I want to know what we're going to do, cause I'm sticking around to fight, but I really want to know how things stand and what's going on, cause this is the only source of income I've got for my daughters." And that fella never says a word, at meetings or anywhere, so I mean it was good. [...] Since I joined, we hadn't been through a critical situation like that.
> GUSTAVO, co-operative member, August 2014

∴

> If a really big decision for the hotel has to be made, [...] then there's a course of action, aside from any niggles we might have, that we fight amongst ourselves. When an assembly's held for something that's happened to the hotel, that's the procedure. I mean, we're all agreed on that. Some of us cause we're committed, others cause it suits them, but they're all pulling in the same direction. Now, in terms of our kind of internal issues, when someone thinks there's been some kind of injustice, then some folk do side with one group and some with another.
> FERNANDO, co-operative member, September 2014

The threat of eviction – the issue of the occupancy of the premises discussed in Chapter 3 – led to an internal line of conflicts. Various positions take shape around the dispute over the property, contained in political and productive enterprise projects based on different conceptions of sustainability. This internal focus of conflicts tends to be activated at times of worsening external conflict, that is, when the continuity and sustainability of the co-operative is threatened. On these occasions, the workers' collective tends to unite behind the enterprise project based on a multiplicity of relationship principles. The locus of this conflict is the board, as it is the job of the board to handle the political, legislative and judicial issues around the ownership of the premises, a parameter by which it is judged.

Moreover, the board also failed to deliver on the binding promise to develop administration in line with expectations. Late payments to suppliers and members, and overdue payments of services were elements mentioned by workers to explain the unease surrounding the board's administration. Last, the workers attribute their de-legitimisation to the changes it enacted in the forms of decision-making and the circulation of information, as well as the organisation of the work, upsetting the customary ways the co-operative and its members operated, and establishing elements of the hotel's disciplinary regime prior to the recuperation and formation of the co-operative. This board's president is also remembered by some members as "authoritarian," as the man who tried to run the co-operative like a "businessman" (Alejandro, co-operative member and leading figure in a co-operative organisation, January 2016). Furthermore, under his administration, the availability and circulation of information decreased, as did the frequency of assemblies:

> Everyone was dead unhappy about this way of carrying on. Cause we were used to being told about everything here. For example, "Such and such a thing is happening tomorrow." So anyway, there didn't seem to be much information, and when there isn't a lot of information, people get edgy. [...] They wanted to know when they'd get paid or wouldn't get paid, or whether this was going to get done or not. So anyway, all that started a whisper, and in places like this, when there's smoke there's fire, you'll eventually run into problems. Cause if you let the rumour spread and spread, it's like cancer: it gets really really big.
> FERNANDO, co-operative member, September 2014

In terms of how the labour process was organised, this board established a rotation system, which was seen as a major imposition, and even went to the lengths of sending registered legal letters to two members, pressuring them to report for their newly assigned posts. Several members felt that the rotations reflected interpersonal relationships based on *"amiguismos"* or "favouritism":

> Someone being given a post that benefits someone they like more cause they're more loyal to them, and that harms someone else: that's one of the injustices you see most [...] Not in all cases, it isn't a general law. On the other hand, that might not happen in a private company, cause there's always a manager and then a top-dog manager and then a top-top-dog manager, all the way on up to the owner. So, it's harder to do that.
> FERNANDO, co-operative member, September 2014

It is interesting to think that the female members who received the legal letters are both 'founder members' and that one of them had also headed the list that won about ten votes less than the winner of the last election. This approach was then extremely disruptive, being the first time that a measure of that kind had been used and because there was a perceived intention to harm anyone who might challenge for power.

The crisis of the board was thus hastened and ultimately triggered when some of its members started resigning. Against this background, it was decided after several assemblies to remove it, after which a provisional board was formed, which would act until early elections were called. Its objective was to steer the transition: in other words, to avoid the complete dissolution of the removed board in order to overcome the administrative difficulties involved (for example, the change of authorised signatures) and ease the institutional crisis. It was decided it would consist of the surviving members of the defunct board and former presidents of the co-operative who were elected by assembly.

Faced with the up-coming election, there were attempts to form a united list "so as not to tear the co-operative apart [...] cause if there was already one half in favour of one and the other half in favour of the other, it would get very nasty" (Ana, co-operative member, November 2014). These attempts proved fruitless, and, in the end, two lists were submitted: one headed by the president of the recently removed board and another made up of some of the former presidents who were part of the provisional board. The latter won the election and won re-election in 2015. On that occasion, of the nine positions that made up the board, only the two speakers were modified.

I would like to draw attention to one particular feature of this new board that expresses an outcome of the conflict described. The president is the 'founder member' who, as a secretary, had taken over the presidency after it had been abandoned by the elected candidate. The vice-president is the 'new activist worker' who had previously been president. In addition, the nine-post board is comprised mainly of 'new members' and 'youngsters.' In this sense, while the conflict that led to the removal of the fourth board and the call for early elections was not informed by these social categories, it is striking that, for the first time, in opposition to this one, a board was formed that achieved a mix of 'founder,' 'newcomer,' 'activist' and 'youngster' members. What is more, it successfully saw out its term and won re-election. I believe this is bound up with the unifying power of the worsening of the conflict over the property and the opportunity it constituted for hegemonic construction, in Ernesto Laclau's (2009) definition as the ability to universalise a particularity. Here, I mean the ability to universalise an enterprise project.

A second outcome of the conflict around the running of the co-operative is the expansion of the participation of 'new' and 'young' members in key bodies in decision-making and control of the productive process. It should be remembered that the relative weight of interpersonal relationships is a wake-up call when it comes to the supposition that the divides observed in the social relations of production in Chapter 4 can be activated unmediated in conflicts. Thus, despite identifying the potentially opposing groupings of 'founder members–new members,' 'youngsters–oldsters,' the positions in the conflict in question are not only informed by such categories but are also influenced by perceptions around previous administrations, the conditions of conflict over the occupancy of the premises and interpersonal relationships.

This confrontation shows the dynamism of these self-management experiences and their potential to reverse unequalising processes. However, it would be wise here to introduce a nuance, or at least a question mark. The same board's re-election could not only explain a hegemonic construction process around an enterprise project, but also the embryonic establishment of a grouping of members considered apt to lead the co-operative and the possible fixing of a leaders–led cleavage.

In short, unlike the labour dispute where the personifications of capital and work clash mainly around the conditions of the consumption and exchange of the labour force, my analysis makes it possible to argue that a main line of conflict in this co-operative becomes the dispute over the running of the enterprise and the control of the 'expanded' productive process, and that the board is the locus of this dispute. María Inés Fernández Álvarez (2012b) points out that there are different jobs in recuperated enterprises which include not only the production of the specific good or service, but negotiations and collective actions too. With Julian Rebón (2015), I share the idea that the function of management is politicised in a second sense. Let us not forget that, in the case of the co-operative, the first sense concerned the debate and dispute over management, whereas this second sense is to do with the fact that directing and running a recuperated enterprise results in organising and co-ordinating work and service provision, as well as managing the conflict over the occupancy of the hotel and establishing connections with social and political actors.

That said, this expansion of the productive process not only involves the effective inclusion of new activities, but also that they are perceived as such by the workers. For them, activities that were probably taken on by the employer in the private-capital enterprise can represent new tasks. Here, I would contend that the productive process in the recuperated enterprise is expanded: as well as production in the strict sense, it involves a series of activities, processes and struggles specific to the recuperated enterprises. The external dispute over the occupancy of the premises is central to activating an line of conflict around the enterprise's political and productive projects, supported mainly by certain leaderships, and with the co-operative's members demonstrating mobile and flexible affiliations that vary according to interpersonal relationships.

Last, I would like to reflect on the conflict over the running of the co-operative. This does not imply a breakdown of political association, and this is an extremely important point, as recuperated enterprises are still shaping their institutions. Even though the conflict leads to the removal of a board, shared norms enable new elections to be held and the co-operative to continue on its course, in addition to the prospect of consolidating an enterprise project.

To describe this process of building autonomous, democratic co-operation, we can apply Mouffe's (2007) view of agonistic conflict relations in human societies, which, in her case, focuses on national political systems. According to the author, democracy implies the conflicting co-existence of different viewpoints. Conflicts may occur in the guise of antagonisms, where the opponent is conceptualised as an enemy to be eliminated deploying a logic of exclusion and exclusivity. Or they may occur through agonistic relationships, namely, struggles between alternative projects based on common values, rules and institutions, deploying a logic under which converge a multiplicity of contradictory interpretations and projects. This notion differs from antagonism because it involves considering the opponent as an adversary and results in a struggle for hegemony. The characterisation of our conflict in agonistic terms enables us to cast light on the dispute without losing sight of the fact that it is inherent to the political and to the construction of hegemonic enterprise projects where adversaries are equals.

The democratisation of the function of management not only generates disputes around the running of the enterprise but also establishes the need for the workers to build procedures for collective self-regulation (Calloway, 2016): collective practices for organising work that replace the disciplinary regime of traditional capitalist enterprises (Dejours, 1992). Collective self-regulation includes, among others, such dimensions as the technical division of labour, the qualifications and training policies, the forms of control, tempos and intensity, and the rotation schemes. As well as regulating and organising the labour process, these collectively defined, sustained procedures integrate the labour collective. As Melina Perbellini (2016) states, the formation of a workers' collective entails the invention and implementation of common work rules, without which it is impossible to talk about a collective, but merely of a group of people. This is the subject of the next section.

2 Regulations, Sanctions and Exclusions: From 'Founder Members' to '*Founderer* Members'

In the practice of self-management, workers construct shared rules as a result of both emulation and innovation. In this regard, one member claims that the hotel "is not a company, it's a co-operative but, either way, the rules are the same as a company" (Rosa, co-operative member, August 2014). Another member notes, on the subject of sanctions, that "before taking a decision or getting something settled, it's always about talking, proposing a change" (Gustavo, co-operative member, August 2014).

> It's a process each recuperated enterprise adopted independently. At first it was like "What do you mean we aren't going to do things right when we're all honest, committed, hard-working compañeros?" Well, no. So, in our case, we set up three eight-hour shifts, we sign in, we've got our items in the monthly wage packet, which are for punctuality, presenteeism, natural issues, cause in practice we were falling short, so we imposed stricter regulations on ourselves to make the hotel run more smoothly. Obviously, we took it on as a decision based on experience. In the early days, we'd say to each other, "See you all tomorrow at nine," but we wouldn't all get in at nine.
> ALEJANDRO, co-operative member and leading figure in
> a worker co-operative organisation, August 2016

That said, the collective creation of common rules and their compliance – with the consequent integration of the labour collective – prove to be shifting sands on which tensions and conflicts between the workers play out. In this section, I focus in particular on the exclusion of members from the recuperated hotel. Exclusion is the last and final sanction used in a co-operative and involves the termination of the relationship. It is also thus about what the labour collective decides not to integrate. Before going any further into the conflict, it is worth reviewing the regulatory instruments in our case study.

Being part of the whole means that self-determination hinges on obeying self-imposed laws through participation in the collective. Under the Co-operatives Act No. 20,337, the instruments par excellence to regulate the work process are the by-laws and internal regulations. Whereas by-laws are mandatory and legislate over general issues in the worker-co-operative form, internal regulations cover the operation of the co-operative and are adapted to the specific features of the sector and branch of activity. Both instruments have to be approved by member assembly and by the INAES. At the time of our co-operative's formation, the hotel's members submitted by-laws based on the model provided by the INAES and internal regulations that included elements of the former employers' regime mitigated by amendments introduced by the new workers collective. However, like most recuperated enterprises, the co-operative's implementation of its internal regulations is flexible, and work regulations become asystematic and disorderly (Bauni and Fajn, 2010). In this sense, our case study displays internal regulations that are "de facto" or "dispersed through proceedings" – different from formal ones – consisting of usual and customary practices, assembly resolutions and extended board meetings, and memos for the hotel's different sectors to communicate with each other:

> Things that kind of mark the hotel's regulations were established de facto. [...] there's de facto regulations as it wouldn't take much to reconstruct [...] through the memos and resolutions of the board and the assembly, but you have to get some bloke to study the whole ten years of the co-operative to be able to systematise it and say, "These are the co-operative's regulations."
> ALEJANDRO, co-operative member and leading figure
> in a co-operative organisation, January 2016

As a result, various regulatory devices have been established in the co-operative over the years: three work-shifts, a clock to clock in and out, refreshment breaks, bonuses in the wages for punctuality and presenteeism, memos for cross-sector communication through supervisors, graduated sanctions (cautions, warnings, suspensions up to thirty days, exclusions) and others.

By 2010, the board started up an integration and development project of internal regulations, which had four chapters: 1) general co-operative issues; 2) board issues; 3) area co-ordinators and sector supervisors; and 4) members' rights and obligations. Though they were drafted, the regulations were not approved by assembly, as no agreement was reached amongst members. In their stead, the amendments to the by-laws were approved a year later. Their main reform was the incorporation of posts in the board in line with the design of a new organisation chart which included area co-ordinators. This amendment, however, did not incorporate the work regulations formulated over the years in a single document.

So, we can see that the collective production of rules in the co-operative is a dynamic, erratic, asystematic process. In terms of effective compliance with the rules and sanctions, the fact that all the workers are members and that family ties are uppermost is seen as a limitation in the establishment or application of any kind of rule:

> If it's private, it's like all a bit despotic, the orders stand and it works pretty well. [...] I come from other hotels and have worked in this area all my life, and I've always studied how people behave when they're tired. So, what happens? I mean, when it's co-operative, when we're all good people, all *cumpas* [compañeros], all friends together, how do you go about giving someone an order when they're a friend of yours and have turned up drunk? What do you do, kick them out? You know their wife and their kids, cause they invited you to lunch. You don't kick them out. And that time it takes you while you're in two minds about what to do and what not to do is where it all goes wrong. It's very hard. [...] Divisions or amiguismos stem from affection, love, gratitude. Cause he brought me in or his cousin's cousin brought him in, or the cousin of the cousin as brought him. There's always a thank you, there's always people you're fond of. And then you fall into that trap yourself; by that I mean it happens to me too. You become friends with someone and it's gutting to have to tell them they've cocked up or they're doing something wrong; or when you know they're going to be kicked out and you have to keep your mouth shut or tell them. It's gutting cause it's someone you like, but you have to agree that the guy isn't going backwards or forwards [doesn't fit in]. But it happens to all of us. But, in a private business, that doesn't happen cause everything's a lot colder, everything's more orchestrated by someone upstairs who's constantly got their beady eye on you.
> FERNANDO, co-operative member, September 2014

The construction of rules aside, the issue is whether the workers' collective upholds them. This problem area has been raised and discussed by both recuperated enterprise workers and social researchers. Accusations and counteraccusations about indiscipline, dispersion, absenteeism and lack of commitment, responsibility and involvement with the co-operative are often heard in recuperated enterprises.

What hypotheses has the research into recuperated enterprises tested in this regard? To understand the lack of commitment, participation and responsibility, María de los Ángeles Di Capua et al. (2011) point to the persistence of the 'salariat habitus,' whereas Perbellini (2016) proposes the formation of a 'torn habitus' as a result of the dislocation of salaried expectations and predispositions from their new position as self-managed workers. These researchers postulate the formation of an opposition principle between leaders and led that emulates the classical labour division of the private-capital enterprise.

Juan Pablo Hudson (2011) notes that, as a result of divergent work backgrounds, the several imaginaries around work allow us to analyse the formation of such opposing generational groupings as *'laburantes'* [grafters] and *'pibes'* [kids]. The product of different work socialisations, the weight of the trade among 'senior' as against 'new' workers proves to be central (Perbellini, 2016). Even work socialisations differentiated across each sector of the original enterprise could rehabilitate the old cross-sectoral competition in the co-operative and generate divides along trade lines, as Maxime Quijoux contends (2011). Last, the persistence of a hierarchical view typical of the traditional capitalist enterprise may set those who perform leadership tasks – board and administration – against the rest of the workers (Deux Marzi, 2014; Perbellini, 2016).

That said, who in our case study does and does not respect the collective rules? How do the accusations and counteraccusations inform their non-compliance? In Chapter 4, I showed how the most extreme indiscipline, irresponsibility and disinclination for work and the trade are often attributed to the 'young' members. In contrast, this indiscipline or lack of commitment is conceived by the 'youngest' members themselves as a result, on the one hand, of 'disillusion' faced with a lack of receptiveness to their opinions in decision-making bodies and, on the other, of the weakness of sanctions and the absence of a boss:

> I don't know if it's a lack of interest or if people are disappointed when they say, "No, we can't sort this out, they won't listen to me, this is my opinion and they go and do something else"; then your interest starts collapsing, and that's reflected in the work. It's tiring, cause you spend the whole day sorting stuff out. I'm not saying it's irresponsible or nasty or anything, but it does get you down. It happens mostly with the youngsters.
> LAURA, co-operative member, May 2011

> There being no boss, you start losing your sense of responsibility. Knowing you're not going to get sanctioned or anything, you start leaving all the work to your compañero. Cause you know you won't get told off or anything.
>
> JORGE, co-operative member, August 2014

Still, as I have already mentioned, we can see that the supposed generation gap seems to be more closely related to the work background in the co-operative than members' ages or different socialisations in the world of work:

> What I was talking about was a generation gap in the co-operative between those as have just come in and us as have been here from day one. That happens to all co-operatives cause it's something basic, it's fine, it happens cause it's only normal. There's compañeros too as have never digested this. But they've been here throughout the process and all that. They've put more into the idea of actually owning a job than having a way or working or a philosophy of work. There's colleagues as have been working with us, then they get offered a more tempting job and they're off. Each one of us looks and comes here depending on how they think.
>
> OMAR, co-operative member, May 2011

I contend that 'generation' is about different linkages with the productive organisation, not merely the ages of workers: in other words, it represents generations of work as cohorts entering the co-operative. This assertion draws on Pierre Bourdieu's contributions (1990) around the category of youth. Bourdieu states that certain conflicts often perceived as generational actually occur through people or age groups forming around different relationships with the school system. So, the unifying element of a generation is established by the common relationship with a particular state of the school system. In our case, 'generation' seems to refer to different relations with the productive organisation. The categories of 'new' or 'young' members are thus often used interchangeably because the members who joined after the recuperation ('newcomers'), as opposed to the members who founded the co-operative, tend also to be younger than the latter. Accordingly, in our case study, I believe that a central oppositional divide between workers prevails in these tensions, constituted by participation in the enterprise's recuperation.

Similarly, the interview excerpt below also shows that, while disciplinary conflicts might be expected to feature 'young' or 'new' members and subsequent exclusions to occur mostly among these members, this is not necessarily the case. Members who recuperated the enterprise and founded the co-operative can also show a lack of commitment and perpetrate serious offences:

> Like in every process, there were compañeros here – I'm saying this not to put anyone down but cause it's part of reality, you can't hide it – who, even though they've been here from the start, even though they're founders, have made monumental cock-ups against the co-operative, against themselves and their own compañeros [...] which is typical when you're employed by someone else [...] but not in your own company.
> ALEJANDRO, co-operative member and leading figure in a
> worker co-operative organisation, January 2016

So, transgressions are present in the daily (re)production of labour regulations and can be a cause of exclusion: from accumulated suspensions for arriving late to stealing from the co-operative or violence against another member, via falsifying medical certificates to justify absences. Although the application of sanctions, and within them exclusions, is the job of the board, the co-operative's by-laws provide that the member concerned may appeal against the measure by assembly. We have records of the case of a member accused of theft who, after being excluded by the board, managed to have the decision reversed by calling a members' assembly and collecting the necessary votes to remain in the co-operative:

> That's how the procedures work. The board asks you for a defence and makes you aware of different situations: "You've missed the co-operative for such and such a reason, we're asking you for a defence to determine what sanction we can apply to you if need be." So, well, you do the defence and the board rules on it, "We're suspending you for seven days," or "We're excluding you." But you, even if you've been excluded, you still have the right to ask for an assembly to overturn the decision. If the member agrees, sorted. It has actually happened. There have been lots of members who've made mistakes and never asked for assembly. [...] I've been through one in my case. Cause of this other compañero, I got dragged into it myself. And I asked for the assembly. They'd excluded me, I wrote my note, asking the compañeros for an assembly to explain the sanction, so well, you've got to get 20% of signatures, I think, for the assembly to be called. Then they give you a date for you to appear and state your case before the compañeros. Then the compañeros decide whether your sanction's right or not. That's why they always say the assembly's the last one to rule on things. [...] There were somewhere between 60 and 70

compañeros: 48 compañeros voted for me, and fifteen or twenty against. […] So, I stayed. At the assembly, I was accused of having taken some money, but I hadn't taken the money. So, just imagine, almost 70% of the assembly present voted that I hadn't made any kind of mistake …

GUSTAVO, co-operative member, August 2014

I would like to focus here on the exclusions of four of the co-operative's 'founder members' in 2014. Among those excluded were the 'founder member' whose board had been removed and the 'founder member' whose daughter had been questioned about her legitimacy to hold the position of secretary on the board. These signs of past tensions, as well as the oppositions discussed above between 'founder members' and 'new' or 'young' members, lead us to a series of questions. How far can the conflicts around work regulations leading to the exclusion of 'founder members' be linked to the conflict over the running of the enterprise or, more generally, to the political dimension of this experience of self-management? Are the application and degree of sanctions associated with the characteristics of the offences and the transgressors? Inasmuch as work regulations also refer us to the formation of a labour collective, how does this conflict explain a 'refoundation' of the co-operative or an integration of the labour collective that excludes certain 'founder members'?

Let us look back over the grounds for exclusion of these 'founder members' during 2014. First, Mariela was accused of keeping donations made to the co-operative. However, this did not appear to be the only reason for the exclusion. The fieldwork led me to the observation that this member was working in the press area – which handled the hotel's institutional and political relations – whose activities were under suspicion, certainly delegitimised. Mariela's departure rocked the press office, which eventually closed shortly after the end of the period studied.

Second, Roberto, who had chaired the removed board, was excluded after being accused of plotting against the new one. The reason for his exclusion was that the board's president was warned of attempts by this member to contact specialists in co-operativism in order to question the co-operative's annual balance sheet. This action was read by the assembly as an individual attempt to damage the board, hence the decision to exclude him.

Third, Ricardo was excluded for entering into individual negotiations with the hotel's legal owner. This member delivered to the co-operative several copies of a letter drafted by the legal owner of the premises raising the prospect of agreeing a return to traditional private management, in which those members interested would be hired by the enterprise as employees. The assembly decided to exclude him on the consideration that no one was authorised to enter into individual negotiations with the former bosses.

Fourth, Osvaldo was accused of falsifying medical certificates to justify absences. While a minor offence – it was even suggested he should opt for reconsideration by the assembly – Osvaldo decided to accept the exclusion stipulated by the board. Last, that same year a non-'founder' member was excluded for using a hotel lounge for a party and charging admission, when it had been reserved and authorised for a family party free of charge. The police were called, and the whole episode proved extremely disruptive.

All in all, in the span of a year, four 'founder members' were excluded. These exclusions are even more conspicuous when we corroborate that the members excluded were not just any 'founder member,' but those categorised as *'founderer* members.' Let's review what it means to be one of the grouping of 'founders,' and then understand what it means to be a *'founderer* member.' Drawing on Rodrigo Salgado (2012), my analysis in Chapter 4 stated that this grouping has an organisational differential in its favour based on the longevity of its relationship, which produces greater social cohesion. This allows it to instil the idea that the struggle for the recuperation of the enterprise involves an investment more than economic, symbolic and emotional that has to be rewarded (Quijoux, 2011).

That said, this symbolic power, reflected in organisational resources and economic differences, comes back like a boomerang to hit a specific sector of 'founder' members, which generates the "stigmatising term" – as Norbert Elias (1996) put it – of *'founderer* members.' With the exception of Osvaldo, these members not only committed serious offences that were regarded as an insult to the co-operative but, as 'founder members,' these offences proved inadmissible: rather than looking after the interests of the project they founded, they jeopardised it. To paraphrase Elias (1996), their offences were further compounded because the anomie is usually located on the side of 'outsiders' – 'new' members – not 'established' ones – 'founder members': the former are generally considered anomic, unreliable, undisciplined, uncontrolled. So, when one of the 'established' or 'founder members' deviates from the norm, or their deviation is suspected, they are sanctioned by the same members of their group through the loss of power and the erosion of personal status.

Regarding the grievances, the cases presented are mainly offences that violate the co-operative's continuity in a context marked by the worsening of the conflict over the premises. Various political and productive projects apart, defence of the source of associational, self-managed work is a strong unifying element in the workers' collective when certain shared rules are broken and jeopardise the co-operative. Above and beyond the offences actually committed, we need to turn our gaze to the characteristics of the excluded members. Our accounts evince longer-standing tensions regarding the *founderer* members.' These include strained interpersonal relations due to the conflicts over the running of the co-operative, the aggravation of their offences, being the ones who recuperated and founded the enterprise in the first place – building and legitimising an organisational differential in their favour on the basis of this – and the emergence of a stigmatising term explaining changes in the balance of power between 'new' and 'founder' members.

Last, how do these exclusions of certain members assimilated to the boss or *'founderer'* of the enterprise involve the 'refoundation' of the co-operative? In the previous section, we looked into the results of the conflict in terms of the reversal of the unequalising process between 'founders' and 'newcomers' as of the board of 2013, which incorporated several 'new' members. Here I noted that, a year later, the exclusion of members categorised as *'founderers'* can be read as part of a process of formation and integration of the workers collective that progressively called into question the differential power of the 'founder members,' especially if these members did not comply with the labour regulations created by all. A new amalgam gradually took shape in the foundry of the workers collective and the refoundation of the self-managed venture.

3   "We Fought over the River Module": The Conflict over Autonomous Work

The design of the Argentina Works Programme provided that, once the beneficiaries were selected, the executing bodies – primarily municipal governments – formed and trained co-operatives through the INAES. The definition of their activities and the allocation of funding were organised in working modules stipulated in agreements drawn up by the National Ministry for Social Development and municipal governments. These were then signed and sealed by agreements between municipal governments and the co-operatives. By 2015, the activities carried out under the scheme included the comprehensive clean-up of the habitat, the afforestation and recovery of green spaces, and painting public buildings and public thoroughfares. To a lesser extent, between 2009 and 2015, co-operatives also engaged in productive activity, building and improving housing and public buildings, as well as ramps and pavements (National Ministry for Social Development, 2015b).

It is worth noting that, in principle, the individual subsidy granted by the scheme was not adapted to fit the assigned activity. That said, despite involving no differences in remunerations, in the co-operative analysed – and in so many others – managing to define the productive activity and the space where it would take place became a major bone of contention in work conflicts. In other words, it was not only important to access the subsidy, but also to gain more autonomy to decide what work to carry out:

> We're in a social organisation where we fight really really hard to be in the neighbourhood. Cause the municipality wanted to send us to clean up the centre of Monte Grande [the main town in Esteban Echeverría District].
> VERÓNICA, co-operative member, October 2012

The demand to carry out autonomous work in terms of the ability to define what work to do and where to do it, thus took centre stage during the early days of the scheme's implementation. Indeed, the signing of the agreements created discord and tension between the municipality and the district's co-operatives, as the criteria for defining activities according to "the municipality's needs" were at odds with the needs and demands of co-operatives. The signing of the agreements was a moment when the full scope of state power in the socio-productive form was demonstrated and, as one municipal official suggested, co-operatives "had no freedom to choose":

> So that was when we started coming into conflict, cause maybe you didn't want to work on clean-ups and preferred painting this, that or the other. That's where they really had no freedom to choose. [...] Cause maybe what they wanted was this whole "cleaning up your own door-step" thing. No, no, that *was* adapted to the municipality's needs, and we made that clear. I think it was like that in nearly every municipality, even though what people wanted was pointing in a different direction, to give or fix or add something in their local neighbourhood. Which is really very understandable too. Why do they send you downtown to pick up bin-bags when you have bin-bags in your local neighbourhood? It's really very understandable.
> Esteban Echeverría Municipality official, June 2016

That said, what exactly were the criteria built by the workers in the co-operative studied to stipulate the kind of productive activity that was most necessary or desirable? When we asked one of the members about her favourite job throughout her working history, she replied: "Here, cause we're closer, and at least we can help the local neighbourhood a bit [...] So we discuss working in our neighbourhood, for people to get to know us" (Luz, co-operative member,

September 2014). This quote shows that the co-operative's members shaped two complementary criteria to define the activity it was to perform.

On the one hand, the help for the local neighbourhood according to its needs; on the other, the search for recognition by local residents. I contend that these criteria are related to the logic of production of this co-operative, the purpose of which is not only the workers' subsistence, but political accumulation by the social organisation to which the co-operative belongs. Consequently, from the perspective of some workers and activists in the social organisation, a job is something done for one's own territory. Put another way, "It wasn't easy, cause he [the mayor] wanted to send us to the centre to collect leaves or sweep up, and we wanted to do work for the local neighbourhood. To work, *work*, not sweeping up" (Paula, Unemployed Workers Movement [MTD] member, September 2011; interviewee's emphasis – see Image 4). These criteria are not only related to the goal of political accumulation but are also linked to the centrality of the meaning possessed by the local neighbourhood in the co-operative members' daily lives: the school and children's community snack-bar, the extended family, and the sporadic, precarious jobs are often located in the vicinity of the shantytown.

Based on these criteria and within the modules outlined by the Municipality and the National Ministry for Social Development, the co-operative decided the activity it wished to carry out was the cleaning of the channel of a river belonging to the Matanza Riachuelo Basin located opposite the co-operative's premises. This involved the submission of projects by the co-operative and adaptation to the municipality's guidelines. While the original idea was to clean the river and the local neighbourhood, and to launch a waste management awareness campaign for local residents, the constraints of the scheme eventually reduced the proposal to the cleaning of the canal.

> We wanted to clean the channel, cause every time it rained, it flooded, cause of it always being blocked like. There was stacks of muck. Every time it rained, the streets filled with water, and the water wouldn't drain. Some went about cleaning up inside the local neighbourhoods too. The business about us wanting to make leaflets so as people would help out with the cleaning and not just dump stuff was also left up in the air a bit too. […] When we submitted the project, it was about cleaning the streets inside the neighbourhood and the river business. Thing is, the module's about the river. So, we fought over the river module. And then out came this module with ACUMAR.
>
> VERÓNICA, co-operative member, October 2012

IMAGE 4   The co-operative's activity
           PHOTO BY DENISE KASPARIAN (JULY 2016)

As the situation stands, we can see that the struggle to define the co-operative's productive activity is related to the presence of two conflicting logics of political accumulation: that of the state and of the social organisation. Since the dominant logic is the state's, the co-operative embedded in the social organisation with the aim of imposing its own logic has to struggle. Yet direct action unmediated by the dominant institutionality (Rebón y Pérez, 2012) does not always occur, though it is possible to resolve certain issues through arrangements and negotiations:

> Cause the government itself also realises it doesn't want the country to see that it's full of problems. […] So sometimes then you get there just with arrangements, we don't have to block [the streets].
> DANIEL, co-operative member, October 2012

Both the co-operative and the government deployed strategies to wage the struggle 'through other means,' which prevented the outbreak of open conflict. For example, while the co-operative delayed the signing of the agreement because it did not involve the working module they desired, the municipal authorities responded to this action by sending formal legal letters summoning the co-operatives to sign the agreements and by applying to the National Ministry for Social Development to delay subsequent payments of remunerations:

> Perhaps the longest conflict came when some of them digging in their heels [resisting], and there were co-operatives that wouldn't sign it, and it was all like "I don't want to be on painting, I want to be on masonry." [...] What we were doing, when the co-operatives delayed the signing of the specific agreement, was holding up the payment to them. The penalty we demanded for them from the Ministry was that: the non-payment of income.
> Esteban Echeverría Municipality official, June 2016

These situations in Esteban Echeverría produced demonstrations outside the municipality's co-operative administration centre protesting about the delay or suspension of remunerations. As we discussed in Chapter 2, during the scheme's early implementation period, demands for remunerations in collective actions featuring these organisations grew. That said, in our case analysis, we see that this demand did not emerge as a contentious dimension in itself once the co-operative was established but was linked to the demand for autonomy around productive activity.

The co-operative administration centre at which the demonstrations were directed is an administrative unit separate from the municipal structure, specially created to support co-operatives. By 2011, this unit comprised approximately 40 people, mostly Argentina Works co-operative members (Boix, Fernández and Marazzi, 2011; Reppeto, Boix and Fernández, 2011). I would like to draw attention to the spatiality of the conflicts. This had been foreseen by the municipal authorities, which was why the co-operative administration centre was located in a building a good way from the centre of Monte Grande:

> That's why the Mayor removes [the co-operative administration centre] [...] from the centre of town, so that the conflicts, when they happen, are a long way away ... the co-operative administration centre is twenty blocks from the centre. So as not to upset the *order* of the middle-classes [laughter]. Forget that, it was done purely and simply with that in mind: keeping them at arm's length.
> Esteban Echeverría Municipality official, June 2016; interviewee's emphasis

The co-operative also participated in an occupation of the co-operative administration centre to demand the payment of remunerations. On that occasion, the police arrived at the administration centre with an eviction order, but the co-operative members would not leave the building until they received an answer to their demand:

> We took the co-operative administration centre cause we had a couple of compañeros who were taken out [of the scheme], who weren't getting paid, so we went and took it. There we approached at eight in the morning, and it was occupied for about twelve hours, till we got the problem sorted.
> DANIEL, co-operative member, October 2012

Last, in 2011, the co-operative managed to secure the cleaning module for the river. In 2012, as it was already carrying out clean-up tasks in the channel, it also entered the ACUMAR River-Bank Clean-Up Programme. This involved receiving a bonus added to the amount of the remuneration contributed by the Argentina Works Programme. While this was a potential source of conflict between different co-operatives to join this second scheme, nothing of the sort occurred:

> The co-operatives that joined were the ones that already did river cleaning. So, fortunately, that definition, that selection didn't create conflict cause they were co-operatives as had already been doing such and such a job, this scheme comes out of ACUMAR that takes them into consideration and so pays them a bonus, but they didn't graft much more than the others.
> Esteban Echeverría Municipality official, June 2016

For a few months, the issues around the co-operative's activity remained stable. But another conflict arose in December 2013. The end of the year was approaching, and it was necessary to furnish the state with information about co-operative members' holidays. The assistant who kept a daily record of presenteeism and work accordingly instructed the co-operative members to draw up the holiday spreadsheet to submit to ACUMAR. The president of the co-operative was responsible for drafting it and taking it to the agency. Then it was announced that the co-operative had lost its link-up to ACUMAR's River-Bank Clean-Up Programme.

> It was 21 December, and I took it to ACUMAR, and the Environment secretary comes and says "The co-operative was left without a contract over irregularities." Being left without a contract means we only get paid 1,200 from Argentina Works and that we don't work at ACUMAR anymore. And I say, "No, I'm sorry, but I was asked for holidays, they never told me this." And he says to me, "Cause of this or that of the other." Know what I mean? They tell you one thing, and then how do you pass that on to your compañeros? Unfortunately, all of us in this thing are making a living from it.
> ADRIANA, co-operative member, January 2015

So, what were the irregularities mentioned by the ACUMAR authorities? What were the reasons for expelling the co-operative from the River-Bank Clean-Up Programme? The ACUMAR authorities contended that the contract had been dissolved as a result of repeated absences from work by the members. The co-operative defended itself by arguing the bad faith of the assistant in charge of recording presenteeism:

> He was passing on all the information wrong. For instance, he knew the ACUMAR inspectors had to drop in, and he'd tell us we had training tomorrow from 9 to 11, so we'd go along to the training session, and the inspector would stop by and say there was no one at the co-operative and mark us down as absent, and we'd say the assistant had told us. Then he'd go, "Oh, I'd forgotten," but the inspector had already been and we'd already been marked down as absent.
> ADRIANA, co-operative member, January 2015

The co-operative also defended other ways of approaching the issue. As most workers were mothers and given the time of year – December is the end of Argentina's school year – their children's timetables had to be taken into consideration. Ignoring such situations and laying down rigid labour regulations went against the rationale of fostering relationships in the social organisation:

> Then the business about calling the inspector, about supervising, about what time they come in. No, if they do that to us, we lose jobs too, cause internally we have to help out a lot of colleagues who have their family *quilombos* [troubles]. And if we adopt their formality, we're excluding a shedload of people. And they don't understand that, cause they're not from around here.
> ARIEL, member of another MTD co-operative, September 2011

Following ACUMAR's decision to distance it, the co-operative carried out a series of collective actions, both institutional and direct. On the one hand, they handed in a petition signed by local residents to the state authorities. On the other, they undertook demonstrations outside ACUMAR's headquarters in Buenos Aires and occupied one of its offices in Esteban Echeverría. These actions were supported by other organisations and co-operatives, which also took part. At first, ACUMAR would not even grant the co-operative a meeting, but eventually the co-operative managed to keep its place in the River-Bank Clean-Up Programme.

> They wouldn't give us the meeting at first. So, we went and walked in. And we wouldn't leave and told them as they had to see us. The police came, but we wouldn't go, cause we could see it looked really nasty. And anyway, we'd submitted signatures from a ton of neighbours from that area, where we clean up the pavements opposite. What we had going for us was that all the residents supported us, cause we work with the residents too, we clean the pavement, here, there and everywhere. We submitted everything, cause we learn loads of stuff through the organisation. A lot of steps coming up, and we're already taking them. We never left the module, we went on working just like before. We still get paid from Argentina Works and ACUMAR, cause we also went to the ACUMAR in the Capital. [...] The whole of our co-operative went. We said that first we'd go as a co-operative, and then the second time, we all went as one organisation. This co-operative went, the other co-operative went, other co-operatives went with us too in solidarity. The negotiation was really tough, but then they said yes, they'd rehire us.
> ADRIANA, co-operative member, January 2015

From the workers' perspective, three elements were central to achieving the desired objective: the learning furnished by participating in a social organisation when it comes to acting in conflict situations with the state, the disruptive nature of the demonstration outside the ACUMAR in Buenos Aires and, last but not least, the support of local residents, the service users. One important reason for this support was that ACUMAR's termination of the contract with the co-operative could lead to the suspension of a service valued by local residents. The logic of solidarity was thus activated, because the state authorities threatened the continued provision of a valued service carried out by the neighbourhood's own residents.

Last, I want to highlight the results of the conflict. As well as keeping the channel cleaning module, the co-operative was able to innovate in its organisation and supervision of the work: co-management devices were established to organise and supervise presenteeism. More flexibility was introduced, and the co-operative established a system of supervision of presenteeism records drawn up by state officials, which I term *presentismo cruzado* [cross presenteeism]. The state employee's presenteeism records were thus complemented by the co-operative's own. Co-operative members made their own spreadsheet in a logbook, in which, along with attendance, they recorded information about the streets covered during workdays, whether or not the refuse lorry had made a collection and other information. The assistant signed the logbook every day, so that the co-operative had back-up against possible discounts, losses of presenteeism and other issues:

> If some conflict or other crops up, out come the papers. Every time we go to get certified – yesterday we went to get certified, and then a week later the cheque comes in and then we only get paid four days after that – we read that everything's fine: the streets, where we're working, all that stuff. And if they put something in red for us, we get our little book out.
> CRISTINA, co-operative member, January 2015

In short, the analysis of the conflict over the definition and maintenance of productive activity – as one dimension of the demand for autonomy, that is, for control of the productive process – we can see that the groupings in conflict continued to be the co-operative workers – who are also members of the social organisation – and the state. This became the locus of the conflicts: the state is the object of the demands for autonomy, which contributes to the unification of the co-operativists. That said, given the socio-productive form described in Chapter 5, in which the state actor is relatively internal to the process, an oscillating relationship is shaped. Whereas negotiations and institutional actions by the co-operative are sometimes possible, the struggle leads in other instances to open conflict and direct action. By involving formal state institutions, this conflict acquired a political character.

Regarding demands, we noted that those relating to remuneration in the case studied were activated in the context of the claim to autonomy and of a conflict that was not always openly expressed but came about 'by other means' as well: negotiations, arrangements, delays in the signing of agreements and the subsequent hold-ups in payments from the Ministry. The conflict then took the form of negotiations and arrangements to the deployment of direct action – the occupation of state establishments – and demonstrations.

Since the development of the productive venture, the logics of political accumulation of the state and the organisation clashed over the definition of productive activity. When it came to maintaining this activity, it was more the need to guarantee the subsistence of the workers than the social organisation's logic of accumulation that underlay the conflict with the ACUMAR. On that occasion, the co-operative's workers were not only supported by the social organisation but the active solidarity of local residents. As users and right-holders, the residents supported the co-operative's actions with the aim of defending the continuation of a locally valued service carried out by their neighbour co-operativists, some of whom were relatives.

The fact that struggles demanding autonomy at work are expressed in the conflict around productive activity demonstrates that the importance attached by the co-operative's members to carrying out this activity in the local neighbourhood is framed by the territorial logics of popular politicity (Merklen, 2005). Succeeding in performing an activity that allows the co-operative a permanent presence in the neighbourhood is central to the political construction of the social organisation in which the co-operative is embedded. The different logics are thus complementary: whereas the social organisation promotes the clean-up of the river as a strategy for political and territorial construction, workers who do not participate in the social organisation's activities reap the benefit from collaborating with the territory and from remaining in the vicinity of the shantytown during their daily work. On the contrary, these logics come under strain in the conflict studied in the following section.

4 Between Subsistence Consumption and Political Accumulation in the Social Organisation

Once the co-operative was formed and its activity defined, another type of conflict ensued. In this case, we can safely say the state ceases to be the locus. In this section, I analyse the conflicts that eventually led to the disassociation of two co-operative members. Whereas in the conflicts analysed so far, it is the co-operative's insertion in a social organisation that allows it to pursue and process them, in these last conflicts this insertion is at the heart of the tensions observed in the group of workers.

The workers in the co-operative would arrive at the social organisation's premises between 8:00 and 8:30 a.m., the tool overseer would open the storeroom and each would take a tool to start work. The blocks to be cleaned would be stipulated beforehand by the works progress supervisor, and everyone began with a particular tool in a fraction of the sector outlined. The work would be done individually and silently, or in small groups sharing conversations. Co-operative members would collect the refuse into piles using rakes.

If they knew a refuse lorry would be sent, they would also bag it. Where there was long grass, this would be cut with machetes or grass-cutters. Another co-operative from an allied social organisation worked alongside our co-operative. They both belonged to the *Frente de Cooperativas sin Punteros* [Front for Co-operatives Without Brokers], which was formed in response to the launch of the Argentina Works Programme. The co-operatives would work together in a spatial sense but not to organise the day's work; instead, they each organised themselves and interaction was rare. The module was also shared with a third co-operative, which usually worked about 800 meters away, so their paths would not usually cross.

At some stage in the morning, the state employee in charge of recording presenteeism would arrive. They would make a note of those present, sign the co-operative's attendance logbook and leave. Sometimes they would inform co-operative members of a delivery of work clothes and ask them for their clothes and shoe sizes; sometimes they would make suggestions about the work. On certain days of the week, another state employee would also visit to supervise the progress of the works and make suggestions about how and where to proceed with the clean-up. In the event of rain or if the neighbourhood was flooded as a result of it, the workday would be called off. If the sector to be cleaned was some blocks from the premises, the co-operative members and tools would be transported in the van purchased for that purpose, which would also pick them up at the end of the day.

At the start of the day, the pace would be dynamic and steady but, by around mid-morning, at which point half an hour was set aside for a refreshment break, I began to notice a slowing of the pace among some co-operative members. This situation was attributed, on the one hand, to the refreshment break: "With the stop for refreshments, we get *pachorra* [weakness] and getting back to work again isn't the same vibe [desire] as you felt at the start" (Analía, co-operative member, November 2012). On the other hand, they mentioned the tedium of the work:

> Even I've come in with serious *fiaca* [extreme reluctance], and you don't feel like it, you look around same as yesterday, you're like taking out the same bag as you collected. [...] I push myself too, cause sometimes I don't feel like it and I'm standing there leaning against a post. [...] The same grime every day, it gets you down a bit.
>
> LUZ, co-operative member, September 2014

The co-operative's stipulated break was half an hour, from 10:30 to 11:00 a.m., when they resumed work until 12:00 noon. But it was a common occurrence after 11:00 a.m. for only one group of co-operative members to return to work, while another would extend the break for another hour until the end of the workday. This difference in work-rate and quantities was perceived by co-operative members as a result of the different predispositions of 'youngsters' and 'elders.' One of the 'young' workers noted that the 'elders' worked harder, and that this caused tensions within the group. However, given the relative autonomy enjoyed by the co-operative during working hours, she said that this difference stemmed from "the demands older people put on themselves":

> There's compañeros as work harder than others. And there's compañeros as make sure you notice and ram it down your throat. [...] And I'll tell you the truth, the people older than us are the ones as work the hardest, more than you do, and you're young. I can see the difference and I feel bad. [...] They like put demands on themselves. You say to them, "No, let me do that," but no, they want to do it, so what can you do. What can we do about it? They're grown-ups now, they're a closed book ... But then they ram it down your throat, which we don't like, cause we're saying "Don't do it," and if you do it anyway, it's cause you want to, nobody's forcing you, but all the ramming-it-down-your-throat is just annoying.
> ANALÍA, co-operative member, November 2012

During one observation of a workday, when my focus was on the dynamics of relations between the two groups, and while sharing a conversation with some 'older' workers, I took down the following field-note:

> In response to my question about work-rate and return to work after the refreshment break, the older women workers told me it's an issue that provokes arguments both on workdays and in assemblies. Sometimes the younger girls answer that they'll do the work for them if they want them to. Elena thinks it's unfair that everyone gets paid the same when they don't work the same. Yet she prefers not to change co-operatives because she already knows how everything works in this one. For example, if you're late for some personal reason, you know you won't be in trouble, and she's afraid of making a mistake or changing her mind if she changes co-operatives as two other compañeras did at the start of the year.
> Field-notes, May 2015

That said, my examination of the working day did not fully explain this tension among the workers. By observing the social organisation's political activities, we discovered that they were often carried out by the 'young' members and that this array of activities was reflected in the present records:

> [I work] on the business of the river that we're cleaning up. But I'm also in the business of the organisation, the business about the community kitchen and all that. I mean, [if I miss the co-operative] they don't record the absence cause I'm doing stuff for the movement.
> VERÓNICA, co-operative member, October 2012

In the course of our fieldwork, I took part in a festival held by the social organisation one weekend in Monte Grande's central square. On that occasion, I only met the co-operative's president and one of the 'young' workers: she told me that "some [compañeras] are on vacation, some are old and can't come, others make and send food to sell at the festival, and others don't come and do nothing." I interrupted at her last remark and asked Analía if all the co-operative's members were also members of the movement, and she answered in the affirmative. Then I asked her how she felt about the fact that some did nothing, and she replied that it annoyed her and that it was always being debated in the assemblies (Analía, co-operative member, Field-notes, February 2016).

Indeed, we can observe that the generational divide – which, at first sight, seems to inform the arguments about each member's work contributions – is constructed on various links with the social organisation that result in different conceptions and assessments about the work. Whereas some co-operative members prioritised their work in the river clean-up, others prioritised their participation in the community kitchen, the demonstrations and other activities carried out by the social organisation.

Notwithstanding the potential significance of the generational dimension for the analysis of any given organisation, we have seen that the operative divide in this co-operative is instead cultural in terms of the various assessments about the work of the organisation's activists and those who focus on the Argentina Works module. In fact, as we saw in the previous section, while the co-operative's inclusion in a social organisation increases the worker community's autonomy from the state, it also creates tensions through the combination of different production purposes. On this point, let us not forget that production in the co-operative is geared to maintaining the subsidy for the workers' subsistence consumption in the framework of logics of political accumulation by the state and also by the social organisation. In short, these discussions might be summarised in terms of a tension between two groupings of members: those who prioritise the logic of subsistence consumption and those who prioritise the logic of political accumulation by the social organisation.

This division of the group of workers is a result of the coupling of the co-operative and the social organisation. In this respect, the points raised by Daniel, one of the 'older' workers, who also participates in the social organisation's collective activities and actions, provides some food for thought:

DANIEL: I'm working here as a builder, which is what I know how to do. And we're trying to put up the community kitchen. And from a long struggle, from a long debate too, cause you know like everyone makes ... You've got to be where you feel best, most comfortable and weighing up what you know how to do and what's best for the movement. Me, doing the river cleaning work, I don't feel comfortable. Cause I think about the movement, and I can see I'm more use here. Cause this [the community kitchen] will be for us, but there, the river, the day the co-operative winds up, we disappear and ...

INTERVIEWER: So how did you all decide where everyone's going?

DANIEL: In the assembly, debating in the assembly. I had that debate and they agreed. And now you see the results, cause before there was nothing, they'd come up to me, look at me and say "*Flaco* [Mate], you didn't do nothing." There's people who come up to me today and look at what I did and what I didn't do. There's always lots of arguments, but the thing is, we make room for arguments too. That's why we are the way we are, that's why we're here. Get everybody participating. Well, some participate one way, and others participate another. Sometimes there are no materials, and they say "Hey, but you've got to get out there anyway." Right, I'm on my way over. But I tell them, "I'll make the fire today, I'll put the water on for the *mate* [yerba mate tea]. Don't ask me to go out and do the ... " And they say, "You never do nothing, you're a lazy bum, you've got to work." And I'm always ready with the reply: "I'm 53, I've already worked. You lot are kids, it's your turn to work now."

DANIEL, co-operative member, October 2012

The state is no longer present in these arguments as the object of the demands. In some cases, the state authorities may even intervene in conflicts as external actors and profit from the situation:

Loads of co-operatives had internal conflicts. They started ignoring authority. Cause what a lot of organisations would do was push the conflict to the brink, saying, "Right, we're not going to work," and that meant risking people not getting paid. And when people realised their income was threatened, they'd decide to wash their hands or whatever and, cause they saw that, through the municipality's co-operative administration centre, the co-operativist started finding a sympathetic ear beyond the organisation, it gave them a bit of independence, and they'd often take on the board and fight it out. Internal conflicts started flaring up, cause of this bid for power, if you will. For us, it was another bargaining tool for negotiating with the social organisation: "Hang on, cause we talked to these fourteen people who don't want you as president, or him as secretary, or him as treasurer."
Esteban Echeverría Municipality official, June 2016

These conflicts described by the female municipal official are avoided when a consolidated collective does not form to oppose the logic of the social organisation's accumulation, nor does the social organisation jeopardise the co-operative members' remuneration. In the case studied, individual conflicts played out as a result of these tensions which led to voluntary disassociations of co-operative members and their moves to other productive units in the scheme.

The first case of disassociation is Viviana, a middle-aged co-operative member who rarely participated in the demonstrations led by the social organisation or any other activity linked to it. Her departure was triggered by difficulties in exercising her duties as treasurer, which involved spending more of her income on work: while the cleaning of the river is only a short walk away, the treasurer of a co-operative must apportion part of their personal income to travelling to the bank located in the centre of the district, without receiving a higher payment. Thus, on one occasion, despite the importance of her signature at the bank for the daily operation of the co-operative, Viviana claimed she did not have the means to make the journey. Beyond its anecdotal value, this situation demonstrates certain tensions between Viviana and the co-operative, which led to her eventually dissociating from it and joining another. However, she also left the second co-operative and eventually joined the third co-operative in the work module.

What then lay behind Viviana's dissatisfaction which had been prompting her changing co-operatives? Two reasons emerge as central, both linked to the tension among members aligning with the logic of consumption and those aligning with the logic of political accumulation. On the one hand, the third co-operative she was attached to was not in the habit of taking part in collective protests. It thus relieved Viviana of such responsibilities usually associated with working in a co-operative inserted in a social organisation. On the other hand, the way income was distributed in the third co-operative resulted in increased individual remunerations at the expense of using this income for other purposes typical of activism in social organisations (the construction of organisations' premises, for example).

The second case of disassociation from the co-operative is Sonia, another 'older' member who was not involved in the social organisation's activities or actions. Her change of co-operative was triggered by a sanction she received following an argument over the payment of the bonus provided by participation in the ACUMAR River-Bank Clean-Up Programme. Let us not forget that this bonus is transferred to the co-operative's current account for it then to make the corresponding individual payments. A misunderstanding over payments led to Sonia and the supervisor in charge of organising them getting embroiled in the shortfall of the share belonging to another member. Under the circumstances, it was decided by assembly to sanction both members, each having to contribute half the missing money. While the supervisor responsible for distributing the individual payments accepted the sanction, Sonia accused the organisation of "stealing from her" (Field-notes, May 2015). After this incident, she decided to leave the co-operative, seeing the sanction as an infringement of her income.

In short, the motive underlying both departures is associated with remunerations, in other words, the conditions under which the work is remunerated. Disassociated members feel the co-operative's purpose geared to providing resources for the subsistence consumption of its members is infringed and strained by organisational logics they do not share. So, while these disassociations are, at first glance, 'personal' and not collective problems, it can be seen in our analysis that the conflicts involve a struggle among productive logics and among conceptions of work that set the river clean-up stipulated under the scheme against the work encompassing activism in the social organisation.

Both disassociations, it should be noted, are facilitated by the co-operative sharing the module with two other co-operatives in the territory. This allows close relations to be established with other social organisations. So, those who perceive that consumption-oriented logic is strained by other logics of accumulation stand more of a chance of reinsertion in another co-operative, a move that involves no change of activity. Another divide in the conflict becomes apparent as a result of paying attention to the logic of accumulation of the territory's various social organisations: while solidarity may at times prevail, they are also related through patterns of competition, especially when the state stops appearing as a common adversary.

5 A Comparative Lens

Both the hotel enterprise and the Argentina Works co-operative are experiences of worker co-operativism with contentious origins, analysed in general terms in Chapters 1 and 2, and, on a micro scale, through our instrumental case study in Chapter 3. The disputed origins of these experiences of twenty-first century co-operativism suggest that, despite explaining forms of adaptive co-operativism (Rebón, 2007) or forced associativity (Hopp, 2013b), they are also linked to social struggles of the working classes, like traditional co-operativism.

How are work conflicts organised once these co-operatives are established? Why do the working classes co-operatively organised fight in the absence of a boss? In the recuperated hotel's case, the autonomous co-operation of workers prompted by the recuperation of the enterprise politicises the function of management, on the one hand, in that it shows – and enables – its disputed character and, on the other, because the productive process expands, and running the co-operative involves not only organising the production of the service and its exchange, but also co-ordinating the political, social and judicial actions needed to ensure the production of the service provided. One of the work conflicts analysed is thus about the disputes over the running of the enterprise, disputes in which two enterprise projects with different ties to the expanded portion of the productive process clash.

That said, enterprise projects are not defining factors in the conflicts surrounding the running of the enterprise. At any rate, both interpersonal relationships, which mobilise project affiliations, and the role of conflict with external forces around legal ownership of the premises are central. While this conflict leads to the formation of an internal divide over how to handle the issue of the premises, its worsening tends to unify the workers' collective and tip the scales towards the enterprise project, which involves multiple relationship principles beyond market exchange. The central role of the conflict over ownership in defining what happens within the workers' collective is therefore clearly in evidence.

In the Argentina Works co-operative's case, a socio-productive form is given shape, resulting predominantly in state domination. The function of management is politicised in the sense that it involves formal state institutions. In the context of a socio-productive form that also makes room for spaces of self-determination, this state domination means that the co-operative – inserted in a social organisation – disputes more autonomy at work and seeks to escape the state subordination created a priori by the design and implementation of the scheme. This dispute is specified in the struggle to define and maintain productive activity in the framework of the scheme. The perception of the state as an external common enemy contributes to the unification of workers.

To begin with, we can contend that what mobilises the labour force's struggles is no longer its unlimited commodification or the conditions of its exploitation during the productive process – two traditional dimensions of capitalist production – but the willingness to increasingly control the productive process. In one case, the dispute plays out between the co-operative's workers – and therefore between adversaries viewed as equals in the struggle to establish a enterprise project; in the other, efforts are made to control this process at the expense of the state. In this sense, we affirm that, as the social space of dispute, the board is the locus of the conflict in the recuperated enterprise over the running of the enterprise, whereas in the Argentina Works co-operative the locus is the state, as the object of co-operative members' demands.

In the recuperated enterprise, conflicts with actors outside the workers' collective (the legal owner of the premises and the different powers of the state) not only bring about the cohesion of workers as a whole but the formation of divides by creating differentiations in the enterprise project. In the Argentina Works co-operative, conflict with the state creates more cohesion and no divides. Given the predominance of state power in this socio-productive form, potential projects and strategies are limited, while a sharper, more unified 'other' takes shape in contrast to the recuperated enterprise.

For its part, unlike the recuperated enterprise, the politicisation of the function of management in the Argentina Works co-operative does not involve the design of different enterprise or co-operative projects. The formation of different assessments of work is linked to the coupling of the co-operative and the social organisation. The co-operative is thus put under strain by the different production purposes (the social organisation's subsistence consumption and political accumulation) creating a variety of conceptions about work. This and the fact that there are other Argentina Works co-operatives in the neighbourhood, and therefore available alternatives, triggers individual conflicts around remunerations, leading to members' voluntary disassociation and moves to other co-operatives. Indeed, once we shift the focus from the state as the object of demands, disputes arise between members and even between social organisations in the struggle for political and territorial accumulation.

Regarding opposing groupings within co-operatives, they turn out to be more horizontal, flexible, multiple and mobile than traditional capitalist enterprises, where the capital–labour antagonism forms more stable and durable identities. I believe that a central element here is the way production is socially organised. The co-operative forms discussed in this book produce more democratic social production relations in worker collectives, even in spite of the state's predominance over the Argentina Works co-operative.

Workers' conceptions about work and production come to be important then, as the socio-productive forms analysed accord a central role to the involvement of their members and therefore to their perceptions and valuations. However, because they are not homogeneous, and workers are immersed in a socio-productive form that promotes non-predominant forms of work in today's societies and imaginaries, such assessments can be expressed in work tensions and conflicts.

In both case studies then, we see that native categories seem to suggest the importance of the generational divide around the different degrees of willingness to work between 'younger' and 'older' workers. However, I have shown that the generation often obscures different links with the productive unit or social organisation, depending on the co-operative form in question. Certain powers, both symbolic and material, are constructed on such links.

In the recuperated enterprise, the linkage with the co-operative – and, more specifically, having participated in the recuperation of the enterprise or not – forms groupings called 'founder members' and 'new members,' indicating that the generation refers to different cohorts entering the hotel. In the Argentina Works co-operative, the link with the social organisation shapes members who, in addition to working in the module, are activists of the social organisation and other co-operative members devoted solely to the module. Let us now look at this in more detail for the conflicts studied.

The formation of autonomous co-operation in the recuperated enterprise points to the need to build collective self-regulation procedures or devices for work that spark conflicts leading to members' exclusion. By analysing this, we explored how the power differential of 'founder members,' constructed on participation in the enterprise's recuperation, becomes a boomerang that, in an unexpected movement, decides their exclusion from the co-operative. We saw that, while the offences committed by members are fairly serious, they are magnified when carried out by 'founder members,' and among this group, by members suffering a loss of legitimacy, as evinced in the circulation of the stigmatising term '*socios fundidores*' [*founderer* members]. In fact, such exclusions demonstrate that inequalities of power in democratic and autonomous productive organisations are not permanently fixed.

In the Argentina Works co-operative, when it comes to defining activity towards the state, the co-operative's multiple logics of production produce no conflicts. The organisation promotes the clean-up of the river as a form of territorial construction framed by a logic of political accumulation. For their part, workers who do not participate in the social organisation's activities identify the benefit of the cleaning activity in helping the neighbourhood and remaining in the vicinity. Even when the continuity of the river cleaning service is questioned, local residents and service users intervene by supporting the co-operative.

The heart of the conflict behind co-operative members' disassociations is the bonus provided by ACUMAR, namely, one of the elements that lends the workers' collective self-determination. The different destinations stipulated for this money bonus and their impact on co-operative members' remunerations create conflicts at the individual level – in the sense that disputes do not involve groupings of members – in which the symbolic power of those who value work as well as activism becomes apparent, since the workers who do not participate in the organisation or share its logic are those who develop a non-conformity which even leads them to disassociation. I therefore believe that the fact that the conflict escalates to a collective dimension, or simply shuts down after individual departures, is connected to the existence of available alternatives, namely the possibility of switching to another co-operative in the scheme located in the same neighbourhood where the income from both schemes – the Argentina Works Programme and River-Bank Clean-Up – remains steady.

That said, analysing the socio-productive form also made it possible to observe that, while it certainly impacts on divides and conflicts, it does not exhaust their understanding. As we managed to ascertain, these work conflicts vary with the specific cultures, assessments and conceptions of the members, the origins and particular stories of the co-operatives, as well as the organisational resources provided by the social organisations and the structures of political opportunity present at various times and in various contexts. All in all, the analysis of conflicts in working co-operatives shows that the unification and 'founding' (in sense of 'alloy' or 'amalgamate') of the labour collectives in response to external forces, usually during constitutive conflicts over keeping and having work, coexist with centrifugal movements to control the productive process and define its purpose.

CHAPTER 7

Conclusions

This book begins with the end. I chose to reveal one mystery only to set up another. I have shown that workers from recuperated enterprises and co-operatives in the *Programa Argentina Trabaja* [Argentina Works Programme] had become actors capable of stating joint claims, which, in the context, even coincided. My challenge was to retrace their steps and understand how they had reached that point, how they had established themselves in the field of production and social conflict, and why workers were waging their struggles without bosses.

The co-operatives 'made in Argentina' and those incubated by the state in conjunction with social organisations could be quite distinct, but what contribution was there to be made in analysing them as paradigmatic experiences of twenty-first-century worker co-operativism? What elements could I draw upon to move towards a theory of the production of co-operative conflict? What facets of co-operativism could be discerned by exploring the seams of its hybrid character in specific experiences?

In the preceding pages, I provided answers – which, as in any research process, are always partial and unfinished – to my question about conflict in worker co-operatives as socio-productive forms not structured on the capital–labour relationship. Below, I articulate my principal findings along two main thematic approaches: first, I provide tools to characterise the new worker co-operativism; second, I contribute towards a theory of unrest in co-operative enterprises without bosses.

1 The New Twenty-First-Century Co-Operativism and Its Struggles Around Work

As my interest lay in forms of co-operativism emerging early in the twenty-first century, I began by outlining a specific universe of worker co-operativism: enterprises recuperated by their workers and co-operatives created within the framework of public policies. At first, the book delved into this bimodal sub-universe, analysing its specific socio-geneses and developments. These first steps in my research were conducted on two levels: one general, one case-studies. A number of central elements emerged through this approach to characterise the new twenty-first-century worker co-operativism: its *contentious socio-genesis*,

CONCLUSIONS

anchored as it is in *demands and claims around work* by the classes excluded from selling their forces of labour and therefore having *nil structural power* and weak *associational power*, and ultimately developed into a specific form of contentious politics, namely the *social movement*.

Enterprise recuperation finds its structuring element in the crisis of the productive unit and in the *infringement of the labour relationship*. Recuperation therefore becomes a workers' collective's response to exploitation relations at enterprise level. That said, in view of the widespread commodification during the turn-of-the-century crisis and within the framework of a society in which the value of work takes the form of a moral economy that makes collective action viable when this work is infringed, a *social movement* took shape based on the confluence of multiple social identities, which drove the expansion and dissemination of enterprise recuperation. I accordingly pointed out that the recuperated enterprise movement comprises two types of work struggles: those seen through the lens of Karl Marx and relations of *exploitation in productive units*, and those mentioned by Karl Polanyi in contexts of *generalisation of commodification* and social dislocation.

In terms of the analysis of *types of power*, I contend that the power of the social groupings on which this movement rests, and their ability to mobilise and instate demands is primarily of a *non-institutionalised associational* kind. This is built on the symbolic strength of the value of work and the springboard of this strength in forming an alliance of diverse social identities that nurtured the movement with political entrepreneurs and organisational resources. Additionally, by occupying productive establishments, these social groups obtain an element of structural power in their favour, since occupation gives them tools to negotiate with their former bosses and legal owners of the premises.

Given that the launch of the Argentina Works Programme was not the product of the struggle of social organisations, public policy-based co-operatives may in principle be considered 'state-induced' (Vuotto, 2011). Nevertheless, the effective formation of certain co-operatives, beneficiaries from social organisations joining the scheme and certain characteristics acquired by the scheme were the product of the *actions of unemployed workers' organisations*.

The Argentina Works Programme was an *institutional window for collective action* by unemployed workers' organisations owing to its focused nature, the questioning of the organisations' mediating role in social policy, and the context of slowing economic growth and political crisis. A *new cycle of protest* thus opened up through the scheme, bestowing the form of a social movement on the struggles of unemployed workers' organisations. Research then helps to tone down the 'induced' character of co-operatives and reveal the struggles underlying their formation. The strength of the unemployed worker movement lies in *non-institutionalised associational power* which, though *relatively weak*, manages to be formed by its constitutive social groups. This associational power is not based on the symbolic weight of a grievance (as it is in recuperated enterprises), but on the ability to mobilise and *disrupt the public order* produced by these organisations through collective action, particularly street closures. What is more, the collective actions developed around the Argentina Works Programme had a net positive effect in organisational terms on the social groupings that comprise the movement, as they helped to create two *union organisations geared to 'labourising' the demands* of the beneficiaries of social schemes with work requirement.

Based on case studies and their comparison, I analysed these constitutive moments of co-operative experiences in depth. In the case of the recuperated enterprise, two findings proved central. On the one hand, by noting that the conflict over the occupancy of the property remains open, I warned about the need to review periodisations that locate such a conflict in the early days of recuperation followed by a period of legal, productive and economic stabilisation. While my analysis does not invalidate this contribution, the case study is thought-provoking in that it points to the *processual and contentious character* of enterprise recuperation, even when the productive units reach a *stage of relative stability.*

On the other hand, behind the running feud with the external forces of the Judiciary and political power, we find a judicial dispute brought by the control and occupancy of the productive unit between the co-operative's worker collective and the legal owner of the property – and former employer – that involves state powers which even – from time to time – become the recipients of the demands. Depending on the socio-political contexts and the state power concerned, the balance tilts in favour of the co-operative or the property's legal owner. We thus saw that the *class cleavage between capital and labour force* does not disappear once the co-operative is formed; on the contrary, it takes the form of a focus of persistent unrest with forces external to the productive unit.

The class content of this cleavage is not based on exploitation relations but on *oppression relations*. By upsetting exploitation and domination relations, workers relativise the power of ownership over the control of productive process and the appropriation of the fruits of labour. However, by excluding them from effective ownership, the legal owner of the property establishes partial

CONCLUSIONS

oppression relations with workers through external conditioning for the final advance on ownership and control of production.

In the case of the Argentina Works co-operative, analysis at the micro level casts light on what the general scale tends to bypass: on the one hand, it makes visible the *interaction of national and local levels of government* in the implementation of the Argentina Works Programme; on the other, it shows the *complementarity of negotiation and confrontation* in the dynamics of co-operative formation. In concrete terms, the worker co-operative succeeded in establishing itself by taking advantage of this mixed dynamic between social organisations and state apparatuses as part of the scheme's launch. Despite observing instances of negotiation with the state authorities, the co-operative's constitutive conflict played out primarily through the collective actions of unemployed workers' organisations.

In this conflict, we also noticed that, while the setting-up of the Argentina Works co-operative meant that the social groups involved sought to enter the *state subordination relationship* implied by the social policy, the dispute was aimed at *relativising, limiting and overcoming* this relationship. So, compared to the recuperated enterprise, the dispute in this case is effectively against the state at various different levels. The conflict is not judicialised yet has a non-institutionalised dynamic driven by the organisations' collective actions.

In short, both experiences of worker co-operativism are grounded in *social struggles* featuring the *working classes excluded* from the chance of being integrated in work, around *conditions of access, consumption and remuneration for work*. Whereas the conflict in recuperated enterprises originates as a *defence* of work, the struggle in social scheme co-operatives is geared towards *access* to work. In either case, the conflicts also dispute the *conditions of their exercise* inasmuch as there is a struggle for self-management and autonomy where external powers are concerned. Accordingly, we see that the disputes did not have the formation of co-operatives either as their claim or their objective, but the defence of work or access to it. For this reason, these co-operatives are categorised as experiences of the 'new social economy' (Pastore, 2010), 'adaptive co-operativism' (Rebón, 2007) or 'forced associativity' (Hopp, 2013b). However, without invalidating such characterisations, the trajectory of this book helps to reinstate these experiences from the dawn of the twenty-first century in the historical line of co-operativism, linked to resistances to the commodification, exploitation and oppression posed by capitalism at various historical periods.

2   What Patterns of Conflicts Are There without Bosses? Towards a Theory of Unrest in Worker Co-operatives

The situation: thesis workshop. My professor proposes an exercise as simple as it is daring. Explaining my research problem in such a way that it can be understood by a family member who has no idea about what we sociologists do for a living. At the end of the day, this seemingly workaday task means putting our concerns and findings in the very eye of the storm, the starkest common sense. He gives us a week to do it.

Enthusiastic about the task in hand, my director and I set about playing with ideas and words. The Spanish word *patrón* can mean either 'boss' or 'pattern.' Could this mean our language only sees regularities and rules in work where there is a boss? Indeed, during that week, I confirm that, in its measurements, the International Labour Organisation (ILO) defines a labour dispute as a conflict between employees and employers that can be measured by the number of strikes and enterprise lockouts experienced by a country in the course of a year. My research proposes we change our eyewear, to provide guidelines in order to grasp more than just strikes over salaried employees' wage claims and working conditions. In a nutshell, my point is that the reader should understand that my research seeks to create tools to find causes and regularities in the struggles of workers without bosses.

Following Erik Olin Wright (1994), this book's central premise contends that the combinations of modes of production impact or structure contradictions, groupings and conflicts. I have therefore set out to explore the hybrid character of co-operatives in order to make the work conflicts that play out in them intelligible. Let us review the main findings.

The recuperated enterprise is a productive form self-managed by its workers, a form in which social power predominates despite the presence of elements from the capitalist mode of production. Evidence of this is that the allocation and use of resources is determined by the power of the autonomously associated workers' collective. Capitalist elements in the mode of organising production can be seen in the venture's orientation towards the production of exchange values. That said, the hybridisation scheme present in the co-operative means that the production of exchange values is geared to worker consumption – for the reproduction of life – and not to accumulation. With Rodrigo Salgado (2012) then, I differ from Wright's conceptualisation (1994), for whom accumulation in workers' self-managed production is built on the parameter of the use of surpluses. I also identified that the sale of exchange values within a capitalist economy does not exclude other economic principles, such as 'reciprocity' or 'redistribution,' as conceptualised by Polanyi (2007). Quite the contrary, these are present and shape a multiplicity of markets (public procurement, co-operative purchasing and so on) that enable the experience to be partially demarketised and given relative autonomy from the conditions imposed by the capitalist market, while still encouraging its sustainability.

The Argentina Works co-operative is a hybrid socio-productive form in which the statist mode of production is dominant and subordinate workers' self-managed production. Evidence of the predominant influence of the state is seen in the way it defines the logic of production and in the fact that it performs the function of management and supervises the productive process. Nevertheless, the existence of a certain social power over the possession of extremely limited means of production lends the co-operative a margin of autonomy.

Unlike production self-managed by workers, the co-operative's activity is not oriented to the market, but to maintaining the subsistence income provided by public policy, and its purpose is mainly defined by the objectives of state political accumulation set by officials. This apart, production is also oriented by the social organisation's criteria of political and territorial accumulation.

I therefore believe that researching the case studies has made significant contributions towards understanding hybrid socio-productive forms from this perspective. On the one hand, although recuperated enterprises display co-operative forms that insert exchange values in the capitalist market for the reproduction of their workers, a characterisation limited to this obliterates other issues. My analysis has made it possible to see that recuperated enterprises constitute productive units interwoven with a multiplicity of economic relations shaping different kinds of markets. In this sense, economic accumulation is not enough; political accumulation is also necessary to reproduce workers' lives.

On the other hand, Argentina Works co-operatives represent ways of socially organising production also aimed at their workers' reproduction but governed in turn by logics of state political accumulation and, collaterally, of political and territorial accumulation by social organisations. These are then socio-productive forms in which the logic of production is strained between workers' reproduction and various forms of non-economic, political accumulation. Based on the characterisations of the case studies, I have outlined the tensions emblematic of these socio-productive forms, as well as potential cleavages in the formation of social groupings. Let us briefly review the main findings.

In the recuperated enterprise, I identified the formation of an organisational divide around the hoarding of organisational resources by the 'founder members,' crystallising in differentials of remunerations. While, in the recuperated enterprise, people usually refer to the cleavage of age groups, I observed that the 'youngsters' were, in fact, a cohort that joined the co-operative later on and did not participate in the enterprise's recuperation and foundation. In contrast to these youngsters, the 'founder members' succeed in consolidating greater cohesion and unity, allowing them to form a symbolic and material power based on participation during the 'heroic period' (Lucita, 2009). Regarding the logic of production in the recuperated enterprise, there is an attitudinal divide based in divergent conceptions about the sustainability of the venture as expressed in enterprise projects embodied by certain leaderships. In terms of the political dimension of production, I identified an organisational divide based on a tendency for members to become permanently fixed in co-operative governance and work co-ordination positions. Groupings of 'leaders' and 'led' could thus be formed, a differentiation in which a supposed generational cleavage between 'young' and 'old' also operates, which in fact alludes to tensions between 'founders,' 'newcomers' and senior non-'founders.'

One of the cleavages in the Argentina Works co-operative takes shape around control of the productive process, potentially setting state authorities and workers at odds. These groupings have contradictory interests when it comes to controlling the productive process given the divergent logics of state officials' political accumulation, on the one hand, and of the complex unit formed through the coupling of the co-operative and the social organisation, on the other.

Furthermore, regarding workers' links to the co-operative and their consequent capacity to appropriate the fruits of labour, I observed the formation of member and non-member groupings. These groupings, however, are attenuated because the coupling of the organisation and the co-operative means that the community of workers is not formed on the basis of the co-operative's formal integration but through those who receive individual subsidies belonging to the social organisation. Regarding the political dimension of production, I identified an organisational divide between 'leaders' and 'led' which is, nevertheless, limited, because the 'leaders' do not abstain from manual work. On the contrary, the 'leader'-'led' groupings are not in accord with a differentiation between manual and non-manual workers. Last, I found an attitudinal or cultural divide around the meanings attributed to work, generating the formation of activist and non-activist groupings.

Having said that, what actually happens in what disputes? Who confronts who, and what are the reasons underlying dissatisfactions with these socio-productive spaces? I now review the work conflicts analysed in the book and then go on to highlight certain significant elements in the construction of a theory of unrest in worker co-operatives.

CONCLUSIONS

In both cases, workers in the constitutive conflicts confront external actors: the legal owner of the property and the various powers of the state in the recuperated enterprise, and the state apparatuses of the Executive in the Argentina Works co-operative. I observe that a more varied external other is formed in recuperated enterprises, ranging from private owners to the three state powers, whereas the invariant locus of conflict in the Argentina Works co-operatives is the Executive at various government levels. So, in both cases, the dispute is politicised, involving as it does formal state institutions as intermediaries or the object of demands.

Whereas, in Argentina Works co-operatives, the state intervenes directly in the conflict, as this revolves around entry into the scheme financed, designed and implemented by state apparatuses, in recuperated enterprises any such intervention is indirect. At certain times, depending on its different levels, the state may mediate in the conflict (let us not forget the early stages of the commercial company's bankruptcy trial and the role of the Judiciary), whereas other times it is the recipient of demands (for example, when demands are made for an expropriation law).

Once the co-operatives are established, other conflicts arise. In the recuperated enterprise, after the class antagonism of production has been dismantled, the function of management is politicised in two senses. On the one hand, the construction of the workers' autonomous co-operation, involving a reorganisation of power in the productive unit, highlights the political dimension of the function of management and its contentious character, namely, the fact that politics is conflict. On the other hand, the characteristics of the recuperated enterprise's origins mean that the productive process expands to encompass not just the tasks needed to provide and market the service, but a series of political, social and legal activities necessary to ensure the co-operative's sustainability and secure occupancy of the premises. In this way, running the enterprise involves making room for such expanded production.

Given the co-operative's medium size and its consequent difficulties dealing with issues in the assembly, the board is the locus of conflict, a space where political struggle over the running of the enterprise is settled. Its characteristics are those of an institutionalised struggle, remaining as it does within the bounds of the co-operative's rules regarding the formation of boards: elections, assemblies for board member removals and other such business. The dispute thus occurs between workers who see themselves as adversaries, equals in the struggle to establish a productive, political enterprise project.

In this context, a kind of work unrest takes shape focused on the dispute over the control of the extended productive process, based on multiple and flexible divides conditioned by interpersonal relationships and the conflict over the occupancy of the property. Although the 'founder member'–'new member' divide applies here inasmuch as the lists of candidates and board members are drawn up around such social categories, these are not the identities that clash over the running of the enterprise; rather, this is down to the clash between productive political projects embodied in personal leaderships. That said, the positioning of members in terms of support for one project or another is linked to interpersonal relationships and to the moments of conflict over occupancy of the property. When conflict worsens, the balance tends to shift in favour of the project that recognises the political nature of enterprise recuperation and the expansion of the productive process to the detriment of the project focused solely on its commercial side.

The dismantling of capitalist domination also establishes collective self-regulation of work as the central theme of the unrest. This self-regulation involves the rules or procedures for the organisation and co-ordination of work established by co-operative members, and which contribute to the formation of a community of workers. In co-operatives, the exclusion of members for serious or repeated failings is established as a final measure. Among the exclusions observed, I focus on those of certain 'founder members.' The exclusion of such *'founderer* members,' beyond any failings or transgressions committed, explains that the symbolic power upon which the differentiation between 'founders' and 'newcomers' is based is not set in stone, but can be questioned, resisted and even reversed. In this sense, the failings take on greater proportions when they are committed by members who recuperated and founded the co-operative, all the more so when these members are undergoing a process of delegitimisation that enables the emergence of a stigmatising term like *'founderer* member,' triggered by the exponential growth of workers joining the co-operative as members and therefore having equal rights.

In the Argentina Works co-operative, there is also a politicisation of the function of management and the conflict, albeit in another direction. As I have pointed out, formal state institutions are central to the socio-productive form that shapes the co-operative, so the productive process immediately becomes political. From the state's perspective, production management in a sense also involves the management of public policy, and so the politics of production are directly state politics. Consequently, the work conflicts that play out there are politicised by virtue of the social relations and institutional context in which they are embedded.

Specifically, the struggle to define and maintain the clean-up of the river is aimed at securing more autonomy in the workplace and escaping the subordination created by the design and implementation of the scheme. This is evidence of another political dimension to the process: performing this activity in the local neighbourhood, and not some other activity somewhere else, not only provides margins of autonomy but deepens the social organisation's political and territorial construction. The constitution of the state as the enemy in this dispute helps to unify the workers' collective.

The locus of the unrest in this co-operative thus consists of the state as the object of demands. That said, the state actor being relatively internal to the productive process shapes a relationship with the state that is not just contentious but oscillates between co-existence and negotiation in the running of the scheme, and the conflict over control of the productive process. As a result, the social organisation's actions succeed in establishing co-management rather than self-management devices, which, in addition to granting the co-operative spheres or niches of autonomy, help to achieve consent regarding the state's domination.

Regarding the conflicts between the workers in the Argentina Works co-operative themselves, and while, in native terms, the tension is conceptualised around youngsters and seniors' different attitudes towards work, the coupling of the co-operative and social organisation creates divergences around conceptions of work among co-operative members and divides regarding the logic of production. Looking beyond the predominant logic stipulated by the state, two purposes of production – though complementary – put a strain on the co-operative: on the one hand, workers' subsistence consumption; on the other, the social organisation's political accumulation. These logics give rise to different conceptions about work, which lead in turn to individual conflicts about remunerations.

I observed that those who dissociate themselves from the co-operative as a result of conflicts are members who only perform cleaning river-cleaning tasks and do not participate in the social organisation's activities. In other words, work, for them, is limited to the co-operative. This brings to light a thought-provoking difference from the recuperated enterprise, where the symbolic and material power of the 'founder members' is questioned, and some are even excluded. By contrast, it is harder in the Argentina Works Programme's productive unit to question the logic of activists, namely, those who prioritise the social organisation's activities over the cleaning services. This is because the coupling of the co-operative and the social organisation means that both the decision-making bodies and the sources of power do not lie solely in the co-operative but primarily in the social organisation.

Moreover, questioning the prevailing logics is less necessary from the perspective of anyone dissatisfied because a central factor in the conflict within the Argentina Works co-operative not escalating to a collective level is the availability of alternatives: there are other Argentina Works co-operatives in the neighbourhood with room for workers. For this reason, they can dissociate themselves from the co-operative that starts the disagreement without losing income. So, while conflict with the state is a central focus of analysis of public-policy co-operatives, when we shift our optic, we see disputes between members and between co-operatives embedded in different organisations.

By way of a summary, in what follows, I make some contributions towards a theory on work unrest in co-operatives. First, I assert that the way production is organised socially speaking has a significant impact on work conflicts. In both types of co-operative, this kind of organising production gives rise to a *democratisation of the workplace* that incentivises participation by their workers and encourages them to express their opinions and conceptions. In the same vein, as well as democratising the workplace, the socio-productive forms analysed *democratise the conflict*: producing more participative, more horizontal dynamics opens up the possibility of expressing disagreements under flexible and varied patterns of relating.

For this reason, the second point of note is that *themes or sources of unrest*, that do exist but fail to be expressed in labour contexts governed by the labour–capital relationship, become important. The co-operative forms analysed tend to encourage workers to question numerous dimensions of the processes. This field sees subjects of struggle emerging, such as a growing will to control productive processes, remunerative income, and working speed and time, or their flipside, leisure time. These themes are based on factors that are not expressed with the same importance or weight in traditional capitalist enterprises. These include workers' various perceptions of their own work, the emergence of different enterprise projects, cohorts of workers in the productive units, as well as networks of *compadrazgo* [comradeship].

Third, I noted that these sources of discontent, dissatisfaction and conflict are not necessarily specific to the co-operative form. In other words, the absence of personifications of capital in work relations does not imply the eradication of conflict, which is inherent in any work relationship involving social co-operation. In today's societies, work is not just a source of social recognition and personal fulfilment; it is primarily a wellspring of resources needed for reproduction of life. Therefore, regardless of the nature of the relationships that frame their work or the way in which production is socially organised, workers will find sources of tension in (invariably relative) deprivations around remunerations, the capacity to control the productive process and hence self-determination, opportunities for personal fulfilment or the availability of leisure time. These are, therefore, *intersecting points of unrest*, even though the unrest seen in co-operatives cannot be studied exclusively using categories from labour unrest studies.

A fourth point is that one of the central differences between work unrest in capitalist and co-operative forms is found in the *opposing groupings* and the *parity of their relations*. I noted that the conflicts activate divides that make up more varied, horizontal, and flexible opposing groupings compared to traditional private-capital enterprises, in which the labour–capital antagonism tends to constitute stable identities and cleavages. As in the sources of unrest, the divides are anchored in the differences between work generations or cohorts joining co-operatives; in different linkages with productive organisations (more or less linked to activism or socio-political participation); in different assessments about work, the productive process and enterprise projects; in interpersonal and 'comradeship' relations and other issues. Unlike labour disputes in capitalist forms of production, I contend that in both types of co-operatives unrest over conditions of consumption of and remuneration for work are not embedded in exploitation relations during the productive process, nor are they geared to blocking unlimited commodification of the labour force.

Fifth, the *possibility of adjustment* or *institutionalisation of the conflict* in co-operative forms became apparent. In general, the channels of resolution are laid down in the same worker-co-operative legal form; despite worsening, confrontations do not overstep institutional channels. For example, in the conflict that led to the removal of a board, even exclusions of members and voluntary dissociations were based on institutional guidelines.

Sixth, it should be remembered that, even giving central importance to the way production is socially organised, other elements that go beyond the socio-productive form and have dissimilar gravitation must be included in the conflicts' chain of causality. I am referring primarily to co-operatives' *socio-geneses* and *particular characteristics of the constitutive conflicts*, but also to workers' different conceptions of their own work, production and politics, the organisational resources they can bank on to express their demands, as well as the social, political and economic contexts that may provide opportunities or constraints for action. In short, I would suggest that conflicts are the result of multiple variables, among which the co-operative form in which production is organised is a central factor – albeit not the only one – when it comes to understanding how they are structured.

Last, *I do not conceive a unilinear analytical schema*. On the contrary, I believe that conflicts impact how democratised the workplace is and, potentially, how production is socially organised. In this sense, for example, I noted that certain conflicts alter the make-up of boards and increase the degrees of autonomy from external powers. In short, they transform the balances of power.

3   From Prelude to Present: A Toolbox for New Research Questions

This is as far as we have got. The book's findings become an immediate toolbox for analysis and a substratum from which to frame new questions. Now, my interest lies in posing two questions that could fuel future lines of inquiry.

In principle, it would be fruitful to extend the comparative schema. For one thing, it would be relevant to integrate recuperated enterprises with wage earners in the analysis in order to observe the extent to which the co-operative form continues to promote a democratisation of work relations, even with the constraints imposed by the wage relation in terms of the equality it fosters amongst workers. For another thing, it would be necessary to analyse state-incubated co-operatives, but not ones taking part in social organisations, in order to establish the extent to which the absence of social organisation impacts the co-operative form's democratisation and autonomy.

The analysis has helped to trace a central tying the experiences of twenty-first-century worker co-operativism in with traditional co-operativism, based on their common link to working-class struggles. It would therefore be interesting to integrate traditional worker co-operativism into the analysis. Given that the democratisation established by the socio-productive form is central to understanding the lines of conflict that emerge, I would like to pose the following question. What would the configuration and dynamics of work conflicts be like in productive units that, in addition to the elements described here, had the will of their members to form co-operatives based on their values and ideologies? What commonalities and differences could be outlined? Where the proposed analytical schema is concerned, broadening the scope of the comparison would help to gauge the relative weight of the elements intervening in the causal chain of conflicts beyond the socio-productive form.

To frame the second line of research, I pick up the book's starting point. There, I positioned myself in a new social, political and economic context ushered in by the change of national government in late 2015. It is now worth asking about the possible changes in the configuration and dynamics of conflicts in the social universes investigated and about the feasibility of these socio-productive forms against a background of changes in the accumulation model and a different structure of opportunities – or restrictions – for collective action.

In the case of recuperated enterprises, with adverse conditions for the domestic market between 2015 and 2019, and in a context of economic stagnation that has deepened with the COVID-19 pandemic and social distancing measures, I ask whether further recuperations are possible. On the basis of what elements will their subsequent developments be consolidated? How have the political and productive projects of recuperated enterprises readjusted, first in a context unfavourable to their development between 2015 and 2019, and then faced with the crisis triggered by the COVID-19 pandemic? Taking into account Erik Olin Wright's statement (2015) that the limitations of low scales and the isolation of individual experiences can be circumvented by liaisons forming a co-operative market, I ask to what extent can this new context help or hinder the consolidation of a co-operative market.

Regarding the Argentina Works Programme, the changes in social policy during 2018 resulted in the elimination of the obligation of work requirements in co-operatives. How did this affect co-operatives created under social policies? What impact did it have on the reconfiguration of the socio-productive form outlined in this book? Bearing in mind that social empowerment in these experiences is linked to the dynamics of relations between social organisations and the state, to what extent did changes in government shift the balance of social power by altering these dynamics?

On another front, this change of scenery has promoted large-scale collective actions featuring organisations of recuperated enterprise and co-operatives under social schemes. Driven by the *Confederación de Trabajadores de la Economía Popular* [Confederation of Workers in the Popular Economy], these kinds of actions even brought about the enactment of the *Ley de Emergencia Social* [Social Emergency Act] of 2016, whose central measure was to establish a complementary social wage for workers in the popular economy. Again, bearing in mind that social empowerment generated by co-operative forms is enhanced by greater degrees of organisational liaison between isolated experiences, I would ask whether these collective actions form a base for deepening the co-operative convergence discussed in this book. Just as there was a shift during the last decades of the twentieth century from popular politicity anchored in the workplace to another anchored in the neighbourhood, to what extent have social policies promoting co-operativism left lasting traces in a 'relabourisation' of popular politicity?

Mindful of the horizons marked out by the perspective of emancipatory social science, analysing institutional and productive alternatives that increase social power always involves the challenge of inquiring into its obstacles and dilemmas. I believe this book has taken up this a challenge with the conviction that work without bosses can illuminate paths of emancipation towards the construction of a fairer economy.

Bibliography

Acosta, M.C., Levin, A. and Verbeke, G. E. (2013). El sector cooperativo en Argentina en la última década. *Cooperativismo & Desarrollo*, 21(102), 27–39.

Adelantado, J., Noguera, J. A., Rambla, X and Saez, L. (1998). Las relaciones entre estructura y políticas sociales: una propuesta teórica. *Revista Mexicana de Sociología*, 60(3), 123–156.

Agencia de Noticias Redacción (ANReD) (25 de febrero de 2006). B.A.U.E.N: Dar la pelea hasta el final. Por L. Castiglioni. Available at: http://bit.ly/36NrQWO [Consulted 6 January 2017].

Agencia de Noticias Redacción (ANRed) (20 November 2009). Urgente: Represión policial en Movilización en Esteban Echeverría por Cooperativas sin punteros. Available at: https://bit.ly/3E0QbKk [Consulted 20 July 2015].

Agencia de Noticias Redacción (ANRed) (18 March 2011). Se presentó la Asociación Gremial de Trabajador@s Cooperativ@s, Autogestiv@s y Precarizad@s. Available at: https://bit.ly/2M7lMAl [Consulted 28 May 2015].

Agencia Universitaria de Noticias y Opinión de la Universidad Nacional de Lomas de Zamora. (25 November 2009). La CTA se movilizó por el centro de Monte Grande. Available at: http://bit.ly/2u1WfTZ [Consulted 20 July 2015].

Alternative Economic Forms survey (2012). Encuesta Formas Económicas Alternativas. Centro de Estudios para el Desarrollo de la Economía Social en América Latina/ Instituto de Investigaciones Gino Germani, Universidad de Buenos Aires.

Antón, G., Cresto, J., Rebón, J and Salgado, R. (2011). Una década en disputa. Apuntes sobre las luchas sociales en la Argentina. In: Modonessi, M. and Rebón, J. (eds.), *Una década en movimiento. Luchas populares en América Latina en el amanecer del Siglo XXI* (pp.19–44). Buenos Aires: Consejo Latinoamericano de Ciencias Sociales.

Arcidiácono, P. (2011). El protagonismo de la sociedad civil en las políticas pública: entre el "deber ser" de la participación y la necesidad política. *Revista del CLAD Reforma y Democracia*, 51, 155–176.

Arcidiácono, P. and Bermúdez, A. (2015). Clivajes, tensiones y dinámicas del cooperativismo de trabajo bajo programas sociales: el boom de las cooperativas del Programa Ingreso Social con Trabajo – Argentina Trabaja. *Revista del CESOT*, 7, 3–36.

Arnold, T. C. (2001). Rethinking moral economy. *The American Political Science Review*, 95(1), 85–95.

Asociación Gremial de Trabajadores Cooperativistas Autogestivos y Precarizados (AGTCAP) (29 September 2012). Qué es la AGTCAP. Available at: http://bit.ly/3b6hEMb [Consulted 10 June 2016].

Balbi, F.A. (1998). *"Esos son acopiadores": moralidad y conflicto en una cooperativa de pescadores entrerrianos. Una etnografía.* (Unpublished Master's thesis in Social

Anthropology). Facultad de Humanidades y Ciencias Sociales, Universidad Nacional de Misiones, Misiones.

Basualdo, E. (2013). *Estudios de historia económica argentina: Desde mediados del siglo xx a la actualidad.* Buenos Aires: Siglo XXI.

Bauni, N. (2011). *La forma de los conflictos laborales de los trabajadores que luchan contra la precarización en la Argentina 2006–2009.* (Unpublished Master's thesis in Social Relations at Work). Facultad de Ciencias Sociales, Universidad de Buenos Aires, Buenos Aires.

Bauni, N. and Fajn, G. (2010). Las regulaciones de trabajo en las empresas recuperadas: orientaciones y alternativas. In: *Gestión obrera. Del fragmento a la acción colectiva* (pp.10–30). Montevideo: Universidad de la República; Nordan-Comunidad.

Bialakowsky, A., Robledo, G., Grima, J.M., Rosendo, E. and Costa, M.I. (2004). Empresas recuperadas: cooperación y conflicto en las nuevas formas de autogestión de los trabajadores. *Revista Venezolana de Gerencia*, 9(26), 229–253.

Boix, M.V., Fernández, J.P. and Marazzi, V. (2011). *Implementación del Plan Argentina Trabaja en Esteban Echeverría. Sistematización de la experiencia.* (Working Paper 60). Buenos Aires: Centro de Implementación de Políticas Públicas para la Equidad y el Crecimiento.

Bottaro, L. (2012). Sentidos, representaciones y prácticas de trabajo en organizaciones comunitarias de la Región Metropolitana de Buenos Aires. Un análisis comparativo. *Trabajo y Sociedad*, 19, 167–187.

Bourdieu, P. (1990). *Sociología y cultura.* México City: Grijalbo.

Burawoy, M. (1983). Between the labour process and the state: the changing face of factory regimes under advanced capitalism. *American Sociological Review*, 48(5), 587–605.

Burawoy, M. (1989). *El consentimiento en la producción. Los cambios del proceso productivo en el capitalismo monopolista.* Madrid: Ministerio de Trabajo y Seguridad Social.

Burawoy, M. (2008). The public turn: from labor process to labor movement. *Work and Occupations*, 35(4), 371–387.

Burawoy, M. (2015). A new sociology for new social movements. *Rhuthmos*. Available at: http://bit.ly/2SdomnV [Consulted 12 June 2015].

Caillé, A. (2009). Don. In: Cattani, A. (org.), *Diccionario de la otra economía* (pp.115–199). Buenos Aires: Consejo Latinoamericano de Ciencias Sociales/Universidad Nacional General Sarmiento/Altamira.

Calloway, C. (2016). Autorregulación de los colectivos autogestivos de trabajadores/as. *Revista Idelcoop*, 218, 11–30.

Castel, R. (1995). *La metamorfosis de la cuestión social. Una crónica del salariado.* Buenos Aires: Paidós.

Castillo, J.J. (2000). La Sociología del Trabajo hoy: la genealogía de un paradigma. Trabajo y Sociedad, 2(3). Available at: https://bit.ly/313RCpb [Consulted 15 February 2021].

Clarín (21 November 2009). Detienen a 15 piqueteros tras un choque con la Policía en el conurbano. By: Debesa, F. Available at: http://bit.ly/2GKhcFx [Consulted 15 May 2012].

Confederación de Trabajadores de la Economía Popular (CTEP) (n.d.). Nosotros. Available at: http://bit.ly/2Oi8UZE [Consulted 15 June 2013].

Coraggio, J. L. (2008). La sostenibilidad de los emprendimientos de la economía social y Solidaria. *Revista Otra Economía*, 2(3), 41–57.

Cortés, R., Groisman, F. and Hoszowski, A. (2004). Transiciones ocupacionales: el caso del Plan Jefes y Jefas. *Realidad Económica*, 202, 1–18.

Coser, L.A. (1961). *Las funciones del conflicto social*. México City: Fondo de Cultura Económica.

Coser, L.A. (1970). *Nuevos aportes a la teoría del conflicto social*. Buenos Aires: Amorrortu.

Cotarelo, M.C. and Fernández, F. (1997). La toma de fábricas. Argentina, 1964. *Razón y Revolución*, 3. Available at: http://bit.ly/3txdeqg [Consulted 17 March 2021].

Dal Ri, N.M. and Vieitez, C.G. (2001). *Trabalho associado: Cooperativas e empresas de autogestão*. Río de Janeiro: DP&A.

Damill, M. and Frenkel, R. (2015). La economía bajo los Kirchner: una historia de dos lustros. In: Gervasoni, C. and Peruzzotti, E. (eds.), *¿Década Ganada? Evaluando el legado del Kirchnerismo* (pp. 1–41). Buenos Aires: Debate.

Danani, C. (2009). La gestión de la política social: un intento de aportar a su problematización. In: Chiara, M and Di Virgilio, M.M. (eds.), *La gestión de la política social. Conceptos y herramientas* (pp.11–34). Buenos Aires: Universidad Nacional General Sarmiento/Prometeo.

Danani, C. and Hintze, S. (2011). Introducción: Protección y seguridad social para distintas categorías de trabajadores: definiciones conceptuales, propuestas de abordaje e intento de interpretación. In Danani, C. and Hintze, S. (eds.), *Protecciones y desprotecciones: la seguridad social en la Argentina 1990–2010* (pp. 9–29). Los Polvorines: Universidad Nacional General Sarmiento.

De la Garza Toledo, E. (2009). Hacia un concepto ampliado de trabajo. In: Neffa, J.C., de la Garza Toledo, E. and Muñiz Terra, L. (eds.), *Trabajo, empleo, calificaciones profesionales, relaciones de trabajo e identidades laborales* (pp. 111–140). Buenos Aires: Consejo Latinoamericano de Ciencias Sociales.

De Sousa Santos, B. and Rodríguez, C. (2011). Para ampliar el canon de la producción. In: De Sousa Santos, B. (ed.), *Producir para vivir: los caminos de la producción no capitalista* (pp. 15–61). México City: Fondo de Cultura Económica.

Dejours, Ch. (1992). *Trabajo y desgaste mental. Una contribución a la psicopatología del trabajo*. Buenos Aires: Humanitas.

Deux Marzi, M.V. (2014). De la recuperación a la consolidación. Análisis y perspectiva del trabajo y sus formas de organización en procesos de recuperación de empresas.

Argentina, 2000–2010. (Unpublished Doctoral thesis in Social Sciences). Facultad de Ciencias Sociales, Universidad de Buenos Aires, Buenos Aires.

Deux Marzi, M.V. and Hintze, S. (2014). Protección y seguridad social de los trabajadores asociativos autogestionados. In: Danani, C. and Hintze, S. (eds.), *Protecciones y desprotecciones (II). Problemas y debates de la seguridad social en la Argentina* (pp. 311–361). Los Polvorines: Universidad Nacional General Sarmiento.

Di Capua, M., Marcheroni, J., Perbellini, M., Solero, C., Tavella, M. and Valentino, N. (2011). Empresas Recuperadas: cooperación y conflictividad. *Revista del OSERA*, 5. Available at: http://bit.ly/39or5Ln [Consulted 15 June 2013].

Dunlop, J. (1958). *Industrial relations system.* New York City: Holt and Company.

Edwards, P.K. (1990). *El conflicto en el trabajo. Un análisis materialista de las relaciones laborales en la empresa.* Madrid: Ministerio de Trabajo y Seguridad Social.

Edwards, R. (1978). *Contested terrain. The transformation of the workplace in the twentieth century.* New York City: Basic books.

Elias, N. (1996). Ensayo acerca de las relaciones entre establecidos y forasteros. *Reis*, 104(3), 219–251.

Enríquez, M. (2016). Bajo el agua negra. In: *Las cosas que perdimos en el fuego* (pp. 155–174). Buenos Aires: Anagrama.

Esping-Andersen, G. (1993). *Los tres mundos del Estado del Bienestar.* Valencia: Edicions Alfons El Magnánim/Generalitat Valenciana/Diputació Provincial de Valéncia.

Etchemendy, S. and Collier, R.B. (2008). Golpeados pero de a pie. Resurgimiento sindical y neocorporativismo segmentado en Argentina (2003–2007). *POSTData*, 13, 145–192.

Fajn, G. (ed.) (2003). *Fábricas y empresas recuperadas. Protesta social, autogestión y rupturas en la subjetividad.* Buenos Aires: Centro Cultural de la Cooperación Floreal Gorini.

Farías, A.H. (December, 2014). Hacia una sociología de las distinciones de las clases trabajadoras marginalizadas. Un ingreso desde el análisis de contenido de redes de sentido de trabajadores marginalizados del sur del conurbano bonaerense (2010–2013). *VIII Jornadas de Sociología de la Universidad de La Plata.* Universidad Nacional de La Plata, La Plata.

Farinetti, M. (1999). ¿Qué queda del "movimiento obrero"? Las formas del reclamo laboral en la nueva democracia argentina. *Trabajo y Sociedad*, 1. Available at: http://bit.ly/2OjSuQp [Consulted 10 May 2016].

Fernández Álvarez, M.I. (2007). En defensa de la fuente de trabajo: demandas y prácticas de movilización en una empresa recuperada de Buenos Aires. *Avá*, 11, 63–85.

Fernández Álvarez, M.I. (2012a). Ocupar, resistir, producer ... sostener. El problema de la sustentabilidad en las experiencias de gestión colectiva del trabajo. *Revista del OSERA*, 7. Available at: http://bit.ly/2GNufWE [Consulted 10 May 2016].

BIBLIOGRAPHY

Fernández Álvarez, M.I. (2012b). "Luchar" por trabajo, trabajar "luchando": prácticas cotidianas de organización y demanda en una empresa recuperada de Buenos Aires. *Papeles de Trabajo*, 23, 11–26.

Fernández, A.M. and Borakievich, S. (2007). La anomalía autogestiva. *Revista Campo Grupal*, 92. Available at: http://bit.ly/31lFPSn [Consulted 29 December 2016].

Finchelstein, D. (2012). Políticas públicas, disponibilidad de capital e internacionalización de empresas en América Latina: los casos de Argentina, Brasil y Chile. *Apuntes*, 39(70), 103–134.

Fonseca, C. (1999). Quando cada caso NÃO é um caso. Pesquisa etnográfica e educação. *Revista Brasileira de Educação*, 10, 58–78.

Gamallo. G. (2012). Desmercantilización del bienestar. Aproximaciones críticas a los derechos sociales y a la política social. El caso de la educación. *Congreso de la Asociación de Estudios Latinoamericanos*. San Francisco: Latin American Studies Association.

Golbert, L. (2007). Argentina: aprendizajes del Programa Jefes y Jefas de Hogar Desocupados. In: Arriagada, I. (ed.), *Familias y políticas públicas en América Latina: una historia de desencuentros* (pp. 401–416). Santiago: Comisión Económica para América Latina y el Caribe.

Gómez, M. (2014). *El regreso de las clases. Clase, acción colectiva y movimientos sociales*. Buenos Aires: Biblos.

González, G.D. (2009). Escenario político-electoral de la provincia de Buenos Aires. *Revista de Ciencia Política*, 8. Available at: https://bit.ly/3toHGCK [Consulted 10 May 2020].

Grassi, E. (2012). Política sociolaboral en la Argentina contemporánea. Alcances, novedades y salvedades. *Revista de Ciencias Sociales de la Universidad de Costa Rica*, 135–136, 185–198.

Groisman, F. (2008). Inestabilidad de ingresos y desigualdad durante la reciente fase de recuperación económica en la Argentina (2004–2007). *Estudios del Trabajo*, 36, 29–47.

Groisman, F. (2011). Argentina: Los hogares y los cambios en el mercado laboral (2004-2009). *Revista de la CEPAL*, 104, 81–102.

Grondona, A. (2012). *"Tradición" y "traducción": un estudio de las formas contemporáneas del gobierno de las poblaciones desempleadas en la Argentina*. (Doctoral thesis in Social Sciences). Facultad de Ciencias Sociales, Universidad de Buenos Aires, Buenos Aires.

Hintze, S. (2013). Las políticas públicas de promoción del trabajo asociativo autogestionado en América Latina. *Revista del OSERA*, 9. Available at: http://bit.ly/31nrgoH [Consulted 10 May 2016].

Hobsbawm, E. (2009). Introducción. In: *Formaciones económicas precapitalistas* (pp. 9–64). México City: Siglo XXI.

Hodson, R. and Roscigno, V. (2004). The organizational and social foundations of worker resistance. *American Sociological Review,* 69(1), 14–39.

Hopp, M. (2012). La sostenibilidad de los emprendimientos asociativos y autogestionados: Reflexiones para la construcción de la Economía Social en Argentina. *Revista Org & Demo,* 12(2), 39–58.

Hopp, M. (2013a). Políticas de promoción del trabajo asociativo y autogestionado en la Argentina actual: un balance. *Revista del OSERA,* 9. Available at: http://bit.ly/37Sfwpp [Consulted 10 May 2016].

Hopp, M. (2013b). *El trabajo ¿medio de integración o recurso de la asistencia? Las políticas de promoción del trabajo asociativo y autogestionado en la Argentina (2003–2011).* (Unpublished Doctoral thesis in Social Sciences). Facultad de Ciencias Sociales, Universidad de Buenos Aires, Buenos Aires.

Hudson, J.P. (2011). *Acá no, acá no me manda nadie: empresas recuperadas por obreros 2000–2010.* Buenos Aires: Tinta Limón.

Hudson, J.P. (2016). Gobiernos progresistas y autogestión en la Argentina 2003–2015: cooperativas no-estatales, sintéticas y anfibias. *Revista latinoamericana de estudios del trabajo,* 34, 91–122.

Hyman, R. (1981). *Relaciones industriales: una introducción marxista.* Madrid: H. Blume.

Itzigsohn, J. and Rebón, J. (2015). The social bases of the solidarity economy transformative possibilities in the global South. *4th Annual Conference of Sociology of Development.* Brown University, United States.

Kasparian, D. (2013a). De alianzas y solidaridades. Las articulaciones no mercantiles en las empresas recuperadas de la Ciudad de Buenos Aires. *Revista del OSERA,* 8. Available at: http://bit.ly/2vI6nlb [Consulted 20 July 2016].

Kasparian, D. (2013b). Enterprises recovered by their workers in Argentina: an assessment of articulations of reciprocity with society. *Journal of Community Positive Practices,* 13(4), 16–31.

Kasparian, D. (2014). Protección social y políticas de promoción del trabajo asociativo y autogestionado en la Argentina (2003–2013): el Programa Argentina Trabaja. *Obets, Revista de Ciencias Sociales,* 9(2), 303–332.

Kasparian, D. (2017a). Pruebas de imprenta: Lucha ¿sin patrón? Un estudio sobre la configuración de la conflictividad de trabajo en empresas recuperadas y cooperativas del Programa Argentina Trabaja, 2017, 336 p. *Sociología del Trabajo, nueva época,* 91, 107–123.

Kasparian, D. (2017b). De la "inducción" a la "cooperativa sin punteros." El conflicto constituyente de una cooperativa del Programa Argentina Trabaja. *Argumentos. Revista de crítica social,* 19, 112–140.

Kasparian, D. (2017c). Conflictividad en el trabajo y clivajes sociales en una empresa recuperada de la Ciudad de Buenos Aires. *Revista Idelcoop,* 223, 110–124.

Kasparian, D. (2019a). Las formas de organización y asociación de los trabajadores de empresas recuperadas en la Argentina (2000–2015). *Século XXI, Revista de Ciências Sociais*, 9(2), 646–673.

Kasparian, D. (2019b). Los patrones de la conflictividad en empresas sin patrón. El caso de las cooperativas de trabajo en la Argentina reciente. *Estudios del Trabajo*, 57. Available at: http://bit.ly/3vOnfB5 [Consulted 1 March 2021].

Kasparian, D. (2019c). Promoción estatal del cooperativismo de trabajo y formas socioproductivas emergentes. Contribuciones en clave emancipatoria a partir de un estudio de caso del Programa Argentina Trabaja. *RevIISE – Revista de Ciencias Sociales y Humanas*, 13, 211–225.

Kasparian, D. (2020a). *Lucha ¿sin patron?* Buenos Aires: Teseo.

Kasparian, D. (2020b). Cooperativismo, políticas públicas y organizaciones sociales: conflictividad en cooperativas promovidas por el Estado en Argentina. *Psicoperspectivas*, 19(2). Available at: http://bit.ly/39kskI7 [Consulted 1 March 2021].

Klein, N. and Lewis, A. (2007). Argentina: sin patrón y sin permiso. Trans. by M. J. Bertomeu. *Sin Permiso, república y socialismo, también para el siglo XXI*. Available at: https://bit.ly/3gLbBzy [Consulted 1 June 2020].

Köhler, H.D. and Artiles, A.M. (2007). *Manual de la sociología del trabajo y de las relaciones laborales.* Madrid: Delta Publicaciones Universitarias.

La Alameda (19 August 2011). Acto fundacional de la Confederación de Trabajadores de la Economía Popular. Available at: http://bit.ly/3bd2rcu [Consulted 25 June 2016].

Laclau, E. (2009). *La razón populista.* Buenos Aires: Fondo de Cultura Económica.

La Nación (4 March 2004). Editorial 11. El dilema de las fábricas ocupadas. Available at: https://bit.ly/2MkyLPk [Consulted 1 June 2020].

Lijphart, A. (1971). Comparative politics and the comparative method. *The American Political Science Review*, 65(3), 682–693.

Lipset, S. and Rokkan, S. (1967). Cleavage structures, party systems and voter alignments. An introduction. In: Lipset, S. and Rokkan, S. (orgs.), *Party systems and voter alignments: Cross national perspectives* (pp. 1–64). New York City: Free Press.

López, P. and Rougier, M. (July, 2011). Nacimiento y trayectoria de la banca de desarrollo en Argentina en el contexto latinoamericano: una mirada de largo plazo. *VI Congreso Argentino de Administración Pública "Gobernabilidad Democrática y Desarrollo Económico con Equidad Social."* Asociación de Administradores Gubernamentales y Asociación Argentina de Estudios de Administración Pública, Resistencia, Chaco.

Lucita, E. (2009). Empresas bajo gestión obrera: la crisis como desafío. *Revista del OSERA*, 2. Available at: http://bit.ly/39bd6mf [Consulted 20 July 2016].

Luxemburgo, R. (1979). *Reforma o revolución.* México City: Grijalbo.

Maneiro, M. (2012). *De Encuentros y desencuentros. Estado, gobiernos y movimientos de trabajadores desocupados.* Buenos Aires: Biblos.

Maneiro, M. (2015). Tiempos y espacios en disputa. Un modelo analítico para analizar la reaparición de las protestas urbanas de los movimientos de trabajadores desocupados. *Quid 16*, 5, 151–169.

Manzano, V. (2009). Piquetes y acción estatal en Argentina: Un análisis etnográfico de la configuración de procesos políticos. In: Grimberg, M., Fernández Álvarez, M.I. and Carvalho Rosa, M. (eds.), *Estado y movimientos sociales: estudios etnográficos em Argentina y Brasil* (pp.15–36). Buenos Aires: Antropofagia.

Marx, K. (2009). Formas que preceden a la producción capitalista. In: *Formaciones económicas precapitalistas* (pp. 67–119). México City: Siglo XXI.

Marx, K. (2011). *El capital. Tomo I: El proceso de producción de capital*. Buenos Aires: Siglo XXI.

Massetti, A. (2011). Las tres transformaciones de la política pública asistencial y su relación con las organizaciones sociopolíticas (2003–2009). *Entramados y perspectivas. Revista de la carrera de Sociología*, 1(1), 9–36.

Mauss, M. (2010). *Ensayo sobre el don. Forma y función del intercambio en las sociedades arcaicas*. Madrid: Katz.

Meister, A. (1974). *La participation dans les associations*. Paris: Les Éditions Ouvrières.

Merklen, D. (2005). *Pobres ciudadanos: las clases populares en la era democrática 1983–2003*. Buenos Aires: Gorla.

Merklen, D. (2013). Las dinámicas contemporáneas de la individuación. In: Castel, R., Kessler, G., Merklen, D. and Murand, N. (eds.), *Individuación, precariedad, inseguridad. ¿Desinstitucionalización del presente?* (pp. 45–86). Buenos Aires: Paidós.

Montes, V. and Ressel, A.B. (2003). Presencia delcooperativismo en Argentina. *UniRcoop*, 1(2), 9–26.

Mouffe, Ch. (2007). *En torno a lo político*. Buenos Aires: Fondo de Cultura Económica.

Natalucci, A. (2012). Políticas sociales y disputas territoriales. El caso del programa "Argentina Trabaja." *Revista Perspectivas de Políticas Públicas*, 2(3), 126–147.

Natalucci, A. and Paschkes Ronis, M. (2011). Avatares en la implementación de políticas sociales. Concepciones y prácticas de las organizaciones sociopolíticas que participan en el programa Argentina Trabaja (2009–2010). In: Arias, A., Bazzalo, A. and García Godoy, B. (eds.), *Políticas públicas y Trabajo Social. Aportes para la reconstrucción de lo público*. Buenos Aires: Espacio.

Neiman, G. and Quaranta, G. (2006). Los estudios de caso en la investigación sociológica. In: Vasilachis de Gialdino, I. (ed.), *Estrategias de investigación cualitativa* (pp. 213–237). Barcelona: Gedisa.

OSERA (2010). Entrevista a Max Quispe Ramírez y Manuel Alzina: La Organización Barrial Tupac Amaru (OBTA): Situación actual y perspectivas futuras. *Revista del OSERA*, 3. Available at: https://bit.ly/3vCPnY7 [Consulted 10 May 2016].

OSERA (2011). Entrevista a Luis Caro, presidente del MNFRT: Modificación de la Ley de Concursos y Quiebras. *Revista del OSERA*, 5. Available at: http://bit.ly/2SgH9Ca [Consulted 10 May 2016].

Página 12 (8 December 2005). El macrismo logró que el Bauen volviera a sus dueños. By: Pertot, W. Available at: http://bit.ly/31fCnJo [Consulted 6 January 2017].

Página 12 (21 August 2007). El padre, el hijo y un espíritu *non sancto*. By: O'Donnell, S. Available at: http://bit.ly/2UiMDyS [Consulted 20 July 2016].

Palomino, H. (ed.) (2003). El movimiento de trabajadores de empresas recuperadas. *Revista Sociedad,* 20–21, 125–146.

Palomino, H. (2008). La instalación de un nuevo régimen de empleo en Argentina: de la precarización a la regulación. *Revista Latinoamericana de Estudios del Trabajo*, 13(19), 121–144.

Palomino, H., Bleynat, I., Garro, S. and Giacomuzzi, C. (2011). Cuestiones actuales sobre el universo de empresas recuperadas y las nuevas lógicas de agregación de los actores. *Revista del OSERA,* 5. Available at: http://bit.ly/2u9Hj6o [Consulted 10 May 2016].

Pastore, R. (2010). Un panorama del resurgimiento de la economía social y solidaria en la Argentina. *Revista de Ciencias Sociales*, 18, 47–74.

Perbellini, M. (2016). *Empresa, organización del trabajo e identidad laboral. Estudio de las empresas recuperadas por sus trabajadores en su etapa de consolidación: análisis de dos empresas recuperadas del área del Gran Rosario.* (Unpublished Doctoral thesis in Social Sciences). Facultad de Ciencias Sociales, Universidad de Buenos Aires, Buenos Aires.

Pérez, V. and Rebón, J. (2016). El retorno del Estado. Valoraciones sociales en torno a las empresas estatales. *Revista Estudios Sociales,* 50(1), 77–104.

Pérez Ledesma, M. (1994). Cuando lleguen los días de cólera (Movimientos sociales, teoría e historia). *Zona Abierta*, 69, 51–120.

Piaget, J. (1986). La explicación en sociología. In: *Estudios sociológicos.* Barcelona: Planeta-Agostini.

Polanyi, K. (2007). *La gran transformación. Crítica del liberalismo económico.* Buenos Aires: Fondo de Cultura Económica.

Programa Facultad Abierta (2005). *Las Empresas Recuperadas en la Argentina.* Buenos Aires: Facultad de Filosofía y Letras – Universidad de Buenos Aires.

Programa Facultad Abierta (2010). *Informe del III Relevamiento de Empresas Recuperadas en la Argentina. Las empresas recuperadas en la Argentina. 2010.* Buenos Aires: Facultad de Filosofía y Letras, Universidad de Buenos Aires.

Programa Facultad Abierta (2014). *Informe del IV Relevamiento de Empresas Recuperadas en la Argentina. 2014: las empresas recuperadas en el período 2010–2013.* Buenos Aires: Cooperativa Chilavert Artes Gráficas/Facultad de Filosofía y Letras, Universidad de Buenos Aires.

Programa Facultad Abierta (2016). *Informe: Las empresas recuperadas por los trabajadores en los comienzos del gobierno de Mauricio Macri. Estado de situación a mayo de 2016.* Buenos Aires: Secretaría de Extensión Universitaria y Bienestar Estudiantil, Facultad de Filosofía y Letras, Universidad de Buenos Aires.

Quijano, A. (2011). ¿Sistemas alternativos de producción? In: De Sousa Santos, B. (ed.), *Producir para vivir: los caminos de la producción no capitalista* (pp. 369–399). México City: Fondo de Cultura Económica.

Quijano, A. (2013). El trabajo. *Revista Argumentos*, 72, 145–163.

Quijoux, M. (2011). *Neolibéralisme et autogestion. L'expérience argentine*. Paris: Éditions de l'IHEAL.

Rebón, J. (2007). *La empresa de la autonomía. Trabajadores recuperando la producción.* Buenos Aires: Colectivo Ediciones/Ediciones PICASO.

Rebón, J. (October, 2015). El carácter social de las empresas recuperadas. Apuntes para un debate necesario. *Pathways to a cooperative Market Economy Meeting*. Instituto de Investigaciones Gino Germani, Facultad de Ciencias Sociales, Buenos Aires.

Rebón, J. and Kasparian, D. (2015). La valoración social de las cooperativas en el Área Metropolitana de Buenos Aires. Una aproximación a partir de la investigación por encuesta. *Cayapa. Revista Venezolana de Economía Social*, 29, 11–37.

Rebón, J. and Kasparian, D. (2018). El poder social en la producción. Una aproximación a partir de las empresas recuperadas por sus trabajadores. *De prácticas y discursos Universidad Nacional del Nordeste Centro de Estudios Sociales*, 7(10), 9–33.

Rebón, J., Kasparian, D. and Hernández, C. (2015). La economía moral del trabajo. La legitimidad social de las empresas recuperadas. *Trabajo y Sociedad*, 25, 173–194.

Rebón, J., Kasparian, D. and Hernández, C. (2016). The social legitimacy of recuperated enterprises in Argentina. *Socialism & Democracy*, 30(3), 37–54.

Rebón, J. and Pérez, V. (2012). Notas acerca de la acción directa y el cambio social. In: *Las vías de la acción directa* (pp. 21–43). Buenos Aires: Aurelia Rivera.

Rebón, J and Salgado, R. (2010). Empresas recuperadas en la Ciudad de Buenos Aires. Un balance desde una perspectiva emancipatoria. In: *Gestión obrera. Del fragmento a la acción colectiva* (pp. 189–209). Montevideo: Universidad de la República/Nordan.

Repetto, F., Boix, M.V. and Fernández, J.P. (2011). *Cómo fortalecer el Argentina Trabaja. Aprendizajes de Esteban Echeverría.* (Public Policies paper/Recomendation N°95). Buenos Aires: Centro de Implementación de Políticas Públicas para la Equidad y el Crecimiento.

Resumen Latinoamericano (n.d.). Argentina. ¿Qué es la CTEP?. Available at: http://bit.ly/2OggX9m [Consulted 22 June 2016].

Rosanvallon, P. (1979). *La Autogestión*. Madrid: Fundamentos.

Salgado, R. (2009). *Entre la innovación y la reproducción social: el carácter emergente del orden socio productivo en las Empresas Recuperadas de la Ciudad de Buenos Aires.* (Unpublished Master's thesis in Social Sciences). Facultad de Ciencias Sociales, Universidad de Buenos Aires, Buenos Aires.

Salgado, R. (2012). *Los límites de la igualdad. Cambio y reproducción social en el proceso de recuperación de empresas por sus trabajadores.* (Unpublished Doctoral thesis in Social Sciences). Facultad de Ciencias Sociales, Universidad de Buenos Aires, Buenos Aires.

Salgado, R., Kasparian, D., Hernández, M. C., Díaz, M.E. and Ferramondo, M. (2012). Función de dirección e igualdad en las Empresas Recuperadas de la Ciudad de Buenos Aires. *La revista del CCC,* 14–15. Available at: https://bit.ly/2NsyivN [Consulted 22 July 2020].

Schnapper, D. (2004). *La democracia providencial.* Rosario: Homo Sapiens.

Senén González, C. and Haidar, J. (2009). Los debates acerca de la "revitalización sindical" y su aplicación en el análisis sectorial en Argentina. *Revista Latinoamericana de Estudios del Trabajo (RELET),* 14(22), 5–32.

Sennett, R. (2003). *El respeto. Sobre la dignidad del hombre en un mundo de desigualdad.* Barcelona: Anagrama.

Silver, B.J. (2005). *Fuerzas de trabajo. Los movimientos obreros y la globalización desde 1870.* Madrid: Akal.

Simmel, G. (1904). The sociology of conflict. I. *American Journal of Sociology,* 9(4), 490–525.

Singer, P. (2007). Economía Solidaria. Un modo de producción y distribución. In: Coraggio, J.L. (ed.), *La economía social desde la periferia. Contribuciones latinoamericanas* (pp. 59–78). Buenos Aires: Universidad Nacional General Sarmiento/Altamira.

Smith, V. (1995). El legado de Harry Braverman. La tradición del proceso de trabajo veinte años más tarde. *Sociología del trabajo, nueva época,* 26, 3–28.

Soldano, D. and Andrenacci, L. (2006). Aproximación a las teorías de la política social a partir del caso argentino. In: Andrenacci, L., *Problemas de política social en la Argentina contemporánea* (pp.1–43). Buenos Aires: Prometeo.

Stake, R.E. (2013). Estudios de casos cualitativos. In: Denzin, N.K. and Lincoln, Y.S. (eds.). *Manual SAGE de Investigación Cualitativa Vol. III: Estrategias de Investigación Cualitativa* (pp. 154–197). Barcelona: Gedisa. (Original work published in 1994).

Svampa, M. and Pereyra, S. (2004). *Entre la ruta y el barrio. La experiencia de las organizaciones piqueteras.* Buenos Aires: Biblos.

Tarrow, S. (1999). Estado y oportunidades: la estructuración política de los movimientos sociales. In: McAdam, D, McCarthy, J. and Zald, M. (eds.), *Movimientos sociales: perspectivas comparadas. Oportunidades políticas, estructuras de movilización y marcos interpretativos culturales* (pp.71–99). Madrid: ISTMO.

Tarrow, S. (2009). *El poder en movimiento. Los movimientos sociales, la acción colectiva y la política.* Madrid: Alianza.

Thompson, E.P. (1979). La economía moral de la multitud. In: *Tradición, revuelta y consciencia de clase* (pp.62–134). Barcelona: Crítica.

Tilly, C. (1978). *From mobilization to revolution.* Nueva York City: Random House.

Tilly, C. (2000). *La desigualdad persistente.* Buenos Aires: Manantial.

Tilly, C. (2008). *Contentious politics*. Cambridge: Cambridge University.
Tilly, C. and Wood, L. (2010). *Los movimientos sociales 1768–2009*. Madrid: Crítica.
Valdueco, I. (2012). *Método comparativo*. Available at: http://bit.ly/2UewIBz [Consulted 20 July 2015].
Vasilachis de Gialdino, I. (1992). *Métodos cualitativos I*. Buenos Aires: Centro Editor América Latina.
Vázquez, G. (2014). ¿Son sostenibles los emprendimientos asociativos de trabajadores autogestionados? Algunas reflexiones a contramano del sentido común. *Voces en el Fénix*, 37, 130–137.
Vuotto, M. (2011). *El cooperativismo de trabajo en la Argentina: contribuciones para el diálogo social*. (Working Paper 217). Lima: International Labour Organisation/Programa Regional para la Promoción del Diálogo y la Cohesión Social en América Latina.
Williams, M. (2014). The solidarity economy and social transformation. In: Satgar, V. (ed.), *The solidarity economy alternative: emerging theory and practice* (pp. 37–63). Durban: University of KwaZulu-Natal.
Wright, E.O. (1994). *Interrogating inequality*. London: Verso.
Wright, E.O. (2000). Working-class power, capitalist-class interests, and class compromise. *American Journal of Sociology*, 105(4), 957–1002.
Wright, E.O. (2006). Compass points. Towards a socialist alternative. *New Left Review*, 41, 93–124.
Wright, E.O. (2012). Transforming capitalism through real utopias. *American Sociological Review*, 20(10), 1–25.
Wright, E.O. (2015). *Construyendo utopías reales*. Buenos Aires: Akal.
Wright, E.O. (June, 2017). Pathways to a cooperative market economy – June. *Pathways to a cooperative market economy meeting*. Department of Philosophy, Sociology, Education and Applied Psychology, Università degli Studi di Padova, Padua. Available at: https://bit.ly/3bWotzn [Consulted 15 February 2021].

Official Documents and Reports

Autoridad Cuenca Matanza Riachuelo
[Matanza Riachuelo Basin Authority]

ACUMAR (2015a). Informe. Available at: http://bit.ly/3b4XWkb [Consulted 18 March 2016].
ACUMAR (2015b). Sistema de Indicadores Anexo- Datos del Indicador: C12 Cooperativistas abocados a la limpieza de márgenes por jurisdicción en la CMR, por semestre. Available at: http://bit.ly/3r5tGfT [Consulted 17 February 2021].

BIBLIOGRAPHY

Jefatura de Gabinete de Ministros de la Nación
[*Chief of the Cabinet of Ministers Office*]

Memoria detallada del estado de la Nación, Año 2012. (1º de marzo de 2013). Buenos Aires: Presidencia de la Nación.

Ministerio de Desarrollo Social de la Nación
[*Ministry for Social Development of Nation*]

Documento de Acceso a la Información Pública del Ministerio de Desarrollo Social, 27 April 2010. Available at: http://bit.ly/31nvvt9 [Consulted 12 March 2016].

Documento de Acceso a la Información Pública del Ministerio de Desarrollo Social, 7 December 2010. Available at: https://bit.ly/3hemRGs [Consulted 12 March 2016].

Documento de Acceso a la Información Pública del Ministerio de Desarrollo Social, 4 November 2011. Available at: http://bit.ly/31hxbUS [Consulted 12 March 2016.].

Ministerio de Desarrollo Social (2010). Argentina Trabaja. Programa Ingreso Social con Trabajo. Guía informativa.

Ministerio de Desarrollo Social de la Nación (2015a). Programa de Ingreso Social con Trabajo. Síntesis de resultados e impactos. Después de cinco años de sus primeros pasos. ...

Ministerio de Desarrollo Social de la Nación (2015b). Situación actualizada de las cooperativas mixtas, perfil de los titulares y aspectos evaluativos al primer semestre 2015 (Resultados de Actualización de Datos titulares activos 2014).

Ministerio de Economía y Finanzas Públicas de la Nación
[*Ministry for Economy and Public Finances of the Nation*]

Ministerio de Economía y Finanzas Públicas de la Nación (2009). Informe de la Contaduría General de la Nación. Cuenta de Inversión 2009. Available at: http://bit.ly/2vD46Yh [Consulted 12 February 2016].

Ministerio de Economía y Finanzas Públicas de la Nación (2010). Informe de la Contaduría General de la Nación. Cuenta de Inversión 2010. Available at: http://bit.ly/3b3Awvl [Consulted 12 February 2016].

Ministerio de Economía y Finanzas Públicas de la Nación (2011). Informe de la Contaduría General de la Nación. Cuenta de Inversión 2011. Available at: http://bit.ly/2RRbvvT [Consulted 12 February 2016].

Ministerio de Economía y Finanzas Públicas de la Nación (2012). Informe de la Contaduría General de la Nación. Cuenta de Inversión 2012. Available at: http://bit.ly/2RPenJG [Consulted 12 February 2016].

Ministerio de Economía y Finanzas Públicas de la Nación (2013). Informe de la Contaduría General de la Nación. Cuenta de Inversión 2013. Available at: http://bit.ly/31lFRdc [Consulted 12 February 2016].

Ministerio de Economía y Finanzas Públicas de la Nación (2014). Informe de la Contaduría General de la Nación. Cuenta de Inversión 2014. Available at: http://bit.ly/31fG9SA [Consulted 12 February 2016].

Ministerio de Economía y Finanzas Públicas de la Nación (2015). Informe de la Contaduría General de la Nación. Cuenta de Inversión 2015. Available at: http://bit.ly/31lLUhF [Consulted 12 February 2016].

Regulations

Legislation

Act no. 1,914 of Creation of the Special Commission for Monitoring the Process of Normalization of the Conflict of the Former Bauen Hotel. 2005. Available at: http://bit.ly/2UifoeM [Consulted 17 February 2021].

Act no. 27,224 of Declaration of Public Utility and Subject to Expropriation of the Premises of IMPA. Year 2015. Available at: http://bit.ly/2OA126b [Consulted 17 February 2021].

Competition and Bankruptcy Act no. 26,684. 2011. Available at: http://bit.ly/2GN6NZO [Consulted 17 February 2021].

Cooperatives Act no. 20,337. 1973. Available at: http://bit.ly/2ueQFgO [Consulted 17 February 2021].

Social Emergency Act no. 27,345. 2016. Available at: http://bit.ly/3lvDJcB [Consulted 17 February 2021].

Resolutions

Administración Nacional de la Seguridad Social
[National Social Security Administration].

Resolution no. 784/92. 1992. Available at: https://bit.ly/3tzuBXd [Consulted 17 February 2021].

Comisión Nacional de Trabajo en Casas Particulares
[National Committee for Private Household Work].

Resolution no. 1/15. 2015. Available at: http://bit.ly/2ubf9aU [Consulted 17 February 2021].

Consejo Nacional del Empleo, la Productividad y el Salario Mínimo, Vital y Móvil [National Council for Employment, Productivity and Minimum Living Adjustable Wage].

Resolution no. 2/09. 2009. Available at: http://bit.ly/3b2FJUj [Consulted 17 February 2021].

Resolution no. 2/10. 2010. Available at: http://bit.ly/2S6zfuS [Consulted 17 February 2021].

Resolution no. 2/11. 2011. Available at: http://bit.ly/31gc1Xm [Consulted 17 February 2021].
Resolution no. 3/11. 2011. Available at: http://bit.ly/39oEnYc [Consulted 17 February 2021].
Resolution no. 2/12. 2012. Available at: http://bit.ly/31eEgFY [Consulted 17 February 2021].
Resolution no. 4/13. 2013. Available at: http://bit.ly/2tqlQWk [Consulted 17 February 2021].
Resolution no. 3/14. 2014. Available at: http://bit.ly/3b2w5Rn [Consulted 17 February 2021].
Resolution no. 4/15. 2015. Available at: http://bit.ly/31nDDtF [Consulted 17 February 2021].

Instituto Nacional de Asociativismo y Economía Social [National Institute of Associativism and Social Economy].

Resolution no. 183/92. 1992. Available at: https://bit.ly/38QJBZ2 [Consulted 17 February 2021].
Resolution no. 4,664/13. 2013. Available at: https://bit.ly/3eOvfMD [Consulted 17 February 2021].

Ministerio de Desarrollo Social de la Nación [Ministry for Social Development of Nation].

Resolution no. 3,182/09. 2009. Available at: https://bit.ly/3BTgC2R [Consulted 17 February 2021].
Resolution no. 1,499/12. 2012. Available at: https://cutt.ly/bWHBKUD [Consulted 17 February 2021].

Ministerio de Trabajo, Empleo y Seguridad Social de la Nación [Ministry for Work, Employment and Social Security of the Nation].

Resolution no. 1,002/09. 2009. Available at: http://bit.ly/3b6wBOj [Consulted 17 February 2021].
Resolution no. 1,297/10. 2010. Available at: http://bit.ly/2S5E9by [Consulted 17 February 2021].
Resolution no. 1,350/11. 2011. Available at: http://bit.ly/2RQNPaM [Consulted 17 February 2021].
Resolution no. 958/12. 2012. Available at: http://bit.ly/2UovDXI [Consulted 17 February 2021].
Resolution no. 886/13. 2013. Available at: http://bit.ly/2udNIgx [Consulted 17 February 2021].
Resolution no. 1,062/14. 2014. Available at: http://bit.ly/31lTd95 [Consulted 17 February 2021].

Statistical Sources

Instituto Nacional de Estadísticas y Censos (2010). *Censo Nacional de Población, hogares y vivienda 2010*. Argentina. Available at: http://bit.ly/3lojHBo [Consulted 17 February 2021].

Instituto Nacional de Estadísticas y Censos. *Encuesta Permanente de Hogares Continua Trimestral*. Argentina. Available at: http://bit.ly/2P34jxI [Consulted 17 February 2021].

World Bank. *Tasa de Crecimiento Anual del Producto Bruto Interno de Argentina*. Available at: http://bit.ly/3tuMTZR [Consulted 17 February 2021].

Cited Interviews

- Interview with former head of FECOOTRA (May 2013).
- Interview with Raúl, leading figure in the recuperated enterprise movement (September 2016). Conducted by Natalia Bauni and Julián Rebón in the framework of the project "Talleres para el fortalecimiento de la autogestión en cooperativas de trabajo" [Workshops for the Strengthening of Self-Management in Worker Co-operatives]. Programa de Cooperativismo y Economía Social en la Universidad [Cooperativism and Social Economy at the University Program], Ministerio de Educación [Ministry for Education], call 2014.
- Interview with Mariano, member of a recuperated food factory (October 2017). Conducted in the framework of the project "Factores positivos en el sostenimiento y consolidación de empresas recuperadas" [Positive Factors in the Sustainability and Consolidation of Recuperated Enterprises]. Programa de Cooperativismo y Economía Social en la Universidad [Cooperativism and Social Economy at the University Program], Ministerio de Educación [Ministry for Education], call 2016.

Interviews – Case Study: Worker-recuperated Enterprise
- Interview with Mario, co-operative member (September 2006). Conducted by Julián Rebón.
- Interview with Alejandro, co-operative member and leading figure in a worker co-operative organisation (August 2011).
- Interview with Darío, co-operative member (August 2014).
- Interview with Graciela, co-operative member (August 2014).
- Interview with Gustavo, co-operative member (August 2014).
- Interview with Jorge, co-operative member (August 2014).
- Interview with Mariela, co-operative member (August 2014).
- Interview with Rosa, co-operative member (August 2014).

- Interview with Violeta, co-operative member (August 2014).
- Interview with Fernando, co-operative member (September 2014).
- Interview with Adrián, key informant (October 2014).
- Interview with Ana, co-operative member (November 2014).
- Interview with Alejandro, co-operative member and leading figure in a worker co-operative organisation (January 2016).
- Interview with Alejandro, co-operative member and leading figure in a worker co-operative organisation (August 2016). Conducted by students of "Sociology of Organisations" of the Department of Sociology, Universidad de Buenos Aires.
- Interview with Iván, academic researcher (February 2017).
- Interview with Matías, former leading figure in the recuperated enterprises movement (April 2017).

Interviews conducted in the framework of the project "Programa de fortalecimiento socio-institucional para empresas recuperadas" [Socio-institutional Strengthening Programme for Recuperated Enterprises]. Programa de Voluntariado Universitario [University Volunteering Programme], Ministerio de Educación [Ministry for Education], call 2010:

- Interview with Laura, co-operative member (May 2011).
- Interview with Omar, co-operative member (May 2011).

Interviews – Case Study: Worker Co-operative under the Argentina Works Scheme

- Group interview with co-operative members (January 2015).
- Interview with Cristina, co-operative member (January 2015).
- Interview with Adriana, co-operative member (January 2015).
- Interview with Esteban Echeverría Municipality official (June 2016).

Interviews conducted in the framework of the project "Trabajo, redes territoriales y acción piquetera. El impacto del Plan Argentina Trabaja (PAT) en un movimiento de trabajadores desocupados del Gran Buenos Aires" [Work, Territorial Networks and Picketer Action. The Impact of the Argentina Works Programme on an Unemployed Workers' Movement in Greater Buenos Aires]. Consejo Nacional de Investigaciones Científicas y Técnicas [National Scientific and Technical Research Council], call 2012–2014:

- Group Interview with MTD members (May 2010).
- Interview with Carlos, member of an AGTCAP organisation (September 2011).
- Interview with Paula, MTD member (September 2011).
- Interview with Ariel, member of the other MTD co-operative (September 2011).
- Interview with Daniel, co-operative member (October 2012).
- Interview with Verónica, co-operative member (October 2012).
- Interview with Analía, co-operative member (November 2012).
- Interview with Luz, co-operative member (September 2014).

Index

accumulation   120, 134, 137, 155, 214
  economic   215
  model of   1, 23, 222
  non-bureaucratic political   12
  of means of production   12
  political   120, 135, 137, 155, 156, 161, 162, 164, 192, 193, 198, 202, 204, 207, 209, 215, 216, 219
  politico-bureaucratic   12
  statist   155, 162, 215
  tension between consumption and   123
agonistic   181
agrarian strike   61
Alliance for Work, Justice and Education   58, 58n5
antagonism   89, 102, 104, 162, 168, 181
  capital–labour   207
  class   101, 104, 135, 217
  labour–capital   221
  potential   136
  structural   6
  structured   7
antagonistic
  interdependency   101
appropriation   7, 10, 11, 12, 86, 89, 101, 102, 105, 112, 113, 114, 136, 143, 150n5, 162, 212
  collective   145, 162
  collective self-   10, 134
  differential   115, 119, 136
  egalitarian   120
  social   110, 112, 143, 148
area co-ordinator   117, 130, 183, 184
Argentina Metal-Working and Plastics Industries (IMPA)   22n2, 27, 29
Argentina Works Programme (PAT)   1, 8, 9, 15, 16, 17, 18, 43, 47, 49, 53–56, 59–60, 62, 63, 64, 64n8, 66, 69, 70, 73, 89, 90, 92, 93, 94, 95, 96, 97, 98, 99, 101, 104, 140, 142, 142n3, 143, 145, 148, 149, 150, 150n5, 152, 154, 155, 162, 166, 190, 195, 200, 209, 210, 211, 212, 213, 219, 223
  demand around management of   70
  demand of incorporation to   70
  demand over remunerations in   72, 73
  early implementation   65

emergence   65
eroded continuity   66
Argentinian Federation of Self-Managed Workers' Co-operatives (FACTA)   43, 44
assemblies   25, 80, 118, 125, 126, 127, 128, 129, 130, 133, 156, 159, 160, 171, 172, 177, 179, 183, 187, 188, 189, 201, 202, 203, 217
  by   179, 183, 187, 205
  extraordinary   126
  formal   127
  frequency of   127, 178
  members'   171, 187
  neighbourhood   26, 79
  ordinary   126
  participation in   133
  popular   20, 108
  weekly   160
  workers'   130

beneficiaries   ix, 51, 52, 52n2, 53, 53n3, 54, 59, 64n8, 65, 65n9, 66, 67, 68, 70, 72, 73, 92, 93, 95, 142, 145, 149, 153n7, 190, 211, 212
board   112, 117, 118, 126, 127, 128, 129, 130, 131, 132, 133, 134, 137, 157, 160, 163, 168, 169, 171, 172, 173, 174, 175, 176, 177, 178, 179, 180, 183, 185, 187, 188, 189, 190, 204, 207, 217, 218
  extended   126, 127, 183
  meetings   131
  members   116, 117, 128, 129, 130, 132, 133, 158, 168, 169, 218
  new   169, 179
  removal of   169, 181, 221
born and bred   109, 110
Burawoy, Michael   13, 14, 98, 161
by-laws   111, 132, 133, 173, 183, 184, 187

camps in public thoroughfares   71, 72
capitalism   4, 14, 24, 32, 39, 101, 213
  industrial   6
case study   76
  multiple instrumental case study   15, 16, 17
  representativeness   16

INDEX

civil associations   58, 59
  non-governmental organisations   58, 110
cleavage   x, 3, 9, 10, 12, 13n6, 15, 19, 89, 104, 135, 136, 138, 164, 167, 180, 212, 215, 216, 221
clusters   46
collective action   x, 1, 13, 14, 15, 17, 22, 25, 26, 28, 29, 35, 38, 44, 47, 57, 60, 63, 65, 66, 67, 68, 70, 71, 73, 79, 84, 88, 91, 94, 96, 98, 99, 180, 194, 197, 211, 212, 213, 222, 223
Collective Brand   40t.3
commodatum   36, 86, 87, 144
commodification   13, 14, 24, 34, 50, 111, 168, 207, 211, 213, 221
  limiters of   14, 35
  of the labour force   13, 111, 168, 221
  resistance movements to   13, 25, 31
  widespread   25
commodity   4, 6, 11, 23, 32, 50, 61n6
  fictitious   13
Competition and Bankruptcy Act   36, 37, 38, 42, 45, 84
comradeship   9, 163, 220, 221
Confederation of Workers in the Popular Economy (CTEP)   69, 70, 73, 223
conflict   9
  as a catalyst for creativity and innovation   9
  class   102
  democratisation of. *See* democratisation:of conflict
  in worker co-operatives   210
  judicialised   89, 96
  pathological view of the   9
  social   ix, x, 6, 9, 13n6, 14, 15, 57, 176, 210
conflicts
  constitutive   18, 21, 49, 76, 82, 88, 89, 97, 98, 99, 101, 102, 135, 166, 209, 213, 217, 221
  work   3, 6, 8, 10, 15, 16, 18, 19, 123, 138, 152, 164, 166, 167, 191, 206, 209, 214, 216, 218, 220, 222
consent   7, 8, 12, 161, 168, 219
consumption   8, 12, 13, 32, 33, 106, 111, 120, 135, 137, 152, 154, 155, 156, 162, 164, 180, 204, 205, 213, 214, 221
  capitalist   6
  domestic   1
  of the labour force   111, 113

  subsistence   202, 205, 207, 219
contentious action   ix, 9, 58, 63, 64, 65, 66, 73, 90, 93
contentious interactions   73, 98
contentious origins   47, 49, 75, 105, 206
contentious politics   28, 211
control
  bureaucratic   161, 162
  classic   162
  direct   162
  of the productive process   147, 162, 168, 180, 198, 216, 219
  of the productive unit   136
  simple   161
  system of   168
Convertibility Plan   23, 23n3
co-operation
  autonomous   125, 134, 135, 164, 168, 206, 208, 217
  despotic   168
co-operative   2
  amphibian   74
  claims-based   2, 22, 49, 73, 74
  in agriculture   1
  in consumption   1
  in public utilities   1
  incubated   49, 74, 75
  induced   18, 96, 211
  integrated   2, 73
  new   x
  non-state   74
  state-incubated   2, 74, 210, 222
  state-induced   2, 49, 73, 74, 211
  synthetic   74
  worker   1
Co-operative Graphics Network   46
Co-operative Textile Network   46
co-operatives
  Co-operatives Act 20,337   111, 126, 157, 183
co-operativism   ix, x, 2
  adaptive   viii, 27, 46, 96, 98, 206, 213
  historical experiences of   2
  new   3
  new twenty-first-century worker   210
  new worker   1, 166
  old-school Argentinian   viii
  on history   1
  traditional   27, 43, 45, 74, 222

training and education about 154
twenty-first century 206
twenty-first-century worker 210, 222
worker ix, 5, 6, 49, 206, 213, 222
Coraggio, José Luis 121
Coser, Lewis 9, 176
crisis
 2001–2002 29
 economic 60, 211
 neoliberal viii
 of 2001-2002 5, 21, 23, 51
 of the COVID-19 pandemic 16, 223
 of the productive unit 21, 24, 88, 97, 211
 political 60, 64, 211
 widespread viii, 24, 26, 30, 59
Cristal Avellaneda 5
cultural incorporation of recuperation 21, 34, *See* cultural installation of recuperation
cultural installation of recuperation 5, 35, 36, 45, *See* cultural incorporation of recuperation
cycle of protest 63, 73, 211

deindustrialisation 23, 26, 57
delegation 129
democracy 11, 26, 181
 a more participatory representative 133
 delegated 126
 direct 126, 130, 133, 160
 internal 12, 160
 representative 130, 160
 social viii
democratisation 164, 168, 222
 of conflict x, 220
 of labour relations 8
 of participation 164
 of production x, 138
 of the function of management 125, 181
 of the workplace 34, 220, 221
 of work relations 222
demonstrations 2, 18, 20, 25, 28, 38, 42, 44, 45, 47, 63, 71, 72, 73, 84, 91, 94, 100, 152, 160, 164, 173, 194, 197, 198, 202, 204
direct action viii, 25, 25n4, 78, 93, 104, 193, 198
direct producers 4, 10, 120, 134

dispossession 4, 25, 98, 102
divides 3, 10, 13, 13n6, 15, 19, 89, 136, 138, 164, 167, 180, 185, 207, 209, 217, 219, 221
Down to Work Socio-Productive Projects 40t.3, 53, 59

Elias, Norbert 115, 116, 189
emancipation viii, 19, 223
emancipatory 4, 106
 social science x, 3, 223
 strategies 4
eviction 39, 83, 84, 85, 88, 112, 122, 127, 173, 177, 178, 195
exploitation 4, 7, 25, 101, 102, 103, 114, 119, 134, 136, 168, 211, 212, 213, 221
 conditions of 13, 207
 guarantee of 13, 98
expropriation
 bill 83, 85, 86, 173
 law 28, 36, 38, 42, 45, 112, 135, 217
 of labour insertion 98

Factory Without Bosses (FaSinPat, formerly Zanon) 5, 36n8, 37n8, 174n2
Famel 39
Federation of Food-Production Organisations 47
Federation of Self-Managed Meat Co-operatives and Related Industries 47
Federation of United Worker Co-operatives (FECOOTRAUN) 43
Federation of Worker Co-operatives of the Argentinian Republic (FECOOTRA) 17, 27, 28, 43, 46, 47
Fernández de Kirchner, Cristina ixn1, 33, 36, 52n1, 53, 61, 66, 69, 124
forced associativity 96, 98, 206, 213
FREPASO (Front for a Country in Solidarity) 58n5
Front for Co-operatives Without Brokers 63, 69, 71, 90, 99, 200
Front for Victory ixn1, 52n1, 91n7

governments
 critical of neoliberalism ix
 Kirchnerist ix, 48
 municipal 59, 60, 64, 64n8, 68, 70, 72, 96, 140n1, 150, 190

INDEX

national 44, 45, 49, 58, 59, 60, 61, 62, 64, 68, 74, 222
officials 20
progressive ix
Greater Buenos Aires Graphics Federation 26n5, 47
groups, social 10, 12, 100, 101, 106, 135, 138, 163, 211, 212, 215
antagonistic 135

hegemony 7, 125, 161, 180, 181
heroic period 83, 88, 114, 216

income
distribution 23n3, 32, 148, 149
redistribution 53
industrial relations system 6
innovation viii, 4, 10, 14, 35, 59, 167, 182
interpersonal relationships 138, 172, 176, 179, 180, 181, 190, 206, 217

Jetcoop 39
Justicialist Party ixn1, 52n1, 58, 58n5

Kirchner, Néstor ixn1, 52n1, 61, 63, 69

labour
control 7
disputes 3, 6, 7, 8, 168, 221
force 3, 6, 7, 8, 13, 14, 23, 29, 38, 50, 89, 97, 98, 104, 111, 113, 117, 119, 129, 135, 144, 154, 168, 175, 176, 180, 207, 212
hierarchies 9
market 7, 13, 23, 33, 50, 52, 56, 60, 97, 98, 100, 102, 115, 141, 142, 149, 162
process 7, 13, 125, 136, 161, 178, 182
legal custody 80

Macri, Mauricio 16, 45, 47
management
co- 161, 198, 219
function of 6, 8, 22, 115, 125, 129, 133, 135, 137, 168, 169, 180, 206, 207, 215, 217, 218
self- viii, ix, x, 12, 22, 26, 27, 34, 35, 37n8, 44, 45, 48, 49, 52, 81, 83, 103, 104, 105, 106, 106n1, 108, 111, 114, 125, 126, 133, 134, 161, 162, 165, 180, 182, 188, 213, 219

market exchange 12, 112, 113, 123, 150, 151, 155, 164, 206
Marx, Karl 13, 211
Marxian 25
Marxist ix, 6
Marxist tradition 101
neo-Marxist x, 7
Mataderos Flexible Packaging 36
Matanza Riachuelo Basin Authority (ACUMAR) 140, 140n1, 143, 150, 156, 195, 197, 209
means of production
accumulation of. *See* accumulation:of means of production
ownership of the 10, 22, 35, 46n13, 102, 105, 110, 111
possession of the 120, 134, 151, 156, 164
use of the 103, 144
member
disassociation of 199, 204, 205, 207, 209
exclusion of viii, 10, 12, 98, 101, 102, 103, 111, 114, 136, 145, 181, 182, 187, 188, 189, 190, 208, 218
founder 82, 83, 106n1, 114, 115, 116, 117, 118, 119, 120, 130, 131, 135, 136, 138, 166, 170, 172, 173, 179, 180, 188, 189, 190, 208, 215, 216, 218, 219
founderer 166, 189, 190, 208, 218
non- 164, 216
recuperator 107, 108
Metal-Workers' Union (UOM) 22n2, 47
Micro-Credit Programme – National Micro-Credit Commission 40t.3
Ministry for Labour, Employment and Social Security 33, 41, 41t.3, 44, 45, 70
Ministry for Social Development 17, 40t.3, 41, 53, 55, 64n8, 72, 91, 95, 143, 150, 190, 192, 194
mode of production ix, 4, 168
alternative 4
articulation of 10, 106
capitalist 4, 8, 125, 214
interpenetration of 10, 19, 106, 134, 155
statist 19, 150n5, 215
moral economy 14
of work 14, 24, 35, 100, 211
Movement for the Social Economy (MOPES) 27

246

National Association of Self-Managed Workers (ANTA)   43, 44
National Confederation of Worker Co-operatives (CNCT)   43, 47
National Co-operative Metal-Workers' Network   47
National Institute of Associativism and Social Economy (INAES)   2, 27, 36, 41n10, 111, 122n12, 126, 172, 183, 190
National Movement of Recuperated Enterprises (MNER)   27, 43
National Movement of Worker-Recuperated Factories (MNFRT)   37, 38, 43, 44
neoliberal
    hegemony   ix, 52
    neoliberalism   ix, 50, 70
    policies   47
    reforms   1
    system   viii
non-market liaisons   80, 86, 113, 174, 176

occupancy   18, 81, 85, 86, 88, 89, 98, 102, 103, 104, 112, 122, 126, 129, 133, 135, 137, 142, 144, 173, 175, 176, 178, 180, 181, 212, 217, 218
occupation   22, 22n1, 26, 28, 39, 79, 80, 83, 88, 99, 101, 171, 195, 198, 211
opportunity hoarding   114, 115, 119, 120, 135, 163
oppression   3, 102, 103, 212, 213
    non-exploitative   101, 114
organisational assets   114, 115
organisational resources   9, 78, 85, 115, 119, 120, 135, 136, 145, 189, 209, 211, 215, 221
overseers. *See* supervisors
ownership
    legal   110, 173, 206
    of the means of production. *See* means of production:ownership of
    private   11, 35, 102, 144
    social   11, 27, 111, 112, 120, 143, 144, 148
    state   11, 87, 144, 148

Perón, Juan Domingo   46, 139
pickets   57, 58, 71, 100
Pigüé Textiles   36n8, 37n8, 174, 174n2
Plan for Unemployed Heads of Household   51, 52, 58

INDEX

Polanyi, Karl   13, 211
    Polanyian alliances and social conflicts   25
    Polanyian struggles   25
political entrepreneurs   25, 26, 28, 45, 78, 88, 211
political opportunity structure   9, 24, 63, 209
political processes   15
politicisation   8, 9, 61, 103, 168, 169, 175, 180, 206, 207, 217, 218
politics
    local   66, 155
    territorial   59, 63n7
possession
    de facto   102
    formal   9
    social   112, 120, 134, 144, 145, 148, 151, 155, 164
power
    associational   100, 101, 211, 212
    social   4, 10, 19, 134, 144, 214, 215, 223
    state   37, 162, 191, 207, 212
    structural   100, 101, 211
    symbolic   45, 101, 189, 209, 218
    working-class   100
production
    immediate destination of   11, 120, 150
    logic of   11, 105, 137, 150, 156, 162, 192, 215, 216, 219
    purpose of   11, 12, 152, 155
    relations of   10, 14, 19, 26, 105, 180
Productive Union of Self-Managed Enterprises (UPEA)   44
Programme for Productive Recovery (REPRO)   32
Promotion of Independent Employment and Productive Structures   41t.3
property relations   10, 22, 79, 101, 104, 105, 109, 120, 134, 135

Radical Civic Union   58n5
reciprocity   11, 121, 123, 124, 137, 151, 164, 174, 176, 214
recuperated enterprise movement   20, 21, 25, 28, 29, 45, 47, 77, 79, 86, 99, 100, 108, 211, 240

INDEX

redistribution 11, 12, 123, 124, 137, 149, 150, 162, 176, 214
regulations
   collective self- 181, 208, 218
   internal 18, 183
   regulated markets 11
Renacer 5
repertoire 28
   of actions 99
   of collective actions 28
   of labour protests 26
   of performances 71
   of recuperation 33, 34, 35
   of unemployed workers' organisations 71
roadblocks 25, 71, 72, 73, 100, 101
rotation 108, 122, 129, 130, 131, 132, 137, 163, 169, 178, 182

sanctions 182, 183, 184, 185, 187, 188
schemes
   to promote worker co-operativism 6
   to set up co-operatives 6
schemes, cash transfer
   with work requirement 56
schemes, social
   with work requirement 49, 73, 212
schemes, social protection 56
schemes, temporary employment 51, 56, 57, 58
schemes, workfare 49, 59
self-determination 12, 103, 104, 122, 156, 159, 160, 161, 162, 164, 183, 206, 209, 220
Self-Managed Work Programme 33, 41t.3, 45, 116, 121n11
self-management. *See* management:-self
Silver, Beverly J. 13, 14
Simmel, Georg 9
Singer, Paul 4
social and solidarity economy ix, x, 2, 6, 12
social change ix, x, 10
social classes 101, 139
social dislocation viii, 14, 25, 32, 34, 211
social economy 2, 4, 40t.3, 41, 46, 52, 121, 122, 124, 125, 148, 213
social form of production 19
   hybrid 10, 19, 105, 134, 138, 162, 215
social formation 4, 6, 8, 10n5

Social Income with Work Programme. *See* Argentina Works Programme (PAT)
Social Monotax 40t.3, 53, 56
social movement
   fragmentation 99
   movementist 28, 42, 47, 99
   resistance movements to commodification. *See* commodification:resistance movements to
syndicalism 45
socio-genesis 3, 9, 13, 15, 17, 18, 21, 24, 26n5, 28, 36, 45, 46, 47, 49, 60, 62, 210, 221
socio-productive form. *See* social form of production
state
   apparatuses 96, 98, 161, 213, 217
   bodies 41, 93, 110, 161, 167
   domination 160, 161, 164, 206
   institutions 9, 198, 206, 217, 218
   Judiciary 38, 84, 88, 89, 98, 173, 177, 212, 217
   legislators 20, 26, 45, 61, 83
   officials 26, 68, 94, 157, 162, 198, 216
   powers 103, 207, 212, 217
   representatives 164
subordination 97, 101, 102, 104, 151, 207, 213, 218
subsidies 16, 20, 33, 58, 74, 80, 81, 83, 94, 96, 116, 121, 121n11, 149, 154, 155, 171, 190, 191, 202, 216
subsistence 152, 155, 192, 199, 202, 205, 207, 215, 219
supervisors 116, 117, 126, 128, 130, 131, 132, 137, 158, 159, 161, 163, 168, 183, 199, 205
sustainability 9, 12, 42, 56, 121, 122, 123, 124, 135, 137, 155, 174, 175, 176, 178, 215, 216, 217

take 84, *See* occupation
Tarrow, Sidney 15, 63
tension between self-management and delegation in recuperated enterprises 133–134
The Little Pigs 39
Thompson, E.P. 14
Tilly, Charles 15
   and Wood, Lesley 28

trades unions   26, 57, 86, 100
   association   69
   delegates   20, 147
   organisation   73, 113, 147, 212
   social movement syndicalism. *See* social movements:syndicalism
   trades unionists   26
   union rapprochement   45, 47
Tupac Amaru Neighbourhood Organisation   48, 49

Unemployed Workers Movements   57, 90, 91, 92, 93, 94, 96, 140, 144, 192, 196, 241
Union Association of Co-operative, Self-Managed and Precarised Workers (AGTCAP)   69, 73
Universal Child Allowance   32n7, 33, 40t.3, 52n2, 53, 56, 62, 72
unrest   210, 212, 216, 217, 218, 219, 220, 221

value
   exchange   6, 120, 134, 150, 155, 214, 215
   surplus   6, 7, 13, 114, 125, 161
   use   6, 13, 125, 150, 151, 155
Vuotto, Mirta 114, 21, 304, 44, 49, 85

wage
   earner   6, 108
   labour   2, 6, 14, 122, 149, 154
   legal minimum   32n7, 33, 53, 56, 66, 72, 121n11, 154

Minimum Living Adjustable Wage   66, 238
non-wage relationships   ix
relationships   3, 6, 8, 138
undermining the wage relationship   21
Women Make   54, 55
work
   access to   97, 154, 213
   as a commodity. *See* commodity:fictitious
   associational and self-managed   42, 46, 52, 53, 56, 59, 62, 63, 126, 149
   autonomous   191
   conditions of access, consumption and remuneration for   8, 213
   conflicts. *See* conflicts:work
   place   7, 13, 18, 22n1, 25n4, 158n8, 161, 218, 220, 223
   process   130, 161, 183
   workfare. *See* schemes, workfare
   working conditions   x, 27, 97, 121, 154, 156, 214
Workers' Confederation of Argentina (CTA)   43
workers' self-managed production   19, 134, 162, 164, 214, 215
Workers' Solidarity Union (UST)   44
Working Programme   51, 56, 58, 58n4
World Bank   51, 58
Wright, Erik Olin   x, 8, 10, 10n5, 11, 12, 105, 114, 135, 150n5, 155, 214, 223

Yaguané   27, 28

Printed in the United States
by Baker & Taylor Publisher Services